SUCCESS ATTRACTS SUCCESS

FREDERICK DODSON

COPYRIGHT

The Copyright of this work lies with the author. Any unauthorized reproduction without the authors written consent, will be handled legally.

Copyright © 2017 Frederick Dodson

All rights reserved.

ISBN: 1537536540

DISCLAIMER

The author is not responsible for effects readers have or allegedly have from this book, just like a driving school instructor is not responsible for his students driving. Furthermore, the information provided in this book is not a substitute for conventional medical assistance.

CONTENTS

CONSCIOUSNESS IN BUSINESS 1

1. The World's Simplest Business Plan 1
2. Do what you Love and Love what you Do 4
3. Be of Service to Society 5
4. Empathy is Stronger than Sales 6
5. The Law of Attraction works better than Marketing 8
6. Taking Initiative 12
7. Specialization Prospers 14
8. Synergy 16
9. Self-Education 18
10. Why would Anyone Choose You over Others? 19
11. Five Steps to Professionalism 20
12. The Power of Focused Productivity 23
13. Everything is Useful 27
14. Turning time wasting Meetings into Productive Brainstorming 28
15. The Power of Habits 30
16. Creating and Breaking Routines 32
17. How Habits of Limitation are Created and Broken 34
18. Creating Unstoppable Momentum 35
19. Levels of Career 37

20.	Moving from Employment to Self-Employment	38
21.	Overcoming Unemployment	40
22.	Dedicating your Life to a Higher Purpose	42
23.	Reality Creation for Companies	43

HIGHER LEARNING 55

1. Creativity Training 55
2. Four Stages of Competence 69
3. You have the Capacity to Learn Almost Anything 72
4. Why it's not only OK but Perfectly Good to be WRONG 76
5. Experiential Learning 77
6. Information vs. Transformation 80
7. Enlightened Education 81
8. The Power of Curiosity 83
9. Turning Difficult Students into Super Learners 84

HOW TO SKYROCKET YOUR SUCCESS 87

1. Simple, Simple, Simple 87
2. Being Authentic 92
3. If you're not Growing, you're Declining 94
5. Stretch Yourself 98
7. Stop Rewarding Negativity 100
8. Your True Vocation 102
9. What Failure Teaches you about Success 103
10. What Sports can Teach you about Success 104
11. In which League do you Play? 105
12. Children Try until they find out What Works 107

13. Learn from People who have Already Achieved what you Want 107
14. Overcome Procrastination 108
15. Your Job as a Work of Art 109
16. People with Enthusiasm 110
17. Techniques to Pass Exams 112
18. The Illusionist 114

SUCCESS AND LIFE MASTERY 117

1. Habits of Mentally Strong People 117
2. Authentic, Aware and Shamelessly Successful 120
3. Life in Balance 128
4. Stop Trying so Hard 131
5. Life Outside the Comfort Zone 133
6. Components of Success 134
7. How I went from being a "Loser" to being a Success 136
9. 30 Things you can Improve in your Life 141
10. A Fork in the Road 142
11. Ten Things Sports can Teach you about Success 145
12. Be a Skilled Person 148
13. Start Strong, Finish Stronger 150
14. Non-Linear Success Dynamics 151
15. Creative Success 155
16. Simple Success Tools.. 157
17. On Having Goals 157
18. Let your Subconscious do Most of the Work 158
19. Something to Look Forward to 158

20. Accepting What Is but being Eager for More 159

21. Should Life Be Easy or Challenging? 161

22. Your Bucket List 166

23. Follow your Goal whether you Feel Like it or Not 167

24. How to get Yourself to Write a Book 169

25. Going for the Win 173

26. Spheres of Fantastic Success 174

27. Let Go of Past Success 176

28. Do what you Love and Love what you Do 179

30. Success Attracts Success Audio Series 180

WILLPOWER AND SELF-CONTROL 181

1. Homeostasis and the Law of Attraction 181

2. Developing Mental Toughness 184

3. Breaking Negative Momentum 191

4. What will it take to Make You Lose your Calmness? 192

5. Mindfulness and Refraining 194

6. Discipline and the Law of Entropy 194

7. Ten Ways to Increase your Willpower 196

8. Break on Through to the Other Side 197

9. Emotional Releasing increases Willpower 199

10. Other Factors that Increase Willpower 200

11. The Self-Control of Human Statues 201

12. Free Your Mind from Unfinished Tasks 202

13. Decisions 205

14. Divine Will & Personal Will 206

- 15. The Proactive Mindset 207
- 16. Free Will vs. Destiny 209
- 17. Changing Patterns... 211
- 18. The Value of Repetition and Practice.. 213

TAKING ACTION AND PEAK PERFORMANCE 215

- 1. How to Change your Behavior... 215
- 2. Sustained Action makes you a Different Person....................... 219
- 3. Weekly Awareness Page... 222
- 4. Peak Performance... 225
- 5. A Rapid Change of State 227
- 6. It's not About what you Own, it's About what you're Able to Do 229
- 7. Healing Workaholism 230
- 8. You Don't need a Crisis to Awaken.. 232
- 9. How to Form New Habits 235
- 10. A Disciple of Discipline 237
- 11. Using Negative Motivation to Reach Goals............................. 238
- 12. Actions, Expectations and Consequences................................ 240

TRUE POWER 243

- 1. Maintain Your Momentum.. 243
- 2. Personal Power.. 245
- 4. How to Rapidly Empower Yourself.. 259
- 5. Confront the Bully.. 261
- 6. The Right Dose of Adversity 262
- 7. From Victim to Victor 265
- 8. The Momentous Power of Repetition 267

    9. The Champion's Mindset 269

    10. Fearless.. 269

INTEGRITY TRAINING **275**

    1. 10 Factors that strengthen your Integrity:............................ 275

    2. Being an Upright Person 276

    3. How to increase the Power of your Word............................ 277

    4. Don't trust the Alarmist 280

    5. The End of Groveling 281

    6. Walk Away or Try Harder? 282

    7. Projected Expectations vs. Authentic Speaking................... 283

ABOUT THE AUTHOR **288**

1

CONSCIOUSNESS IN BUSINESS

1. The World's Simplest Business Plan

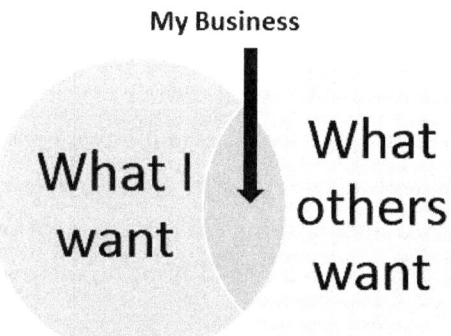

The image above has been my entire Business Plan and Strategy for the last 25 years. And it works. I don't know what the bank would have said if I'd presented this to them as my entire plan. My work takes place within the intersection of what I want and what others want. **Any** lack of achievement in Business is due to being outside of that intersection.

Let's first look at "what others want". Any money you make comes from others. Obvious, right? There's no income to be had when you're isolated and alone. The greater your network of friends, associates, clients, and prospects, the more income potential there's. **Anyone** who runs a successful Business must provide something people **want** to pay them for. First, they give something of value, then they receive income in return (exceptions to this rule are extortion, gambling and theft).

"Do what you want" and "follow your bliss" is only one half of the equation. The other half is to **follow other people's Bliss**, not only yours. If your Bliss is taking pictures of swans, that's great, but you have to ask yourself whether anyone else wants to pay for your swan photography. If not, then swan photography isn't your business, it's your hobby, and you'll need to find another job or business to support yourself. I've seen a lot of people attempt the "follow my Bliss" dictum for years, because that's what many self-improvement gurus teach as "the ultimate key to success". They're taught that it will make their business skyrocket, only to be disappointed and say: "Fred…I have been following my bliss for years. Something isn't right. My business is still not working". To which I ask: "Well…what's in it for me? What's in your business for me? It's nice that you're following your bliss, but I'm not interested in your swan photographs". When people approach your Business, their egos are always asking "What's in it for me?" Unless they are the Dalai Lama they aren't saying "I hope he's happy".

That doesn't invalidate "follow your bliss": If you're not doing something that brings you joy, your life feels like slow motion suicide. "What I want" is the other 50% of a prosperous and fulfilling business. If you're not doing what you like, exhaustion and bad vibes are the reward. **If you do something you enjoy, like and want, you have the energy to follow through** for many years and decades.

Once you have found a vocation, business, venture, project, service, product that both you and others love, you have the potential for success. "What I want" is the energy you give to yourself (first) and "What others want" is the energy you give to others (second).

Some will say "I don't know what I want" or "I don't know what people want". Imagination is the root of creation. If you can't imagine a business that fulfills both you and your customers, then you won't be running your own business. In that case, look into other ways of making a living. Where does lack of imagination come from? It comes from lack of energy. Lack of energy in a business context is often caused by being overworked or fearful.

What causes people to want to do business with you or buy from you?

Usefulness.

Beauty.

Perceived Value.

Ascribed Meaning.

Status or History.

Perceived Scarcity.

Linking positive states to whatever it's you do.

I had an old watch that I found. It was a pilot's watch from WWII that I had tucked away on a shelf for years. One day, while cleaning out the shelves, I thought "Well…this looks rather novel." So I took it off the shelf and placed it on a bookcase for viewing. More time went by, until it finally occurred to me: a watch like this might be rare and valuable. I found nothing about it on the Internet so I decided to try a little experiment. I decided to list it on eBay for $6,000 as a "vintage" and "retro" watch. It didn't get a bid the first time around, so I just kept listing it on eBay week after week, believing "One day someone is going to believe and perceive that it's worth that money, and buy it". Mind you, I had no idea how much it was really worth. It could have been worth no more than a few hundred dollars, but I was experimenting (which also means there was no attachment to outcome – an important state in business dealings). Finally, after about 8 weeks, there was a bid on the watch…for the $6,000 starting price. What happened then was remarkable: others started bidding and the price rapidly went up to $7,000, then $8,000 up to the final selling price of more than $9,000!

This taught me an important lesson about **perception**: once one person had bid, the item was *perceived* as being of high value. Before that, there were no bids for weeks, now suddenly there were dozens. It needed someone willing to raise the bar. An old watch that was worth nothing to me was suddenly worth something to others. In other words, it might take a while to get your business running, but **once it takes off, there's no stopping it.**

2. Do what you Love and Love what you Do

When you choose a vocation that you love, persistent focus comes easily. However, just like life itself, every profession has a few challenges or undesirable tasks. Duality and Contrast are the nature of reality and even the projects you're most passionate about will contain obstacles on the path. That's why it's not only important that you do what you love, but also that you love what you do.

If you haven't yet found the job of your dreams, "Loving what you do" becomes especially important. An energetic person feels good in a wide variety of circumstances. Not enjoying your current work gets you stuck in it (**what you resist will persist**). By pushing against unwanted work ⌐ ⌐e energy that would otherwise be available to attract a new job. If you're not in a good flow with your old job you won't be in a good flow with your new one. Many complain about what they do, but then continue doing that job! The only empowering solution is to either **Love what you do, or Leave it**. If you don't feel you can leave the Business, then Love it **until** you can leave it for something better. The real work is inner work. Stop blaming society, bosses, and co-workers for your state and work to feel well from within, no matter what you're doing. If you feel happy about what you're doing today, you'll begin to attract better opportunities. Everybody talks about "doing what you love", but it's **loving what you do** that magnetically takes you to what you love.

3. Be of Service to Society

Balance your passion with the market's demand. Respect all expressions of reality whether you agree with them or not. Be kind to all of life, including yourself, at all times. Making yourself more extensively of service to mankind and appreciating life is a quick way to ascend spiritually as well as become a success. You can cultivate so much care for people and projects that you begin to fly high. The purpose of any sort of venture is to serve others and in doing so to elevate those you serve and yourself. In this holographic universe, what you do for others **is** what you do for yourself. **If you make a large number of people happier, success is guaranteed, no matter what field you're in**. Even if you're not an entrepreneur or boss but an employee, you can upgrade your status with a new self-definition: **not to define yourself as an employee but as a service provider**. The service you provide as an employee is to customers, clients, colleagues and supervisors.

If you're only in it for money and survival you'll perform at a mediocre level and fail. Instead learn and study what people want. The prevailing myth in our society is that rich people are greedy and ego-driven, but if you look closely you'll find that this isn't true for long-term success because in order to become rich you need to provide something of benefit to many. Any shift from service-to-others to merely making money will be followed by a decline in success. Think about it: who do you give your money to? Which products, institutions and people do you spend on? And what do they all have in common? They all offer something that is of service to you.

You don't need to study economics if you understand these basic truths. Such study could even become a distraction as one loses sight of the forest by studying all the trees. In fact, to get rich I recommend someone doesn't study economics, but instead how to identify and meet others' needs and desires..

Check your intentions. Ask yourself right now:

"What kind of business am I in, and why am I in this business? How is what I'm doing contributing to society? How can I better serve others? How can I make it a joy to serve?"

Many people say "Thank God it's Friday", "I look forward to vacation", and "I'm looking forward to retirement". Those are clear indicators that you haven't found the success-vibe yet. The success-vibe **loves** to serve. When I'm on vacation I enjoy it, but I also miss my work. If you can reach the point where you **miss** your work, you have transcended the treadmill, you have mastered the game.

4. Empathy is Stronger than Sales

If you have empathy, you truly enjoy what you do and you have something of value to give, you don't have to worry about "closing a sale" or "the right marketing strategy". Those are secondary considerations. Business is all about people and exchanging trust, exchanging value, exchanging energy and **having a good time providing mutual benefit**. If you're focused on "making sales" or "getting customers" your priorities are mixed up. To increase your business success, simply become more enthusiastic about other people. Try to find something you like about **everyone**.

Sales training teaches people what to say, but what you say determines no more than 10% of your communication with others. More important than what you say is what you think – because people perceive your thoughts and energy subconsciously. If you feel awkward or inauthentic, that energy will be transmitted. That's something you don't learn in any sales training, management course or university. Intend to find something you like about the person you're dealing with no matter what. Do you like their looks, their hobbies, their life, their expertise, the words they use, their tone of voice, their interests, their attitude? Everybody has something to like. What did you do the last time you got along well with someone? You probably turned on your empathy transmitter. That energy carries your communication and words. It's not only the words, it's how you say them. Some of this is transmitted through your body language. More of it's transmitted non-physically.

Developing empathy means you no longer try to "sell" something. Who likes a salesman? Nobody does. We are suspicious of salespeople. Instead you build relationships with people and build trust. People spend money on what they trust. Even if your service or product are vastly superior to others, you won't be selling any of them if people don't personally know or trust you and if you can't demonstrate the trustworthiness of your service or product. Empathy means that when you sell a vacuum cleaner to an elderly lady, instead of boring her with the technical details of the machine you'll talk about what she is really interested in. That may be whether a certain spot on her rug can be removed or maybe she just wants to talk about her neighbors. If she wants to talk about her neighbors, let go of your need to explain technicalities and listen to her. Developing empathy with her, she is much more likely to purchase your vacuum cleaner than if you try to force-feed your sales pitch.

Stop transmitting frustration, depression, boredom, and anger onto others. Just stop. With an employee, boss, spouse, friend, or customer, practice shifting your state and attitude. Shift it again and again and again. People will want to work with you because of your state. If you're in a good state, you're able to shift them to a higher state, too, and that's what getting together is really about. It's not about money, services, or products. Those are all just excuses to get together and improve your state. By looking at what everything is really about, you create a positive energy field, and that attracts good business. You can't fake a good mood because your energy vibration is always instantly communicated. Practicing mood adjustment is the most worthwhile thing you can do to improve your business.

5. The Law of Attraction works better than Marketing

At the corner of East 76th Street and 5th Avenue in Manhattan, there are three hot-dog stands. The last time I was there I bought drinks at one of them for several days. One day I realized that I was always going to the same one. I even waited in line for "the one" although there was no line at the other two. Being inquisitive, I asked myself why I was **subconsciously drawn** to the same guy, although he had exactly the same products…water, coke, Gatorade, etc.…as the other two. And it was simply because he seemed friendlier than the others. The other two looked grim and impatient, as if I would be inconveniencing them by buying some water.

This called for further investigation. I sat at a nearby bench for a full hour and counted the number of people who made a purchase at each of the three stands. I wanted to know if it was only me or whether there was more at work here, the three hot-dog-stands being a microcosmic representation of **all** Business. Sure enough, the happy hot-dog seller outperformed the other two. In that hour he sold to 25 people. The other one on the same side of the street sold to 11 people. The one across the street sold to 14 people.

In other words, no matter where you look, you'll see the **Law of Attraction** at work.

I write about it here because some of my students have no confidence when I say "Don't focus so much on business, sales and marketing, focus on improving your own energy and identity, look at the Law of Attraction". The three hotdog stands all had the same "marketing": They looked the same, sold the same items, and were at the same location. Whether they had the same prices or not I don't know…and I didn't care. I had chosen my hot dog stand based on subconscious attraction.

Not to completely undermine your belief in marketing – it does belong in any successful business, but there's more going on in the semi-invisible realm of energy. If you have looked into marketing you have probably been told that the key to your success lies in putting ads in the paper, getting endorsements, building a presence on social media, running Google AdWords campaigns, optimizing Google rankings, crafting landing pages for your website and increasing their conversion rate, getting more traffic to your website, engaging in direct mail marketing, phone marketing, email newsletter marketing, etc. When business-oriented students ask me about these things, I say that I don't really care much about any of that. I say:

"Good marketing is marketing that's not recognized as such."

I'll write a good article that helps someone. That's good marketing. It's not recognized as "marketing" because by the conventional definition, it isn't. If your product or service are good, people will be as naturally and effortlessly attracted to it as people were to the hotdog stand. If someone endorses my work, then it's not because I paid him or her to do so, but because they *really* like it.

Not long ago I received the following email (excerpts quoted):

"I'd like to help you with your marketing. I noticed you only have 4,000 Fans on Facebook. The big names have hundreds of thousands. That doesn't reflect well on your business. I can show you how to run successful ad campaigns. You should also (just in the beginning) consider buying Facebook fans to make it look better".

No offense to the person who sent me that email, but I could fill an entire book listing what's wrong with it. The entire mindset is repellent to success. First of all, the number of fans someone has on Facebook denotes quantity, not quality. If I look at my highest sources of income in 2014 they were entirely unrelated to Facebook…or even the Internet. As a Business owner you could ask yourself: Would I rather have one good follower or 10,000 uninterested ones? Quantity isn't the ultimate measure of success. Sure, it's one measure. If your product nets you $1 and you sell a million units, then you're a millionaire, but you could also offer just *one* product for $1 Million and sell it to only one person and you're a millionaire too. I mention this because many of my readers aren't in mass market products but rather in "niche" businesses.

Second, why would I run "ad campaigns" on Facebook? Facebook is where people go to relax, connect with friends and engage in light reading. Nobody goes there with the Intention "I want to be spammed with ads". So **why contradict people's Intention**s? That's not good marketing. Good marketing **aligns with people's intentions**.

Third, "purchasing Facebook fans" sounds embarrassing. I've noticed how a few big name coaches might have 80,000 "Fans", but below the fan count on their Facebook pages there's also a counter indicating how many people are "talking about" a brand or product. If someone has that many fans but only 5 are "talking about" it, that's just funny. It shows that this company or business purchased some of their "fans". Sure, "fake it till you make it". But as I very clearly say in my books, the "fake it" part should be **as real as possible**. The correct credo is "Live it until you make it". If there's no basis, no belief, and no reality to your "faking it", the faking it will harm you, not help you. Example: 22 years ago, before I had published a single book, I called myself "an author". I was "faking it". But there was a **real** basis to my claim because I was already writing books with the strong belief that they would be published.

Later, when I finally did invest money into Facebook ads, I got this email:

"Hi, I noticed you make Facebook ads for your articles. I'm a marketing expert and I can help you with that. You're wasting your money. Facebook ads should not be directed to your articles, they should be directed to your products and services!"

What followed was a long proposal on how he would help me boost my income. I would that he's not a very successful marketer. Why? Because my intention was to advertise my articles, not my products. I don't advertise my articles to get a return on investment, but so more people get the knowledge. My income sources lie elsewhere. This "marketer" couldn't imagine I just wanted to do some good with no expectation of return.

I'll leave it at these few examples, even though it would be tempting to de-construct a number of other marketing myths. Your marketing, of course, should depend on what kind of people you want to attract. I'm in a business where I wish to attract **conscious** people, which automatically excludes most forms of marketing. As already stated, the better and more real your products or services are, the less marketing is required. If your products/services are fairly worthless to people, that's when you need aggressive marketing. Coca-Cola has no nutritional value, hence it can only be sold with ongoing, super-expensive marketing. Google Chrome is naturally superior to Internet Explorer, so Internet Explorer will need a lot more marketing to compete with Chrome. Or it could take the much easier path: to improve the product! You can tell that someone at Microsoft had the mistaken belief that Firefox and Chrome outperforming Explorer was "just marketing", but that's not true. The truth is that Microsoft's browser simply wasn't as quick and efficient as the competition until Microsoft Edge was released in 2015, replacing Explorer.

The Law of Attraction mindset doesn't ask:

"What should I **DO** to attract many customers?"

Instead it asks:

"Who could I **BE** to attract good customers?"

All three hotdog sellers were *doing* the same things but *being* someone different.

If we were to place a super-sexy person in one of the hotdog stands, would that increase sales even more? Possibly, but not necessarily. Context is also important. "Super-sexy" isn't expected from a hotdog seller and may come across as incongruent, especially to those purchasing hotdogs for their families. The "happy and chubby uncle" type might be best suited for the task. It's something that could be tested in an experiment.

6. Taking Initiative

I remember a student who was applying for a job. Out of the blue she had the idea to send her application as a video. She got the job. Nobody had **ever** sent a video as an application to the company before. She was the *first* to do it. Sometimes it can take a few runs of initiative to get something right but in this case initiative was rewarded immediately.

Years ago when I worked as a language teacher, I laminated the papers and lessons of the day to make them waterproof, then I took my students, a group of 7, to hold our lessons at a lake. Exhilarated by the new experience, the students' performance increased tenfold. They are still talking about that special lesson over a decade later. On that day I did something that had never been done in that language school before and it made a fantastic impact that is remembered. The fact that they still remember it shows that these people haven't seen much initiative in the years since then. That's how little initiative there's in society. We follow the same old patterns over and over, whether they are exciting or not. At one point in my former career as an English teacher I was featured in an article published in a popular newspaper titled "Is this the best English teacher in the country?" That's when I knew my innovations and initiatives had paid off.

If you're waiting to be discovered,

Waiting to be noticed,

Waiting for a pay raise,

Waiting to get a gig,

Waiting to get customers,

Waiting to be recognized,

Waiting to be paid,

Waiting to be praised,

Waiting to be employed…

You're wasting your time!

The world owes you nothing. Take **Initiative**. Other ways to express the idea:

Just Go.

Just Start.

Be the first to…

Ready, Fire, Aim!

Stop Waiting and Do Something.

Go Ahead.

Lead the Way.

Make something out of nothing. Start anywhere on the map. Making a mistake is better than doing nothing at all.

Taking initiative, I have also made several mistakes but these have not kept me from enthusiastically moving on. Admit a mistake early, let it go and do better next time. Initiative is fearless.

7. Specialization Prospers

Specialization prospers because holding focus on one thing for a long time accumulates energy. When you specialize in doing one thing and doing that one thing really well, you radiate confidence and people sense your expertise. Your expertise is something of value to others because they haven't focused that long and solicit your help because they know that you know every aspect of your work.

When someone tells me my books are too expensive, I say: "Nonsense. They are the accumulation of 20 years of focusing on this subject. You can save many thousands of dollars in workshops through the proper application of any one of my books". I wouldn't have this confidence had I not specialized in my field and learned *everything* there's to know about it. People have said that my asking $3.4 million for one year of full time coaching with me is too much, but because I know in my heart that what I can offer in 365 days of personal coaching will benefit the person for not only one lifetime but several, the price still seems too low to me. Getting someone to a point where they no longer have to reincarnate to this planet is actually worth billions. ;-)

Spreading your attention too widely can water down your service or product, making it unclear what value you're actually offering. Do one thing until you have completely mastered it before expanding into other lines of business. If you offer a service or product, narrow it down to a few simple choices for your customers to make. Research has shown that where there's too much choice, no choice will be made. For example, I coached an auto dealer on growing his business a few years ago. Our coaching went for 5 months and he paid $20,000 for my coaching. His sales were down compared to previous years and he had no idea why. Apart from telling him that his building desperately needed a paint job in order to increase the dealership's energy level, I noticed that there were way too many cars in his main showroom. It's alright to have numerous different models and colors in his outside parking lot, but the main showroom should only feature a few carefully chosen cars. In his building it was crowded…there were 10 cars in there (in addition to the 35+ cars outside) and we could hardly walk between them.. I told him to park them all outside and only feature his two best cars of the month in the main room. Sales went up immediately from that point. Of course there are hundreds of factors that can influence sales, but in this case less choice was the key. His $20,000 investment in coaching paid for itself through increased sales within only a few weeks.

Narrow down your field of expertise to one, two or three things and do those very well before moving on. If you have done nothing other than build furniture for a decade, you automatically attract everything and everyone having to do with that. Such is the power of focus. People know that and they will approach YOU to get furniture and not the guy who sells furniture and clothes and also cosmetics.

8. Synergy

The expression "It's all about your network and connections" isn't just a cliché. It's true and always has been. This bears repeating because the obvious is often overlooked. In the cliché, this expression is used to mean "In order to succeed you need connections to the higher ups". That's not necessarily true. Connections are important because of the **Synergy** they generate. In nature, two things connecting often combine to create something greater than the sum of the individual parts. For example Sodium and Chlorine make salt. In and of themselves Sodium and Chlorine are of little use. The same is true of almost all Elements: they only reach their full potential in *combination* with something else.

The dictionary defines Synergy as follows:

*"**Synergy**, in general, may be defined as two or more things functioning together to produce a result not independently obtainable"*

Achieving business success in isolation is difficult. In order to make it big, you must provide something people think is valuable. Money making is energy *exchange*, not a solo project. You must connect with others on a deeper level to exchange energy with them. If you think you can stay emotionally safe and unnoticed and make a lot of money, good luck. Becoming successful means you or your product or service become known by very many people as well as you knowing very many. That also means you have to put yourself out there, show up, become a public figure.

The people you connect to aren't only your customers. They are your friends, competitors, partners and peers. Release negative judgment about them and you'll see that *each person* in your life has resources, knowledge, expertise and ideas that *you don't have*. These people are in your life for a reason. Other human beings usually don't subtract from your experience of life, they add to it, sometimes in ways you don't expect.

It's no coincidence that businesses similar to each other locate near each other. You'll find a bank district, a jewelry district, a clothing district, etc. in most cities. And you'll even find entire cities that specialize in something, such as Los Angeles specializing in entertainment, New York in banking and Milan in fashion. It's not true that you have to get away from the competition; in fact, the opposite is true. You should not only **keep your competition close** to you but even co-operate with and benefit from your competitors. All the chocolate shops are in the same street because of the synergy effect and because people specifically go there to buy chocolate. That's why the Internet, with all its connectivity, has and will continue to greatly contribute to the prosperity of mankind.

Connections summon appreciation and the energy of appreciation summons higher prosperity. If you appreciate your job you're willing to tell people about it. How many people do you know and how many know you? Who knows what you do? How many do you know well enough that an energy field of appreciation is established between you and them? The longer your list of good, nurturing connections, the better off you're. Try to imagine a lone wolf having business success. It's challenging, isn't it? You're not the center of the world. Other people have fantastic ideas, resources and power and can be blessings in disguise.

Never value money over relationships. Money is generated by love, by what others give you and you give in return. If you value money over relationships, you'll run out of love and in time run out of money.

Notice how those who keep talking about money usually don't have it and those who keep talking about their friends, family, partners and colleagues are better off. You can actually prove this through statistical research. Hard facts never contradict but always confirm metaphysical truth.

Relationships are more important than money because business is a matter of reputation, interaction and communication; of being connected, exchanging energy, talking and listening, giving and receiving. To keep the energy exchange in a state of flow, don't exaggerate money's importance. Money isn't the ultimate goal, it's only a means. There are other exchanges of energy that can make you financially more abundant than just money: Exchange of Smiles. Exchange of Information. Exchange of Joy. Exchange of Care. Exchange of Objects. These are all aspects of wealth that are ignored by people desperately chasing money for its own sake. Even though economic literature is rife with tales of cheaters achieving success for a while, I have never seen cheaters *sustain* their wealth and health – one or both always suffers. Have this be a week's Affirmation:

"I love people and treat them kindly"

This is a more sustaining Affirmation than "I'm rich". No trickery or cleverness in the world can replace a sense of love. All the money in the world is of no use if you have nobody to share your joy with.

9. Self-Education

Business success is linked to education, and by that I don't necessarily mean college. Many of the most successful business people never finished college. Bill Gates didn't, Steve Jobs didn't, Mark Zuckerberg didn't, James Cameron didn't, Tiger Woods didn't. Each of these people has an extremely high level of *Education* in the truest sense of the word. It's how ave **educated themselves** that makes them what they are. They have invested the time to learn a number of relevant skills in perfect combination to achieve amazing results. I repeatedly emphasize the power of focusing attention and one benefit of doing so is that you can learn anything you want if you have the *energy* to focus.

It pays to be well versed in many different skills, even if one specializes in only one area. **Learning** is the passion of the successful. They never stop learning. They are good at a wide variety of things and this shows in their energy field. They have that special "aura".

What skills do you have? Are you good at e-commerce or web design? How many languages do you speak? What instruments do you play? Have you ever run a business? What adventurous travel have you experienced? What sports do you do? What courses have you taken to expand your knowledge and awareness? What education are you giving yourself? What systems of thought are you familiar with? What jobs have you done? What crafts are you good at? What is something new you have learned in the last few weeks?

10. Why would Anyone Choose You over Others?

The single most important question you can ask yourself as a business person:

Why should anyone choose my business over all others?

The answer to this question is your "Unique Selling Proposition" (USP). Your business or career will only take off once you have identified your USP to your own full satisfaction and can then communicate it to a targeted group of people, your customers. If I have no reason to choose you over anyone else in your niche or category, then I won't choose you, I'll give my money to someone else. It's really as simple as that. Whether you own a boutique or whether you're a musician or the CEO of a multinational company, if you fail to answer that question you won't succeed. Even if you have heard and asked yourself that question before, it's good to consider it on a regular basis. I highly recommend you research this. Use Google and type in "famous USPs" or "best USPs" and see what comes up, then, summarize your own unique and beneficial offering until you can convince both yourself and others that there really is nothing better in your category than what you sell.

11. Five Steps to Professionalism

If you want your business or career to be perceived as more professional, you need to be an expert. Here are 5 universally applicable steps to **internalize** for that purpose.

1. Professional Status is half real, half fake

Professionalism is a mix of your *real* and true skill and expertise and other people's *perception* of your skill and expertise. Being a Pro is 50% skill and 50% a self-styled creation of public image. That means there are some real and unreal components to being seen as a Pro, an Expert or an Authority Figure. For example Eckhart Tolle's status as an "enlightened teacher" and "internationally recognized authority figure on everything spiritual" is mostly self-created. Large parts of his life were spent in a state of depression and unemployment before he began calling himself a spiritual teacher in the mid-1990s and began communicating his message. Today, only 20 years later the New York Times hails him as the "most important spiritual teacher in America". Of course his public image isn't 100% crafted…he also worked on himself, underwent an inner transformation and read an awesome number of books on the subject, thus building his credibility as an expert. His books contain little that wasn't already discussed in depth in previous literature of course. In his case, it's the attractive repackaging that made all the difference.

Let's take another example: The most famous marketing expert today is probably Seth Godin. Like so many before him, little of what he writes in his bestselling books is actually new. Much of it was already known in the 1960s, 70s and 80s. His massive success is again not primarily due to what he says or does, but in who he is being, his deliberately crafted persona. Like so many others, he has "celebritized" himself. I coined the term "celebritize yourself" to describe what self-marketing really means and how it's mainly based on public illusion.

My own "reality creation" expertise is derived from 20 years of working as a "reality creation coach"…but 20 years ago I had zero education or experience in the field. My beginnings were therefore completely self-styled and self-defined.

To become a **Pro** you need to learn skills and study your field in depth to build "real" expertise (people will sense whether you know your things or not), but on the other hand you need to learn to brand yourself or "celebritize" yourself as well, and that is a function of imagination. What you can or can't become is mostly limited by your imagination and level of courage.

2. Sincerity and Focus

Whatever career you're in, you can get even more sincere about it, and even more committed. Only when you have fully committed to a path, without focusing on alternative paths or "escape hatches", can you develop momentum and charisma in that field. Choose your field wisely but then stick to it so that over time you can build initial skills and then build upon that which you have already built. Your project or career will be based on very strong foundations, clearly defined principles and streamlined systems that create consistent results – the hallmarks of a Pro.

Getting Sincere with what you do also means striving to be the best in your line of work. I ask myself:

"If I'm not going to be the best in this field, what's the point of doing it?"

That question has served me well. Even if I'm not the best and even if I never will be the best, the aspiration creates the inspiration needed to improve. Another thing you could do is look at the very best people in your field, study them, learn from them…and then intend to become better than them! In the Evolution of Human Consciousness, perfection is never reached and there's always room for improvement. That's the beauty of the Universe – it's never finished and can always get better.

3. Super-Prioritize

Prioritize by frequently saying "No" to that which doesn't align with your overall vision and saying "Yes" to that which does. Sift and filter the realities aligned with who you really are and reject the things that aren't aligned. While this may sometimes be painful to yourself or others, it's beneficial in the long run. No matter what line of work you're in, one of your priorities ought to be to provide true value and flavor to other people and customers/clients. People want to experience life more fully and any sort of product, service or work you do can focus on that overall goal. Companies and individuals who forget that basic premise, eventually go broke. A Super-Prioritized person will be seen as a Pro.

4. Act as if there's no Yesterday or Tomorrow

Act as if there's no Yesterday or Tomorrow – but with Integrity. This entails many things, too numerous to list here. One of them is to look at your Boss, Employees, Customers etc. with fresh eyes…as if there were neither a yesterday to base your opinions of them on, nor a tomorrow where you can make up for failing to treat them kindly or clearly communicating with them today. Tomorrow has no power to act, influence and create tomorrow. All that power is only available today. If you knew for a fact that there's no yesterday, you could view things with fresh eyes. For example, if you think you "already know everything" you create a lot of blind spots…weaknesses you can't detect in yourself but others can, then you need to rely on others' feedback for an accurate reality check. If you knew for a fact that there's no tomorrow you would implement the "life you always dreamed of" today, not some day. The road called someday leads to a village called nowhere.

5. Fascinated People are Fascinating

Simply put, if you're bored by your work, others will be, too. If you would like people to be more interested in you, then be an interested person. Fascination draws attention. **Attention is the true currency of the 21st Century**. If you can generate fascination with something within yourself, you can also generate fascination in others. You can trash all of the business literature you have if you know how to maintain a high level of fascination with life and transfer that fascination to others. You can literally sell **anything** if you're fascinated, amazed and enthusiastic about it. Enthusiasm is a palpable energy force that attracts people like a brightly shining light. So even if you're "only" selling vacuum cleaners door to door, you could make a fortune from them if you were actually fascinated by them. The only problem: who is actually fascinated by vacuum cleaners?

12. The Power of Focused Productivity

Here is an absolute fact: there's no "secret" to success. Either you focus attention and **disregard distraction**, or you don't. I see many beautiful, talented, brilliant souls waste their attention (and thus their precious life energy) on distractions offline and online. Online they'll get lost in Facebook, Twitter, and a myriad of other time and attention-suckers. Why? Because it's easy. Because it's entertaining. Because they have no goal. They'll fill their heads with Trivia and "News" of "World Events". But how much of that trivia and news is actually valuable for your personal growth and contribution to the world? Would you like to be the person who passively watches the news or would you like to co-create the news of the day? Would you like to feel helpless and indignant about world events or would you like to shape the future yourself? When you get yourself to focus on one thing (and only one thing) at a time – forget multi-tasking, something peculiar happens: You get into **flow**. You're less easily distracted. All those distractions become less interesting. This kind of dedicated focus can sometimes actually be felt as a kind of vividness around the third eye, the forehead, and the eyes as if those areas are activated. **If you don't determine your focus, others will.**

My #1 productivity tool is **Attention Lists.** These are an all-in-one freestyle hybrid mix of to-do-lists, errand lists, reminder lists, intention lists, and things to release lists. I don't need a Task Management or Productivity app or computer program to write my Attention List, a simple piece of paper and a pen or a computer page are fine. Most digital task managers, with their endless options and folders, actually disperse attention rather than focus it.

When someone gives me a good idea in conversation, I write it down immediately (on a Notes page in my iPhone). When there's an errand that needs to be done, I write it down. When I have an intention, I write it down. All of these things are on the very same piece of paper or page, so it looks kind of crazy and incomprehensible to an outsider. If I'm practicing a week of gratitude, then the list will include things I have been grateful for on that day. If I'm practicing accounting, then the list will include money spent and made for that week. If I have an idea for an article on my website, I put it on the list. If there's some strange code I need to unlock my phone just in case I forget its password, it's on that list. If I've been procrastinating cleaning out my garage, it goes on that list and it stays on the list until it's done, no matter when. If I read something interesting, I put it on the list. If that piece of data is no longer interesting after some time, I remove it. Otherwise I somehow **make use** of it. That is actually an important stance of a sifting, filtering, prioritizing, success-oriented mind: If I can't make use of a piece of data, I discard it. That's why I'm not that interested in trivia and news online (except for breaks and relaxation time).

The media presents waves of "news" that you can do nothing about. About the only thing left to do is to sit there passively and be shocked. What's the use of that? It's fundamentally disempowering to constantly focus on things you can't personally change. Sitting in front of the TV ranting about some conflict in some country will do nothing to change it. If you want to do the world a service, then uplift your own consciousness! That will have a ripple effect that will uplift the consciousness of the world, making the event of war less likely.

The productive mind asks: **How can this piece of information be utilized, salvaged, exploited, used, and applied for the betterment of myself and others?** That is why, in contrast to the "news", I insist that every article written on my website must be either of some practical usefulness or uplift and inspire. These articles may not be as entertaining as others, but long term they change a readers overall attitude and reality for the better.

Priority and To-do Lists are criticized by many because "they never get done" or "put me under pressure" or some other nonsense, but I insist they are of great benefit for productivity because they **sort attention.** Once you have put an item on paper or a page, you don't need to worry about retaining it. You have written it down so it won't be forgotten and you no longer have to waste attention and emotion worrying about it. Interestingly, **some things take care of themselves** over time and then they can be crossed off the list or removed from the page. I don't put a time limit on the tasks on my list, and I don't feel guilty if I don't complete tasks in a certain time. Such ideas are neurotic nonsense that one can simply release. Many people want a clear mind and "peace of mind". If that's important to you, then simply clear your mind of clutter by getting it all out on paper, all of it, and then remove whatever you no longer need to pay attention to.

If you find yourself worried about something, it's because you're not focused. If you find yourself jumping from thing to thing it shows that you're not focused. I call jumping from book to book, tool to tool, purchase to purchase, "leapfrogging". In such cases you don't focus on anything long enough to produce energy-momentum, so no results show up. For the productivity-minded, **less is more**.

If you work at the computer or online it's also wise to manage your emails in a sifting and prioritizing way. I cancelled all of my "subscriptions" years ago. I never give my normal email address to places that will send me ads, newsletters, spam and junk mail. 99% of all newsletters contain nothing useful to me. If I want to know something I can find it out on my own and don't need advertisers telling me what to focus on. Filtering attention lets you achieve more and more, and becoming more in-demand requires even more filtering. Any email, actually any external reality, that isn't sincere, loving or aligned with your goals can be deleted without hesitation and with a clear conscience. Everything is energy, everything is vibration and you must choose and filter which vibrations belong in your life and which vibrations don't.

While there are many productivity destroyers on the Internet, there are also numerous productivity facilitators. My all time favorite is actually **WordPress**. It's a time and money saver. With it I have built my website and dozens of other websites for students with a few simple clicks. Anyone can build any kind of website with it for free, with a little focus. A few other time and money savers I like: Fiverr (you don't have to pay hundreds of Dollars for services that only cost $5), Last Pass (you don't have to waste time generating passwords, requesting forgotten passwords or logging into places), Zamzar (you don't have to spend hundreds on file-converters), Google Drive (you don't have to pay Dropbox to store and share files).

Being a reality creator is being a reality filter.

13. Everything is Useful

Everything you want to get rid of, everything you want to overcome, everything you don't want in your day-to-day life, is actually useful. It's only because you refuse to see the useful aspect that you can't get rid of it. Everything you're trying to get rid of is actually a gift of a higher source to you. Wanting to get rid of it's disrespectful toward the gift and yourself. Discover its value, then you'll no longer have to get rid of it (by which its negative aspect disappears). No matter what it's…whether you had an accident or lost someone or something or aren't experiencing this or that…it's useful. Discover its secret benefit. This is a very powerful formula for good living.

When I was young I had an accident that broke my leg. I was in the hospital and realized what a wonderful thing that was because I finally had the time and solitude to do what I had been yearning for so long: To read a lot of books. And the hospital had a fantastic library.

A decade ago I had a phase in which I felt fatigued and tired most of the time. I asked myself: "What secret benefit could this have?" I realized that the fatigue was an indicator. It was trying to help me learn that my lifestyle wasn't appropriate for that which my soul longed for. I changed my lifestyle and the fatigue disappeared.

Around the same time I lost my job. I thought I would be devastated because I no longer had an income safety net, but I remained calm and poised, knowing I'm always provided for. What was the benefit of losing it? If I hadn't lost it I wouldn't be the self-employed and thriving person I'm today.

Everything is useful. Don't try to get rid of things. Instead see how you can modify or use them to your benefit.

14. Turning time wasting Meetings into Productive Brainstorming

Do you feel that many of the meetings you attend fail to create the desired results? Do they leave you frustrated and longing for more? This section will explain why and how to turn your frustration into inspiration.

In my experience, business meetings, team meetings, and committee meetings are mostly wastes of time. They might not be wastes of time if their purpose were to connect socially, but they are often wastes of time when it comes to decision-making, goal-achievement and building your energy state.

Of course social connection and interaction can have a learning effect and some merit, but if social connecting were the intent of business meetings then at least they could be labeled as such and be conducted in more pleasant settings, combined with long and delicious breakfasts for employees, for instance.

The problem with the countless meetings that take place in offices every day is that many of their conclusions could have been decided in just a few minutes. Meetings are frequently called because a team leader doesn't know what decision to make about an issue (although making such decisions is the leader's job). Meetings then become an excuse for delaying decisions. "Let's have a meeting about it next week" is like saying "I'm too tired to think about it or decide right now".

Many who attend meetings don't really have to be there. So they stare into the air, open their laptops, or play with their smartphones to kill time. If you find yourself doing things to "kill time" you're certainly not in a high-energy state. Plenty of meetings lack a clear intention or agenda. That's why so many employees leave meetings asking "What was achieved in this meeting?" and "Why was this meeting held?"

One reason meetings can be counter-productive is because attention isn't focused on the goal but distracted by behaviors of the participants, to "look good" in front of others, to "look better in front of the boss", to outshine perceived competitors or taken as an opportunity to list complaints and excuses why certain things aren't working. Often roles, responsibilities and ranks aren't clearly delineated, creating as many contradictory opinions (vs. facts) as there are people. All this can deplete personal energy and have you feel drained afterwards.

There are two ways to solve this and make team members more creative and productive: the first is simply to conduct fewer meetings or meet in smaller groups. The second is to conduct meetings as brainstorming sessions focused on a particular goal or question to be answered. In this scenario a question is posed and everyone in the group offers their answers to the question and nothing more. There's no posturing, no trying to make oneself look good and others bad, no litany of complaints and misgivings, no small talk. There's just the question/goal and the collection of ideas. After that each idea can be spoken out loud by a reader and voted on with thumbs up. The ideas with the most thumbs up are taken into the minutes of the meeting as potential action steps the team leader may or may not follow up on. That would be an example of a meeting that is focused and aligned with a particular goal. The energy of groups can be useful and productive if it's laser focused on a particular intention or purpose. Without a purpose and the dedication to it, business meetings can just be a confused voicing of various opinions and subsequent agreements and disagreements. Productive meetings require someone to guide a meeting in this manner and re-focus the group on the original intention of the meeting, repeatedly if necessary.

15. The Power of Habits

Creating your Reality means shifting your Habits

Your reality is a habit. Shifting reality means shifting your habit. That's possible when you're aware of what you want **instead** of the habit. Awareness is always the key. If you don't remember that you intended to shift your habit, you continue the old habit. You need to know what you want to replace the habit with and then **remember** to implement the new pattern. For example, instead of giving someone a hard time, turning on the TV, surfing the internet or overeating you could:

* Take a walk and look at the world with childlike curiosity

* Stretch your body

* Take a bath

* Meditate for 15 Minutes

* Create an Intention List

* Check your To-do List

* Ride your bike

* Play with your children

* Lie in the grass watching clouds

* Lie in the grass watching the stars

* Take a class

* Do volunteer work

* Get a massage

* Write a priority list

* Get acupuncture

* Do yoga

* Read a book

* Have sex

* Prepare good clothes for the week

* Learn a language

* Learn to play an instrument

* Learn to cook a new recipe

* Clean your place

* Visit a friend or family member

* Play a board game

* Have a date with your partner

* Finish something you have been putting off

* Learn a new business skill

* Write

* Get involved in your community

* Visit a place of high energy

The list could go on for pages. **You have infinite options.** The idea is to be aware of your options every day and to make wiser choices.

16.   Creating and Breaking Routines

Routines are sets of procedures and habits that are repeated every day, week, etc. You have the ability to create routines and break routines. Both are important skills for life on earth. When you seek to feel more alive and creative, break routines. When you seek to feel more grounded and focused, establish routines.

A few examples of breaking routines:

* Brushing your teeth with the other hand

* Sleeping somewhere new

* Wearing something you don't typically wear

* Suddenly stepping into a building you have passed many times but never entered

* Being friendly to a neighbor you haven't talked to

* Being unfriendly to someone you've been polite to (be selective)

* Sleeping in for many hours (if you haven't done so in a long time)

* Getting up very early (if you haven't done so in a long time)

* Playing music you've never listened to

* Reading a type of book you have never read

* Walking backwards

The boundaries of your reality are defined by your routines that are laid out like train tracks throughout your day. By breaking routines you regain a sense of magic and surprise because you're saying **"Reality isn't defined by those tracks that have been laid out, reality is defined by**

me, right now". Breaking a routine opens up new pathways in the mind and you'll find yourself getting new input and ideas.

A few positive examples of creating routines:

* Create a success-routine of working on your favorite project first thing in the morning

* Eat healthier foods at one or more of your daily meals

* Create a new way of greeting people

* Create a routine of using one new word a day

* Create a routine of having a good thought every morning when you wake up

Routines are created by repetition in conjunction with action, emotion and physical movement. Any sort of new habit you wish to establish will have to be repeated several times before it becomes second nature. That's why the beginning days of a new reality are usually the most difficult. It does take some time to establish a new way of being, but once the effort is invested, the new track gains momentum and a drive of its own, taking less effort. Like pedaling a bike…the first few pedals are difficult, but once the bike starts rolling it gains a momentum of its own and no longer requires that initial effort. It's easier to establish new routines (and with them new realities) if you're accustomed to stopping, breaking or releasing your old routines. <u>Any undesired reality you're experiencing is a routine</u>. It consists of a set of pieces and patterns which are repeated and which together form a behavior. If you can break down a routine to single pieces they may be easier to release. All of your ways of being, moving, talking, behaving, and thinking are routines. **Any of these patterns can be interrupted at any time. By doing so, you create your reality.**

17. How Habits of Limitation are Created and Broken

Many long-term prisoners are reluctant to leave the prisons they have become familiar and comfortable with. Long-term captives or hostages can develop "Stockholm Syndrome" in which they begin to identify with and even fall in love with their hostage takers. Many would rather keep their familiar government in place, even if that government doesn't serve them, than to have a major overhaul. A baby elephant that is tied to a pole for a long time so that it can't move stays inert and immobile once it's freed from the rope. There's no rope, the elephant is free to leave, but it doesn't because it's become habituated to being limited. The same applies to humans. This starts at a very early age. If you lock a baby's belt in its stroller, after a few months you won't have to lock it anymore and the baby will still assume it can't get up. This particular limitation is a useful one, of course, but there are many thousands of limitations humans have learned that may not be quite so positive. My challenge as a reality creation coach is that **most people would rather maintain the status quo than change, even if they say they want to change**. I have met many who, with utmost conviction, insisted that they wanted to change, but when put to the test, averted and stifled that change with all their might. Consciously they'll say "yes, I want to change my reality", but subconsciously they would often really prefer things to remain static.

The baby elephant that has been taught to stay put, the prisoner who has been taught to be dependent on a prison, the child that has been taught not to move in the stroller…they would need to re-learn freedom step by step. One could guide the elephant around, showing it that it can indeed walk beyond its previous boundaries. One might place incentives outside of those boundaries. One might demonstrate other elephants walking outside of them.

To create a new reality involves a change and a possible **upset of the status quo**. That means, before things get better they sometimes have to get worse. Why? Well, if you're living in a building and would like a new building, you may have to tear the old one down. That's a lot of noise, commotion and debris at first. You're letting go of the status quo and going into the unknown. If you want things to stay the same, you're not going to experience a new reality anytime soon. So you have to ask yourself: **What do I want more, that things stay the same or that they change?** Or that they only slightly change? 'Once you have decided for a change, a number of things will have to be sacrificed, especially old beliefs and ways of seeing. Just like the baby elephant, there are a number of things you have been taught and have taught yourself, that no longer apply to your adult life. There are a few limitations that are useful for organized society to function, such as "thou shalt not kill", but beyond those basics you don't need most of your limitations. One of the main causes of not seeing possibilities is lack of imagination. That's why it's good to sometimes ask: "Who says it's to be the way it's? '", "Who says this has to be difficult?", "Who says I have to do my job in this inefficient manner?", "Who says a country has to be run either this or that way?", "Who says there's no way to rise above this issue?", "Who says X isn't possible?" When you realize the answer is "nobody", then with imagination, re-learning and courageous action old habits of limitation crumble.

The best way to keep your senses sharpened on the subject of habit and complacency is to regularly break your routines. Even a small act such as brushing your teeth with the other hand can set new patterns for the day.

18.   Creating Unstoppable Momentum

You can create unstoppable momentum by realizing that it takes about 21 days to create new habits. Thus, you can give yourself 21 day challenges consisting of some specific daily action you take every day for the next 21 days. You can increase that to a 30 day challenge or a 90 challenge or whatever feels empowering to you. If you repeat something for about 21 days the body/mind become accustomed to it as a "new fact of life" and a part of it goes on automatic. Putting positive behaviors on automatic is a good thing because less effort is required to do them. To get you inspired here are some examples of positive 21 day challenges:

* I'll do without my addiction for 21 days (examples: Coffee, Nicotine, Internet, TV, Pornography, Sugar, Alcohol, Carbs)

* I'll participate in sports for the next 21 days

* I'll find a new way to make money every day for the next 21 days

* I'll deliberately practice forgiveness, letting go of negativity and having a positive attitude for the next 21 days

* I'll meditate for the next 21 days

* I'll meet one new person every day for the next 21 days

* I'll choose a new skill and practice it every day for the next 21 days

You can use this technique to create any new habit. After the 21 days (or whatever period you define as your challenge), you don't have to do it quite as often, but should still do it on a regular basis…once or twice a week for example. The first 21 days are a booster rocket to create a "new normal" for yourself. If you miss a day you simply forgive yourself and continue the challenge the next day, perhaps adding an extra day to the challenge to make up for the lapse.

The truth is that you can fundamentally transform your life in a fairly short amount of time with a little intention, commitment and awareness.

You can make creating new habits (and thereby new realities) even easier by first creating the change within, on the mental plane.

Reality isn't what it was in the past. Reality is what I now decide it's.

19. Levels of Career

These are the general Levels of Freedom and Responsibility regarding a professional career. Don't take these levels to mean "from bad to good"- not all people are Entrepreneurs and not all people enjoy higher positions and the extended expectations that go along with them. Instead, this scale is to point out that if your soul's inclination is to be free, you'll tend to be unhappy as an employee, and if your soul's inclination is to be an employee (and hence in a closer relationship with others), you'll tend to fail or be unhappy working for yourself. The higher you go on this scale, the greater the personal freedom and rewards, but also the greater the responsibilities and risks.

1. Slave

2. Worker

3. Employee

4. Self-Employed

5. Business Owner or Entrepreneur

7. Free Person

These are general levels; of course one could make this scale more specific and note hundreds of sub-levels. There's nothing wrong with being a worker or employee if you're happy with that. Many would rather not go through the hassle of self-employment. The majority of my students are employees, self-employed and business owners. Those are the usual consciousness levels I address. Some are unemployed. "Unemployed" isn't shown on this scale because one could either be happily unemployed (level 7, the "Free Person") or unhappily unemployed. It's easier to find employment by increasing your skill, focus and consciousness level.

At the top of the scale are "free persons" who are either older or retired individuals, children or enlightened sages who have left the cycle of work and pay. Enlightened people receive what they need when they need it directly from the Universe and without effort. As this state is really rare, I think most people are better off targeting levels below that, such as becoming self-sufficient. Traditionally, not working is more associated with older, retired people, whereas the young have the energy to work and would be wasted sitting in a cave meditating all day.

20. Moving from Employment to Self-Employment

Employees who are unhappy no matter where they work simply don't belong at that level. As a coach I meet many people whose potential is higher and the constraints of their position bother them greatly. If the challenges of self-employment also bother them, they will be stuck between two levels. If you happen to be in this situation, you have two good options:

1. Make peace with your position of employment and to take that position to a higher version of itself.

2. Have the courage to build a position of self-employment.

The step from employment to self-employment is a leap of courage. One must have faith in invisible and unknown things – because it's unknown how it will turn out for you. The same leap is required to jump from Self-Employment to a level of Entrepreneurship, where you need to risk funds and possibly carry responsibility for other people. The leap of faith is required at every level.

No matter the career-level, it's important to trust in the Abundance of Source and that you'll always have what you need when you need it. If you believe there's something you can't afford or that you're dependent on someone financially, you're holding on to a belief-emotion construct that feels "smaller than" that reality. You need to ask yourself: "Do I want to become the person who is bigger than that? The person for whom such amounts of money are small?" It requires a shift in perspective from "smaller than X" to "I'm bigger than X". If you self-identify with the body-mind you'll feel smaller than most things. If you self-identify with the Universe or its Source, you'll feel bigger than most things.

For those who are certain they would like to move from employment to self-employment, the best path is as follows:

1. Enjoy your current position of employment as best you can (resistance will only prolong your being stuck there). See if you can take your current job to the next higher version of itself, including investing less time while still achieving the same results.

2. Choose a self-employed path that interests you and benefits others (money is only made if you offer what people really want). Begin while still in your old job. Self-employment doesn't begin "someday", it begins today. The only place from which you can affect your reality is today.

3. Take some time to feel the higher state.

If you wish to move from Self-Employment to either Entrepreneurship or your own Company, start delegating and employing, outsourcing and expanding. If you're afraid of or too inert to expand, that means you feel more comfortable at the level of self-employment and must either lose your fear to move up or accept your lot in life. **Great leaps in your career and abundance take place when you begin to dedicate your life to a higher purpose than yourself.**

21. Overcoming Unemployment

If you're unemployed and wish to become employed or self-employed you can start by no longer calling yourself "unemployed". When I was young there were times I was unemployed, but I said to myself: "I'm not unemployed, I'm just currently not interested in working for anyone unless a really good offer comes in". There were also times I was in great financial debt and trouble. In those times I confidently told myself: "My future self is bigger than this and can pay these bills". By adopting new beliefs and attitudes, I changed my destiny. If you're unhappily unemployed, you must list your inner beliefs and then list what you would prefer to believe instead – take charge of your mental conversation!

When I was invited to job interviews I learned early on that I could control the perception others had of me. The interviewer would ask me "What are your salary requirements?" If I could name a high number while keeping a straight face, that salary would be accepted If I named that number with doubt in my heart or while suppressing a laugh or getting fidgety or nervous, interviewers would perceive that "he isn't worth that kind of money".

As someone "unemployed" there are two good routes to go if you want to attract better conditions into your life: Get a job that is authentically good for you, or begin enjoying unemployment. If you can't find the right job immediately, you could at least enjoy the day, today, as best you can. Because enjoying the day, today, as best you can, lifts your mood. And when your mood is lifted, your mind is clearer. And when your mind is clearer you're more likely to attract the right people, the right circumstances, and, if you like, the right job.

Quit seeing yourself as poor. Others may be richer in money, but they are rarely rich in time. "I just don't have the time" is one of the mottos of the employed. But you're **rich** in time. This time of unemployment can be used for your long-term benefit. This time can be used to learn a skill which will later make you more money than temporary jobs would. You can use the time to enjoy things those caught in the 9 to 5 rat race can't enjoy. Make the best of what you already have (such as time) and you'll be given more.

A challenge isn't a boundary, it's a frontier. A boundary and a frontier aren't the same thing. A boundary is a limitation, a restriction, and is felt as such. A frontier is also a demarcation line but its purpose isn't to restrict but to set a baseline for expansion, to define a starting place from which to move forward, if you choose to see it that way. If you become aware of your lifestyle limitations that you blame on unemployment, most likely you're feeling this as a boundary or a restriction, accompanied by some contraction within your body. You may feel tight contraction in your chest, stomach or forehead. If you feel that, release your grip a little. Relax. Open up. Open up to the frontier. And imagine your situation as a frontier, as an opportunity for great things. Imagine embracing your situation because it's the perfect preparation for new times, embracing your situation because it's the perfect stepping-stone to what's next.. Unemployment taught you to be tough and self-reliant. That's the lesson of unemployment. You no longer need to be afraid of unemployment because you already are unemployed.

When you call yourself "unemployed" you're dragging up all kinds of unhelpful mental associations that are stored in mass-consciousness. What do you associate with being unemployed? Never mind. Don't tell me. And quit telling yourself too. Reframe your experience by referring to yourself as a "free person" or "self-employed". See yourself as self-employed. Tell others you're self-employed. This may seem unusual or unreal at first, but the more you define yourself in that way, the easier it becomes. "Unemployed" literally means that you don't have anything to do and that you don't have a purpose, but that's not true, is it? You do have talents, skills, interests, goals and purposes, and by cultivating them, you regain self-respect.

Don't look at what you're reaping today, because what you're reaping today is the result of times long gone. Look at what you're sowing today. *"Keep your face toward the sunshine, and the shadows will fall behind you"*.

22.   Dedicating your Life to a Higher Purpose

The path up the scale for the "already-successful" among you is to dedicate your life to a higher purpose than yourself. Being well-off means you have reached the pinnacle of personal development…but that can't be all there's, right? It isn't. It then becomes time to share your knowledge and skills with others and to create a legacy that will outlast your own lifetime. *"A society grows great when old men plant trees whose shade they know they shall never sit in"*.

At a certain level of maturity, you no longer seek applause and new material things from the world, you just want to do what is for people's highest good.

If you write down your values – the principles and ideas you stand for in life, you won't only imprint them to memory but also create a blueprint or map of self-guidance. If you write down your talents you'll imprint your memory with your worth and the contribution you're able to make (and will thereby also quit selling yourself for less than you're worth). Write down your goals and you'll have a general direction to target your attention. You'll start feeling more stable and determined. Instead of berating yourself for not having achieved past goals, re-define your goals and follow through on them.

Your soul's experiences are unique. That's why there's something that only you can give to the world. No one else can provide that. You can't be replaced. When you have lost your path in life you forget that you can provide that unique viewpoint and energy-field and you even sometimes forget what that unique viewpoint is. It's the combination of painful and beautiful experiences, observations, skills, genetics, and culture that make you unique. Find out what you're able to do better than anyone else and see if you can make a job out of that. And if you say "there's no such job", maybe it's up to you to create a new niche? Don't buy into society's belief that you're replaceable. Don't buy into the belief that you're just another number, just another face in the gray masses. You're a Spirit, you're Divine, you're capable. Reclaim your uniqueness and move forward in showing the world who you are.

23. Reality Creation for Companies

This is a Template you can use for Reality Creation work within groups and companies. Its purpose is to turn scattered focus and uncertainty into streamlined team focus – which can accomplish anything. The Template remains the same, no matter the size of the group or the scope of the Project.

Reality Creation for Groups differs from Reality Creation for the Individual. As more people, resources and money are involved, more specific outlines are required.

The Template:

WHAT?	WHY?	HOW?	WHO?	WHEN?
GOAL (What is wanted?)	PURPOSE (Why is it wanted?)	ACTION (What must be done to achieve it?	ROLES (Who will do what?)	TIME (When will each item be done?)

SUCCESS ATTRACTS SUCCESS

An Explanation of the Template:

1. WHAT?

The first step for any organization is to define its goals so that each and every team member or employee is clear about what is wanted. In this way each part of the company is focused on the end result rather than sidetracks or the unwanted. This may seem like a simple step but you'd be amazed at how many companies have lost track of what their actual goals are. Any organization that is experiencing problems needs to shift attention from problems to goals if it wishes to succeed. Every problem can be rephrased as a desire. Never begin with action steps or to-do lists, but with goals. The to-do-list is of no value if it's not based on a clear Vision of the end result. Furthermore, employees and team members need to be reminded of the organization's goals on a regular basis so that they know what Vision they are working for.

2. WHY?

Many skip this step. However, all action is driven by purpose, by emotion, by reasons-to-act, by motive, by the pursuit of more experience of life. Defining the WHY (rather than beginning with the "How", "Who" or "When") tends to boost people's ability to act. Why is this goal worthwhile? Why is it important? Who benefits? What is your benefit in working to achieve it? Why do you want that? Some object that the "why" behind goals is obvious or that earning a salary is enough reason or that "upper management has their reasons, don't ask so many questions". But as you'll see in the process of using this Technique, group members have a difficult time keeping their focus if they don't know why they are doing something. Even if you personally are able to maintain your focus without reminding yourself of the "why", don't assume everyone else is, too.

3. HOW?

In this step the team defines what specific tasks need to be done for the goal to become a reality. Having a good idea of what actions are required is a further action booster and can make it feel like you're halfway to the goal.

4. WHO?

This step is based on the previous one in that roles can't be defined without knowing the actions. Here you define who will do what. Each action is assigned to a specific person who is responsible for making it happen. Failing to assign responsibilities is one of the most common mistakes I see in the corporate world. Most conflicts I have seen within companies can be traced back to not knowing who is in charge of a certain action or job. If everybody is responsible, nobody is responsible. This step connects each action of list three with a name.

5. WHEN?

This step defines when each item should be completed. The purpose of this step is to give each group member an idea of how long an action should take. Of course each action may take longer or be finished more quickly, but giving team members a rough idea of what is expected will accelerate the process.

A Practical Example

A bicycle shop owner has been struggling. If he doesn't generate sufficient income in the next 2 months he will have to close the shop. His monthly expenses are $6,000, his income is $5,500. In the following example, note that the action steps in the table relate to the goal and the roles beside them, not to the purposes.

GOAL (What is wanted?)	PURPOSE (Why is it wanted?)	ACTION (What must be done to achieve it?	ROLES (Who will do what?)	TIME (When will each item be done?)
The bicycle shop flourishes more than ever. Existing customers return, the number of new	Because we care about bikes and we care about our jobs. Because people need to get out	Make the shop known to 5,000 more people by setting up signs in town, by handing out flyers in	Vincent (signs), Tony (flyers)	By March 31st

customers doubles. The shop's income increases by at least 50%, costs don't increase.	into nature more and exercise more	the next town, by using free Internet resources.		
	Because our service is fast and thorough.	Increasing our repair prices by 10%.	Julie (change price tags in computer)	By March 15th
	Because we have the best bikes in town.	Removing the 15% of our bikes that never sell and instead adding a few fashion- and speciality	Robert (purchasing dept.). Vincent, Tony, Julie, Steven (repair shop) and the Apprentices.	By April 15th

		bikes (Cruisers, Kids Bikes, Tricycles)		
	Because fuel prices are high and riding a bike to work saves money	Staging a bike-race for the town. Offering an additional accessory to each existing customer	Vincent responsible. All front shop employees (Mike, Tony,	By 15th of April for the first week of May Every Day
	Because more than 5000 people in this area rely on our services.			

I have used this template over and over again in various business situations and in many variations, tailor-made for the company I was coaching. The template can be made broader or more specific. A more specific version would, for example, involve a separate timetable in which the exact amount of hours worked each week on a specific action would be shown. Bigger projects would have the "Roles" section be more specific with team leaders re-assigning tasks to their respective teams.

In this example, taken from real life, the idea for staging a bike race in town was a new one that only came to mind once we started the process of writing it all down. The method is a facilitator of new ideas, of productive brainstorming. It later turned out that staging the bike race was the determining factor for an increase in their revenue and that some of the other actions didn't make that much of a difference. But that doesn't mean that the other actions were not worthwhile. Action that is taken with a clear intent, increases the company's energy field. This energy field then attracts new ideas. If the results don't come from those actions specifically, but from elsewhere, it was still the momentum produced by those actions that created the results. It's a mistake to assume that those actions were "not worth anything". The bike shop did indeed thrive and is still thriving today, so it doesn't matter which actions supposedly made a difference and which didn't.

Boosting the Method

A few details on how to boost the method and avoid typical mistakes. This method is for people who are inclined to accept reality as energy.

* Goals are Visions, not Actions. "Staging a Bike Race" isn't a "goal" even though one might say "It's our goal to stage a bike race for this town at the end of the month". It sounds silly in this context, but it's a distinction many don't make. If you ask them why they are doing that, they would state the actual goal: To save the company! To let the company flourish again! A goal is an end result. If you want to boost your method, state a visionary and inspiring end result as your goal and state it in the past tense, as if it's already happened. Do this only if you feel the group is open minded enough to follow the principle of "acting as if". In our example that would be: "The bike shop started flourishing

again. It grew faster than ever as the number of customers quadrupled and our income increased by more than 50%."

* The Purpose section may not seem to have merit from a purely intellectual standpoint, but as you yourself write down as many reasons as possible, you'll feel a slight emotional shift and it's that shift that makes all the difference and sets this method apart from conventional goal setting. If you wish to boost this step, not only answer the question "Why do we want this?" but also "Why do we believe it will happen?" The answers that would then arise might be things such as: "Because we are good at what we do". "Because springtime is in the air and people want to get on their bikes!", "Because we have been in business for 10 years, so another 10 years should be easily achieved". Having emotions and/or mental images associated with the goal is of great value for the subconscious.

* One way to boost the action section is by starting out with a free flowing brainstorming session where all ideas can be voiced without fear of ridicule. It's important that there's no censorship or evaluation of ideas at this stage, that even outrageous actions can be mentioned. All ideas are written down. After the first round is over, the group votes on the actions that feel, look and sound potent enough to be useful for achievement of the goal. Another way to boost the action steps part is through a process called backward planning. Backward planning involves writing down events and actions starting at the end result, then noting what happened right before the end result, and right before that, and right before that, etc., all the way back to the present. This type of Visualization can be extremely effective in inspiring teams to act. Another, even more advanced way to deal with actions is by including acting as if steps into the action list.

* You can boost the "Roles" section by creating new labels, mottos and identities for each team member or employee. "Julie – the numbers

Wizard", "Tony – the race maniac" and by then re-affirming and roleplaying that role throughout the working day. This method is for advanced practitioners only and won't be detailed here.

* Make the timetable more effective by making a schedule or calendar and assigning each action to a day or even an hour. For larger companies this would be a necessity.

Dealing with Obstacles and Objections to using the Method

*If there's disagreement on the goal, rephrase the goal or define a higher level goal (meta-goal) that every team member can agree with. You'll see that this meta-goal contains all the lesser goals people were disagreeing about. If Tony has the goal of having more customers and Vincent has the goal of having more fun in life, the meta-goal is to have fun with the bike shop and its customers. This is a simplistic example, I know, but the principle is the same every time: Find a goal that includes all lesser goals and that everyone agrees with. The final decision lies with the boss, of course.

* If the group lacks reasons, "whys", and purposes then it's either because people aren't accustomed to accessing their playful, emotional side or because the goal isn't inspiring enough to evoke reasons. Either change the goal or ask the group to be a bit more outrageous and poetic. Nothing is gained by holding back feelings or "keeping it rational". The rational mind comes into play later, with the action steps.

*If there's a lack of ideas on what actions to take, this can be traced back to mistakes in the first two steps. Any problem with one step is always connected to weakness in earlier steps. If no action ideas come to mind, it may be because the goal isn't tangible enough. In this case, rephrase the goal or choose one that is more tangible. Yes, the goal should be visionary and inspiring, but not so high in the clouds that it can't be grasped by each member of the group. Another reason no to-do list emerges may be reluctance to speak up or entertaining the idea that certain actions lead to certain results. In this case remind everyone that taking focused action itself is more important than what action that is. This concept is hard to grasp for people cut off from reality as energy. If so, find a more conventional way to make it clear that any sort of aligned action in the direction of a goal is helpful.

* The most common block on roles is that they aren't specifically assigned and that there's ambiguity on who does what. No matter how much trust there's at the outset of a project, this will eventually lead to doubt and blame. Make sure that everyone knows exactly what they are responsible for accomplishing. This will avoid a lot of confusion in the future. In some cases, employees don't want certain roles or prefer others. It's the job of the group's leader to assign roles, and most employees truly appreciate knowing exactly what is expected of them. The leading cause of de-motivation in employees is not knowing what they should or can do. In the rare cases in which an individual prefers a different role, check whether role-swapping with someone else is possible. It's the natural flow of the Universe that there's just the right role for each member of the team. Note that the roles are based on the action steps. Find out who is equipped to take certain actions and assign those actions to that person. Problems would have only arisen if Julie, the accountant, were asked to work in the repair shop and Steven, the repair shop guy was asked to work at the computer. All suffering in life arises from not being yourself, of being something different than what your you're good at. The tree grows naturally if it's allowed to be a tree.

* A common mistake in time planning is that it's done without specifically defining the goals, motivators, actions and roles. If time planning is taught or done in this way, it won't be useful. Project timelines can be thrown off by unforeseen circumstances, but these aren't really an issue if some leeway is built into the timeline and it's not

expected that everything rigidly comes to pass as planned. Nothing can ever be planned with precision and not all risks can be foreseen. Expecting precision at every step is a recipe for disappointment and ultimately failure. In my view, project planners that attempt to control and micro-manage every small detail of a project are mistaken and should focus on the big picture while the smaller pieces take care of themselves. Should an unforeseen circumstance come into play, the timelines are simply shifted – nothing more, nothing less. A more advanced approach to time planning, but one that is often not appropriate on a group level or in conventional business, isn't to define any specific timing but only the goals/motivations, actions and roles and allow the employees to do things in their own time. This is recommended with employees of a higher caliber. A variant would be to only define the end-date (as done in our example), without the specifics of when and how long the employee has to stay at work. I prefer this method because each person has their own speed and method. On a personal, non-group level I never define a timeline or end date for anything, I just but focus on the joy of action itself, leaving it up to life when it would like to show results.

2

HIGHER LEARNING

1. Creativity Training

This chapter teaches a series of methods to unleash the creative intelligence of the Supermind – deeper aspects of consciousness than the surface thoughts of everyday life. Don't use these techniques as chores but playful toys to experiment with, as the steward of your own mind.

"Lack of ideas" is the most prevalent modern illness. It isn't even recognized as such, as if the deep hypnosis of dullness we walk in, were somehow "normal".

Method 1: Notice what isn't Here, Notice what is Here

Apply For: More Ideas, Unsticking Attention from the Present Focus

Duration: A few seconds

We tend to put the most attention on what is right in front of us and on habitual mind content, not anywhere else. With this technique you **deliberately** notice what isn't there. What is someone **not** doing? What is an object **not**? What isn't in your surroundings? This is different from the mind's usual escapism from the present moment. It will enhance your Imagination. The exercise is best done on walks, during routine parts of the day (such as commuting to and from your job), at home, at work or anywhere else for that matter. If, for instance you're meeting someone supposedly "really important" you can release some of your attention stuck to them by remaining aware of all the other things happening that have nothing to do with that person. If you're watching "the biggest ball game in the world" in a stadium you can take a short break from being glued to the field by noticing what and who isn't there.

The polar-opposite of this technique is just as valuable and important in unleashing deeper qualities of the mind. It's "noticing what is there". You might say, "well, that's a silly exercise, because I do take note of what is around me", but do you really? The average mind is neither here nor there, neither properly focused on what isn't nor properly focused on what is but instead in some kind of vague mental purgatory of repetitive and pointless thought patterns. Bringing your attention more fully to the present by noticing what is here – right here in your surroundings – and what those things look like, sound like, feel like, smell like, and taste like in detail will brighten your perception and increase the quality of your experience, whatever that experience is.

Being able to shift your attention deliberately instead of by default is the key to genius.

Method 2: Setting Time Aside for Art

Apply For: More Creativity, Routine-Breaking

Duration: Hours

Use this method when you're creatively stuck due to repeating familiar patterns of thinking over and over.

You don't have to be a painter or artist to benefit from this, plenty of business people also find themselves stuck in a rut. When using this technique you retreat to a place you can be alone for a while and take various creative tools with you: Empty sheets of paper or a canvas, paint, brushes, pencils, pens, markers. If you want you can also take musical instruments or clay, wood, wires, etc. with you to make sculptures. And then you simply **create, create, create**. For hours, you condition your mind to create and come up with "something out of nothing". The aim here isn't to create works of art that others will like, but to get the subconscious into creative mode. Go crazy with what you're creating. If writing is your preference, instead of painting or sculpting, simply write and write and write whatever comes to mind. Coax yourself into writing on topics you have never written about. Another thing you could do during this art time is to build models – such as model airplanes, model trains, and model buildings.

If you like you can also create an artwork that displays either a particular problem in your life or a particular vision you have in your life.

Create and create and create non-stop until you feel that you have overcome your frustration, your block, your dullness and **feel very alive**. Awaken that boundless creative spirit you had in childhood. Unleash the creative intelligence of the Supermind.

Method 3: Exposing Presuppositions

Apply For: Breaking Negative Beliefs, Mind Opening

Duration: A few minutes to an hour

Step 1: Write a list of your presuppositions (assumptions about the world and life that you don't question). These are things you think are so obvious you haven't given them a second thought. Some of your presuppositions are true, but not all of them are. List especially your presuppositions that begin with *"I can't…", "I should…" and "I must…"* as well as the presuppositions about *"how things work"* (such as "It's easy to gain weight but more difficult to lose it" or "I can only succeed if I'm nice to everybody") and also your assumptions about what you think others expect, need or want. In reality you can't really know what others expect, need or want. For example, certain neighbors never invited me to their place because they *presupposed* I didn't have time for them. It was only when I invited them over, that their presupposition was cancelled.

Finding presuppositions to list is sometimes not that easy because they are like sunglasses you look **through** rather than glasses you look **at**; they're the filters for your life experience. Because you believe them to be true, you fail to question and look into them. Merely listing such deeply held beliefs **as** beliefs (rather than truths) will begin to neutralize their effect on your reality.

Another example: I was chatting with a distant relative of mine who wanted coaching from me but was reluctant to ask for a long time. I never thought of offering him coaching because of three presuppositions I held: a) He can't afford my coaching b) He's not interested in my topics c) He doesn't have the drive to implement what I teach him. All three presuppositions turned out to be **completely false**. It turned out he could easily afford it (despite the rusty car he drove) and he was very much into these topics (despite never talking about them).

Step 2: Challenge each item on your list. Ask questions such as **"Is this really true?"**, **"What if this isn't true?"** and especially **"What would I do if this were not true?"**

Step 3: Go and make it happen (this last step is the essential step). You'll be astonished at how many of your assumptions turn out to be untrue. A student of mine, for instance, had written a book. I said to her "Get an endorsement from a celebrity/expert in your field". Her *presupposition* was that none would be available or respond to her request. She dropped that assumption, acted on my suggestion, and did get an endorsement.

You can look at anything with fresh eyes anew, unblocking your mind from repetitive surface layer thoughts. When you do, more creative thought emerges.

Method 4: Roleplaying

Apply For: Perspective Shifting, new ideas, a new mood

Duration: Minutes to Hours

This enhanced creativity method will give you ideas and insight you would have never come up with in ordinary thinking.

You can access or "channel" higher levels of information by shifting your identity. As "yourself" you have certain habitual ways of thinking and seeing the world, producing similar ideas over and over and over. Shift to another identity/persona/role and you instantly receive **fresh input.** The mere shift in attention allows for new ideas to flow in, rapidly unblocking any creative stagnation you may have had.

Step 1: Write down a question or issue on which you'd like new ideas.

Step 2: Write down the names of various people you admire and respect (as well as some you don't admire and respect, but whose opinion would be useful to hear).

Step 3: Imagine asking each of the people from your list the question. Imagine being them and answering from their perspective. **How would they answer?** Going through each person in turn, complete your list. Don't filter or censor yourself, just write down what comes to mind. You can filter and discard what you don't like later.

The personas you write down can be celebrities, experts in their field or other people whose views you value. Have fun with this and see what comes up. This may very well be the most powerful brainstorming technique in the world, so make use of it!

10 Ways to Boost your Creativity

1. Conflict is Creative

A smart executive not only employs people who are similar to him but those dissimilar. A smart lover isn't looking for a partner similar to him/her but one that is different. A smart professor isn't seeking only agreement but disagreement. There's nothing more uncreative and dull than a room in which everyone agrees with everyone else. Some amount of conflict, competition and adversity breeds creativity. That's why the children of parents who come from two very different cultures usually have a creative touch. The conflict of two cultures within them breeds new ideas or a "third culture" that was unknown before. As an individual, if you only read books you know you'll agree with, you learn nothing new.

2. Don't Wait, Create

When you see that life isn't about what you get but about what you *put out* and that you can *create* instead of wait, you have an attitude that breeds creativity. The world owes you nothing. You don't have to wait on a boss, colleague, paycheck, applause, a spouse, the right time, the right mood, the right place, the right meal…all those things are only excuses and distractions. You don't have to wait for **anything** to get started. Just get started with **something**, no matter what, and see where it takes you. **Ready, Fire, Aim.** Lower your expectations of where the initial step is supposed to take you and allow yourself to be surprised by where you end up.

3. New Actions create new Thoughts and vice-versa

You will notice that when you go to a place you have never been before, your thinking changes. Most people think more creatively on vacation because they are seeing and doing new things and behaving in new ways. If you wish to be a more creative person, do new things and go to new places now and then. Walking on new sidewalks you have never walked before opens new pathways in the mind. New thoughts create new actions and new actions create new thoughts. It also matters **how** you perform the actions. You probably shower every day, but have you ever sung while showering? You probably drink tea, water or coffee every day, but when is the last time you only drank and nothing else? Slight changes in routine go a long way to open your mind to allow new data to stream in. Some of the best ideas and inventions in human history happened in moments the inventors were doing something outside of their usual routine.

4. Make New use of Old Things

Creativity isn't only creating new things but also seeing the old things in new ways, being able to make use of old things in different ways and combining old things with new things or old things with other old things in a way they have never been combined before. The world is abundant with resources that can be used in many more ways than passive people think. In chemistry, when two elements are put together, the resultant third compound is often something entirely more useful than the two original elements on their own.

5. To succeed in one thing, try ten things

Do people that constantly fail at new things annoy you? These are actually creative people that will succeed one day unless they are talked out of it by people who they annoy. Generate hundreds of ideas, try many of them. Most will fail, even if they are brilliant. Some of them will stick and succeed. Remember, the best hitters in the Baseball Hall of Fame only succeeded 30-40% of the time. The same is true of people like Edison or Tesla, who generated many failed ideas and inventions, but did get a few major breakthroughs right. Be like a little child that tries out everything in order to learn what works and what doesn't. Even if your high creativity doesn't immediately support you to make a living or earn money, it usually does pay off long-term. Trust in the long-term process, don't judge by the snapshot of the day. Both success and failure are better than inaction. He who makes no mistakes, makes nothing.

6. Disregard Talkers, be a Doer

Most people talk about what they are going to do, what they plan to do, what they want to do, what they think others should do. Disregard them. You don't need talkers, you need walkers. Creativity doesn't mean to run around with a bunch of ideas and talk about them, creativity means bringing them to life, trying them out for real, applying the ideas, making them physical, doing them! People who continually talk about what happened or will happen are a distraction to the creative process. Find yourself doing things instead of talking about doing things. Don't expect people to praise or applaud everything you do. Don't seek confirmation or agreement from everyone when you do something new. Some tend to ridicule what is new.

7. To be Unconventional, have a firm grasp on the Conventional

An airplane takes off to fly from a stable platform. The Harlem Globetrotters created something new, innovative and creative with their comical style – but they had a firm grasp on normal basketball before they did so. Apple created something fresh and innovative with its iPhone a decade ago, but Apple had a firm grasp on conventional cell phones, programming, software and computers before it did so. Personally, I wrote a groundbreaking book titled "Parallel Universes of

Self" in which I introduced my "Reality Creation" views. I had a firm grasp on traditional psychology, business coaching and eastern meditation practices before I did so. Being knowledgeable in your field will give you the security, the safety net to venture forward into the unknown and present something brand new. If you create something that didn't exist before, people might not understand it at first. They will counter your new ways with conventional and old ways. But if you have a firm grasp and understanding of the old ways, you'll win the argument and be able to convince them of something new.

8. Physical Movement, Mental Silence Activity breeds creativity. Leaving your comfort zone or even adding some deliberate discomfort can get you going. "A little discomfort" doesn't mean you have to go from crisis to crisis, but just a little hunger is a good thing for creativity. As you aspire for something higher, ideas come up. As you dance, sing, paint, write, make, physically move or work out, new ideas come up. I get my best ideas when I let go of everything and just get on my bike, riding my bike, letting go of all impatience, just riding. The state of physical movement while the mind is relaxed is one of the best states for receiving creative inspiration. Dancers know this. Athletes know this. Training your creativity can be done by just writing or just painting or just creating physical things. You swim not by reading about water but by jumping into it. Not by preparing for the swimming pool but by jumping into it. Not by thinking about which end of the pool you enter, but by jumping into it. Not by standing beside the river but by jumping into it. And as you jump into it, its current, its flow takes you…to a new place.

9. Music, Art, Writing, Paining, Dancing, Photography

Listening to music changes your frequency, allowing for the influx of new ideas. Actively painting, writing, dancing, photography or a number of other traditionally creative acts naturally train your creative muscle.

Any of these activities (and dozens more) will benefit you in any other area of life as well. Because of the change in brain frequency, your behavior at home or on the job or anywhere else changes too.

10. Sensory Deprivation

An ancient technique to boost creativity is to deprive yourself of one of the senses to create a new influx of ideas. You might blindfold yourself for a day and only perceive the world through hearing and touching, or you might wear earplugs for a day to see what comes up in a silent space. Depriving yourself of something for a period of time creates a vacuum which **something new** must fill. One of the biggest creativity boosters is to deprive yourself of television for a while :-)

Loving to Play

"We don't stop playing because we grow old, we grow old because we stop playing".

Playing games teaches your body/mind everything there's to know about life. Just like any board or sports game, the game of life has pre-set rules and boundaries. Within those rules and boundaries you're free to decide to do whatever you want. To make it more exciting, there are numerous rulebooks, some of them full of misinformation. Some people seem to arrive on earth already blessed with a talent at the game. Some struggle. Proficiency at the game is measured on many levels.

If you have the idea that life is serious and extremely stressful, **let go of it now** and embrace life as a game. Instead of demanding that the game be this or that way, strive to get better at playing it. Instead of suggesting that the game is a conspiracy, improve your game skill. Losing a few rounds isn't the problem. The question is **how you deal with losing**. The game already exists. You wake up into it every day. How are you going to deal with it?

In any type of teaching, course, or seminar, instruction without playfulness or games teaches nothing. I play ball games, board games and activity games in many of my courses. Most people respond to them well, saying, "Wow…I haven't played in such a long time, I was really missing that". Why do so many stop playing when they grow up? Because they forgot that life is a game and that the game of life can be played. Ask yourself whether you're a piece on the board or the player of that piece, whether you're body or spirit, whether you have a narrow view or a bird's eye view.

A small number of people are so far removed from play that they don't even understand the point of playing games in a workshop context. The way people deal with the games is also the way they deal with life in general. Some don't want to play the game. Some are terrified to play it. Some are eager to play it. Some play it with ease. Some have chosen the wrong game to play, some have chosen the game that is just right for them.

I have considered conducting an entire course through playing games; maybe someday I'll. Whether they realize it or not, what people really want is to test their skills and master their skills through practice. What they really want is to laugh and have fun with others. **What they really want is to play**.

The lesson here is that the next time someone invites you to play, don't reject it because you think it's a waste of time. Play is what your **soul** came here for. Go have some fun.

The Spiritual Secrets of Dance Choreography

Your body movements summon, channel, form, bind, focus and break strands of life-energy.

Dance is a ritual that activates various types of spiritual life force. When the uninitiated watch or participate in a dancing performance they are unaware of the implications and physical reality effects of various movement combinations. Those combos can open and close various gates to spiritual realms.

If this sounds obscure keep in mind that nearly every ancient culture used dance and movement for these purposes. Sufi Dervishes dance to reach an altered state. Tai Chi artists move to achieve an altered state. Indigenous tribes dance to achieve an altered state. That's what dance is all about, even if modern society pretends one can go dancing without a fundamentally spiritual context. Most of the dancing in modern clubs and discos is done randomly, without deliberation and purpose – and still serves to alter the dancer's state. The ancients however, danced to bring about specific results. They may have danced for rain, for sunshine, for a person's healing, for the demise of an enemy or to summon various forces to carry out tasks.

To demonstrate the relationship between physiological movement and psychological state, try the following classic NLP exercise:

State an intention for a state you would like to have, such as **"I'm poised, strong and confident"**.

Right after you state it, take a deep breath and make a hand, arm or body movement such as snapping your finger, knocking on your chest three times or nodding your head. Any deliberate action will do. Repeat voicing the statement, taking a breather and making the same movement several times, until the movement is associated with the state. From now on, anytime you wish to remember (re-activate) the state, **doing the body movement once** will be enough. What previously took 15 minutes to practice can now be achieved in a few seconds.

If something as small as this has such a strong effect, you can imagine how much more is possible through dancing with more intricate choreography. One dance-pattern performed with concentration by a professional group has the power to emotionally shift entire masses of people for the better (or worse). Group choreography can, if you're open to it, hit you like a rippling wave of ecstasy, even more so if you're the dancer (giver) yourself. The mind is like a sponge and you can program anything to it with emotion. A state of arousal is a good time to program new beliefs. Dancing is a good way to achieve a state of arousal.

The Advantages of the Self-Taught

I have no formal education in anything at all. One might assume that's a big disadvantage when navigating through life. But I didn't say I have no education. I said I have no **formal** education.

Allow me to explain: The other day I played table tennis. What made the event special is that I hadn't played table tennis in 20 years! Despite that gap, I won 8 games to 4. I was again surprised by the timelessness of the subconscious – that it could retain a skill that hadn't been used in 20 years. But there was something more interesting: My opponent appeared to be playing "by the book", the way one normally plays table tennis. Because I never had any formal training and had never learned to play "the right way", my style of playing was odd, less predictable, and more creative. His skill was superior to mine but because I wasn't shooting as he might expect, I had an advantage in the game. He sometimes tried to get into a mode of playing as learned in formal training where you hit wide shots back and forth. Having never been in formal training I wasn't familiar with the pattern and never went along with it. I was freestyling! The ball continually landed somewhere other than he assumed it would, and I kept winning.

This got me thinking about Autodidactism. I've met self-taught photographers, self-taught programmers, self-taught entrepreneurs, self-taught musicians, self-taught soccer professionals ("street players") and in every instance I was impressed by their style and creativity. Lacking formal and standardized procedures, their learning will have come from a wide variety of sources, books and teachers as well as from intuition based on experience. Intuition was their greatest teacher. As a result, their styles are more individual and surprising.

I'm not minimizing the value of formal education which has its own advantages. It can provide a strong basis from which to develop one's own style. Not all self-taught people are geniuses, to say the least. And not all things should be self-taught…flying airliners or performing surgery for example:-) Still, the advantages of putting aside formal instruction and going by raw and direct intuition can be enormous – no matter what field you work in.

I know a self-taught electric guitar player who does things with his guitar that nobody else does. He says he taught himself to play with the help of YouTube videos and then just added his own ideas. Doing things that aren't formally taught in music school means he produces amazing sounds that nobody else has. In combination with a few effect tools I know nothing about, he has played sounds to me I wouldn't even recognize as coming from a guitar.

Being self-taught is common among well known entrepreneurs. That's because good business relies on intuition. It doesn't always lend itself to standardized steps that apply universally. You can go to Business School and follow what you learned there and that will give you some amount of expertise, but the more fertile parts of the field can only be accessed by those who develop their own game. You're more likely to win when you invent the game.

What I teach – Reality Creation – also works well when done in your own unique style inspired by your Higher Self. It can't be taught. When I teach Reality Creation Techniques I expect people to develop their own variations over time. That doesn't mean you have to reinvent the wheel. In any field, when you develop your own unique style you naturally also check out what past masters did and learn from their wisdom. From that, you can extrapolate something new. That's how the Universe expands.

2. Four Stages of Competence

Modern cognitive research observes four stages of competence. The conventional method of learning new abilities is to go through these four stages. One could also term them as follows:

1: I don't know that I don't know (Unconscious Incompetence) 2: I know that I don't know (Conscious Incompetence) 3: I know that I know (Conscious Competence) 4: I don't know that I know (Unconscious Competence)

For example, when you learn to drive a car, at the first stage you may be seeing cars drive by and be a passenger in a car, but haven't considered getting a drivers license, have not yet considered your own ability to drive a car. At the second stage you have just started your driving lessons and have, for the first time, taken the driver's seat and realize how little you know about driving. In the third stage you're proud and grateful to be able to drive a car but it still takes a lot of focus and awareness to get it all right. And in the last stage you're a seasoned habitual driver and don't have to pay attention to every detail of driving.

When we say "Ignorance is Bliss" we are referring to the innocent stage of "Unconscious Incompetence". Never having thought about a certain ability, it doesn't bother us that we're unable to do it. "Stress" is usually at stage two, when we become aware of our incompetence (because some have been conditioned to feel pain or shame regarding their inability to do something, they prefer remaining in stage one regarding that subject). Those who push on and learn whatever they are incompetent at finally reach stage three which is probably the most happy and gratifying state – that of having mastered a new skill, a new competence and all the new viewpoints, perceptions and emotions that go along with it. With every new competence, new aspects of the world are noticed. However, this stage may still require a lot of energy to maintain, it may require focus and sustained action to habituate. Finally you reach the final stage in which the learned ability becomes automatic and unconscious. It becomes easy for you. You don't have to focus and invest energy to maintain it. It's "natural" to you. Others marvel at how easy it seems to be to you. By this time, the subject may have lost its fascination and excitement to you. You're able to teach it to others, you're able to demonstrate it, but your true interests lie elsewhere…in areas where you have not yet achieved competence.

An example from my own life: People keep sending me books and websites on the topics I teach (consciousness, reality creation, self-improvement). Not a week goes by where I don't receive some kind of book I'm supposed to read. They are then surprised that I appear to have little interest in reading these books. Why? Because I have been *teaching* the topics for 25 years. I have integrated them at a level of "unconscious competence". My real interests lie elsewhere. I have become confident in these subjects to the point where they are *complete* for me. So the only thing left to do with them is to teach them. My private interests, however, is in everything *I don't yet know*. Looking into the unknown facilitates consciousness expansion and helps maintain a flow state.

Of course there's a faculty of consciousness that bypasses the 4 Stages of Learning: It's called Intuition. Intuition gives you a basic "Unconscious Competence" over all-that-is in the Universe. Intuition gives you the capacity to learn almost anything.

This universal unconscious competence that is called "Intuition" is summoned when you **do and experience something for the first time**. This is why, when learning something new, I don't recommend first reading about it, hearing about it, talking about it, and studying about it, but instead to try and do it. You can then later formally go up the 4 Stages of Competence, but it will be much easier for you because you already have a good experiential sense of it. An example of this: I learned windsurfing about a decade ago. Before taking formal classes to get my license, I hung out with windsurfers at the beach. I got on a board myself, imitated the expert windsurfers, and familiarized myself with the scene. I did a lot of things right intuitively, because I was under no pressure to perform or pass tests. By the time I took formal classes I already understood the subject at an experiential level, my body-mind had already learned it, so learning the theory became much easier. I'm a great fan of "practice before theory", which contradicts the prevalent "theory before practice" paradigm we are living in. The "theory before practice" doctrine of universities and formal education facilities really slows learning down, in my view. If you want o learn something quickly – Ready, Fire, Aim.

3. You have the Capacity to Learn Almost Anything

A lady I know told me of a time during the Bosnian war where she was working as a nurse for the wounded. At one point she found herself in a precarious situation with everyone around her wounded and no help or protection in sight. The war had taught her that in order to survive and help others she needed a calm mind. A calm mind is a clear mind. There was a broken CB radio nearby. She had never handled one, nor used (let alone repaired) anything similar. But by calm examination alone and by what her subconscious had picked up from others, she managed to repair the device and use it to call for help.

There was a nice but unused bike in the basement of my building. A broken bike isn't quite as precarious a situation as that of the Bosnian nurse facing possible death, but the story she told me inspired me to fix the bike myself. My earlier default behavior had been to just take a bike to the repair shop. I wasted plenty of time and money in the past by being too lazy to just **look**. Because we don't just **look**, we often miss how easy things are to learn and do. The bike was easily fixed, even though before, I had so little confidence in my ability to fix bikes that I wouldn't even consider it. Of course, bicycles are simple inventions and anybody can actually fix them, but the truth is that most things are simpler and easier than generally assumed. The nurse needed no lengthy training program, no technical education, no certificate, no degree, not even a trial run to repair and use the radio. This is why living from intuition, rather than the intellect, is much easier. If you're in touch with your intuition and you're in a job interview and they ask you "can you do this?" and "can you do that?" you would just say, "yes!" because you know how quickly you can learn whatever they are asking of you.

You have the capacity to learn almost anything. If you're without mental resistance or fear, not only can you learn almost anything but you only need to see it done once or twice before you can do it yourself. In other words, you need less repetition and hours of learning if you maintain a calm state of mind.

As a teenager I wasn't a good learner. My grades at school were mediocre. My mind was usually wandering and I wasn't interested in any of the subjects being taught. Later, in my twenties, I increased my ability to learn quickly by focusing on the things that interested me, using the powers of fascination and amazement to guide me. By my thirties, I had gained peace of mind. In this state I could learn almost anything whether I was interested or not. My journey of learning went through three stages that are typical in people who seek to raise their consciousness:

Stage 1: Life of Resistance

Stage 2: Follow your Bliss

Stage 3: Unconditional Love

In the first stage of awakening we realize how we aren't enjoying anything, neither this nor that feels good. Then we make a deliberate effort to do the things we love and enjoy. So instead of looking at what isn't wanted and liked, we look at what is wanted and liked. Instead of looking at resistance, we look at things where there's no resistance. Finally, in Stage 3, we not only "do what we love", but love what we do, enjoy what we do. At this point the well being no longer comes from the object, it comes from within. The three stages could also be expressed in this way:

1. Minus-Minus

2. Minus-Plus

3. Plus-Plus

At minus-minus everything is seen as difficult or problematic. Having a job is troublesome, not having one is troublesome. Being married is troublesome, not being married is troublesome. Going to the party is a problem, not going is a problem. At the second stage, attention is deliberately shifted from minus to plus, to the things you like and to things with little or no resistance. And at the third stage, everything you do or everything that happens to you is seen in a positive light. Having a job is great, not having one is great too because it gives you more time. Being married is great because it provides intimacy and familiarity, not being married is great because it provides freedom. Going to the party is great because you meet new people, not going to the party is great because you get to relax. Even ill health or financial-crisis is labeled positively, as in "this is a lesson on what's important in life" or "this is a lesson to awaken", etc.

In a plus-plus state you have the capacity to learn almost anything. You're able to think and do more than you know if you can think more simply. For example, many probably assume they could not build and run a profitable boutique or even build their own website, but if you're reading these words, you can. If you think more simply, calmly and clearly (these three go hand in hand) What is a boutique actually? What is it really? Well, it's just..

a) a room;

b) Hangers with clothes hanging on them;

c) Price tags on the clothes;

d) a cash register;

e) a storage room;

f) some accounting work; and

e) some decoration work

That's all it really is. How easy to set one up! Get a room, some hangers, clothes and price tags and you're done. The secret to its success lies in how well this same old set-up is presented and where it's presented. I say "you can learn almost anything" because most things are much, much more simple than they appear to be. You might say…"but accounting! I know nothing about accounting!" To which I say: Yes you do. You know everything about accounting if you simplify your thinking. Accounting is spending money and making money and comparing the two. So you spend $1 to buy a dress and sell it for $3. That leaves you with $2. That's accounting. And then you say "Yes, but I have no training as a salesperson! I can't do this!", and then I say: Yes you can. Every conversation you have ever had with anyone, is trying to "sell" a certain idea, viewpoint, suggestion, or response to someone. Everyone is "selling" all the time. And then you say "But what if the shop fails? Times are hard!" At this point I start to yawn, because the person I'm talking to is more interested in creating limitations and negative beliefs than in doing something.

"Well, it's not as easy as you think! I've tried opening my own shop before and I failed!" someone recently told me with a frustrated look on his face. He wasn't willing to see that the shop lacked anything interesting, useful or even unique and that he opened it in a place with no other shops. Opening a shop where there are no other shops isn't wise. I won't bother to explain why, it becomes obvious to people who take the time to just **look and learn.** Quick learning is linked to calmness, slowing down, clarity, simplicity, interest, intuition, attention. And to knowing that all things in life are actually simple, even if they are made to look or appear complicated.

4. Why it's not only OK but Perfectly Good to be WRONG

Humans are essentially interested in finding out what is true and good. Once they find what they think is true and good, they tend to become defensive about it. Admitting ones mistakes can feel embarrassing, so many would rather stint their growth than to say, "I was wrong".

"No, don't tell your readers you were wrong about that! It undermines your authority as an author and coach!" someone once told me about something I wanted to publish. I said:

"Don't you see that's the whole problem with the world? People preferring to look good and feel good at all times and at the expense of truth? This is what politicians do all the time. So that it doesn't "undermine their authority" they feel compelled to lie"

I've been wrong about hundreds of things in my life. For example, at the age of 23 I wrote a book called "Astral Travel" (have your energy body leave their physical body to travel around) in which I claimed that *anyone* could astral travel *any time*. I was wrong! I wrote that out of ignorance of various puzzle pieces I gained years later. Not everyone can astral travel any time; if they could, they would. All of my writings, words and actions contain some errors, omissions and mistakes. There's no merit in pretending that humans are infallible. The fallibility of mankind has been known for millennia and described in all poetry, philosophy, religion and psychology. It's the basis of the wonderful tragedy and comedy called life.

Conventional education teaches children the false belief that making mistakes is "not good". Mistakes are punished. So mistakes are avoided and kids try to be "good boys" and "good girls". However, if this mode of education is *overdone,* it can become too restrictive. If I'm not allowed to make mistakes, then I better not **explore, try out and risk** either. But if you don't try or risk anything, you can't experience much of anything, much less success and life results. The most successful people in the world are also the ones who make the **most** mistakes. The best example is a baseball hitter, who makes hundreds of outs in the process of getting a hit that wins the championship, or inventors who failed hundreds of times before they broke through on one invention. But if mistakes are seen as "bad" or reasons to get angry or discouraged, those who make them as a normal part of life won't move forward to embrace even more mistakes and their opposite polarity – successes. **Success and Failure are two sides of the same coin, the go together. If you want one, embrace the other.** You can't have a mountain without a valley. Don't fall into the trap of thinking, "I mustn't make any more mistakes and at my level I mustn't show any weakness" or the even worse mistake of claiming you have no weaknesses or mistakes. Instead, fully confront your weaknesses, admit to them and then invest some conscious effort in correcting them. Otherwise you'll be "right" all your life, but you won't necessarily be any wiser or more successful

5. Experiential Learning

Tell me and I'll forget. Show me and I might understand. Involve me and I'll remember" – Chinese Proverb

Swimming is best learned in the water, not in a classroom or movie theater. Relating to other human beings is best learned among human beings, not as a couch potato. Rapid learning happens through experience. Studies conducted by myself and others show the following:

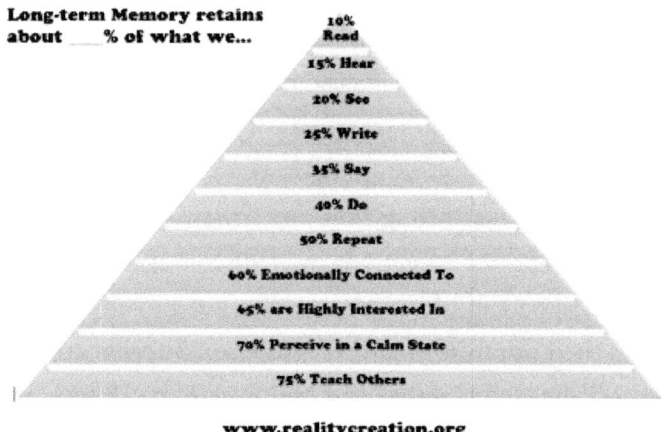

In this Information Age we are so overloaded with data that these numbers are actually dropping. The other day I read a famous marketer recommending: "If you want your blog to succeed, you should write at least 7-10 blog posts a day". I chuckle at these sorts of suggestions because they represent hyperactive, ADHD-like overload. 7-10 blog posts a day? Yeah right. That may be good for folks looking for news-like distraction, but it does nothing for building knowledge. Because:

"Where there are many priorities, there are no priorities".

Not setting priorities for focusing hinders learning. I'd wager that, long term and on average, we retain no more than 5% of what we read. But long term retention of information can be increased if you prioritize, repeat, feel emotionally stimulated or connected to what you're reading, hearing or seeing, if you're highly interested or invested in a subject, when you have a relaxed state of mind while learning and if you apply what you learned.

"Unapplied knowledge is no real knowledge at all"

Let's take the articles I have posted on my website as an example. If you read most of them, I predict you'll be lucky to retain 5% of what I have written. Because the mind perceives internet text as less real than a book or newspaper which is held and touched, the number further drops to about 2%. If the information is read when one is stressed, retention is no more than 1% and the applicability of this information goes toward 0%.

If you re-read material, your retention could increase to 10%. Your memory is also increased if you read the articles in a slow and conscious manner and think about specific ideas on your own. Retention rises further if you take some of these articles "for checking" – you try out, or apply them of your own volition. There's another elevation of memory when you teach them to others or creatively invent your own versions and ways-of-expressing what is written here. If all this is factored in, your retention goes up to 80% or even 90% and your time spent reading a book or website is well spent. If it appears as if you didn't have time to fully experience certain concepts, you should at least write down key ideas you read about. When I read a book I retain more of it by first highlighting important sections (but not too many, prioritization is key) and then writing some of those sections out in a word file. This way I'll have a 20% memory of a book and a 50% memory of its highlighted parts. Now if I also go ahead and implement some of what I read in the book, it's stored.

It's said, "a picture is worth a thousand words". And I agree with that and add: An experience is worth 10,000 words". Anyone who attends a live seminar on these subjects, will have 80% retention or even higher.

An experience is something you go through in real life, something you feel and do. Overcoming one real life challenge with **your own ingenuity** is worth a hundred books. Of course people have been conditioned to consume more than create. They'll consume a movie, which is a good visualization tool, but you should remember that it's doing all the visualizing for you. You're not developing your own Imagination while watching. The only people developing their inner powers are the director, scriptwriter and actors. The Internet is a good information tool but you should remember that it's doing all the thinking for you. You're not developing your own quality thoughts while browsing.

6. Information vs. Transformation

A donkey carrying a bag of books is still a donkey. We live in the Information Age where it's said that "knowledge is power", but there's something more powerful than information, and that's transformation.

I realized this again in a recent Reality Creation course where there were people who had read numerous books and articles – they had all the information – but had yet to experience transformation in some areas of their life. They finally experienced transformation when they created new experiences rather than repeating or sharing what they knew. Knowledge isn't power, applied knowledge is power. Transformation follows action.

One healing, one tangible improvement, one result can surpass the knowledge of 1,000 books. You can have all the knowledge in the world, but will you be able to remember and apply it when it's most needed?

Consider a glass of wine. Reading about it, talking about it, speculating over it, theorizing over it, or building hypothetical constructs over it can't actually substitute for just tasting it. As you taste it you'll truly know the wine, in the real sense of the word "know". And as you taste it slowly and mindfully, you'll know it even more. If mere information were power or knowledge, then Wikipedia and Google would have made everyone rich, healthy and happy. Life transformation is a matter of choosing what knowledge to acquire and then putting it into practice. With mindful practice, anything can be achieved.

7. Enlightened Education

Our unenlightened school system emphasizes information over experience. Too much time is spent feeding all sorts of information to children regardless of whether it's important, applicable, or relevant to our times. A "good student" is one who can copy and memorize what the teacher said and repeat it in tests. Very little time is spent with the process of learning itself, with **learning about learning**. My teachers gave me many things to pay attention to – **not once did they instruct me in the process of focusing attention itself**. Very rarely did a teacher give us the choice of what to focus on by saying: "Children, would you rather look at this subject, or this other one?" Not once were we taught that there are different methods of learning and storing information in our minds. Hardly ever did we go outside and directly experience the subjects discussed. Unenlightened education is similar to reading a book about bicycling without actually getting on a bike, reading a book about fruits without actually eating them, reading about history without actually co-creating it, reading about business without doing it, reading about the body without exploring it, reading about other cultures without seeing them. Information about something isn't the thing itself, the map isn't the territory. Too much information without experience is fundamentally disempowering because children learn to replace information with life itself. Enlightened education would therefore include more physical activity and "going places", not spending 99% of the time sitting on a chair looking at a blackboard or book. That doesn't have to cost very much; I can go outside and actually smell the flowers depicted in the schoolbook, and I'll know more about the flower than a thousand books can tell me. Why do most children look forward to the school bell? Because they get to go outside and experience life instead of theorizing about it.

Enlightened education teaches about Love. Isn't love one of the basics of life? Why isn't it taught in school? Isn't the purpose of school to teach about life? In my time in school there was no mention about the sensations of falling in love, no mention of how to handle relationships with others, no mention of the different types of relationships, no mention of sexuality. That's why there's a massive industry of books and adult seminars on Love – because nobody was taught anything about it in school!

Enlightened education teaches about money. Isn't money one of the things that makes the world go round? I'm shocked at how little people know about money when they leave school…and even college. Why is almost everyone financially ignorant? Why doesn't school teach them basics such as "make more than you spend" and "you can either spend the 100, or invest it and receive 200 back, by which you now have 100 to spend and another 100 to re-invest"? And we haven't even started with the metaphysics of money yet.

Enlightened education teaches about Health. It teaches about the Body. It teaches about the Mind. These are the basic building blocks of life. As it stands currently, most people are a bundle of confusion and insecurity by the time they leave school and only start gathering themselves and understanding how life works by the age of 40. By the time they understand who they are and what they really want, half of their life is already over.

Recently I walked past a schoolyard in an average neighborhood. I stood to examine the state of consciousness there. About half of the students were puffing away on cigarettes – a sign that they were desperately seeking relief from the boredom of their classrooms. About a quarter of them were overweight to obese – another sign that they were desperately seeking some compensation for the wasted time. In an enlightened school system, teachers are paid more, teachers are valued more. By allocating more funds to education than to any other sector of society, the funding flows through to all other things and society saves money in the end. If there was better education there would be less war, hence less money allocated to military spending. If there were more education there would be less poverty, hence less money needed for welfare. More funds allocated to schools, teachers and teacher training would make them more resourceful, caring and entertaining. Teaching can also be entertaining. It's not just reading from some textbook and having kids repeat it. It's also being charming, and humorous.

If more modern learning techniques were applied to schools you could cut learning time in half. That doesn't mean that parents would have to spend more time taking care of their children. The time saved could be used for more creative activities in school. Imagine a school day where Intellectual study only takes 50% of the time and the other 50% is spent on developing specialized skills, writing, painting, singing, dancing, sports, play, games, and meditation. A human being is more than just the recording device we call "the mind".

8. The Power of Curiosity

I don't like the saying "Curiosity killed the cat". Curiosity is the basis of self-improvement. Follow it and your learning never stops. Question everything, not in a neurotic way, but with playfulness. The moment you think, "I know everything" is the moment learning and growth stop. I'll never rest on my laurels. Life is deeply mysterious no matter how much you learn. Even if you learn everything there's to know on Earth, that still leaves an entire Universe undiscovered. Everything I have written makes up a fraction of 1% of what could be learned on these subjects.

Aristotle said "the sign of an educated mind is to be able to entertain an idea without accepting it". That means you can actually stay open to a wide variety of ideas without having to adopt them as your own. If you're able to temporarily occupy different viewpoints, you keep learning.

The opposite of curiosity is apathy. And apathy is what killed the cat, not curiosity.

9. Turning Difficult Students into Super Learners

This section was written for teachers. Some of you struggle with "difficult students" and "problem children". The first step to improving your relationship to that child or teenager is to recognize that your own resistance doesn't help them release theirs, nor does it help you to be an effective teacher. Sure, some children would require more care than you have the time and resources to offer. But there are some who are at a **tipping point**…where their school career could go either way. Those are the ones you can help.

To increase your compassion see them as the bundle of confusion and insecurity that young people often are. See them not as a problem that you have to correct but as the humans that they are. In this unenlightened world humankind is somewhat lost…and the same applies to that child or teenager. Understanding the existential struggle of every human being increases compassion. Approaching the child with the energy of compassion will have a subtle effect on them.

Also note that their rebellion is actually something good. You wouldn't only want to produce little yes-men and -women, would you? A child emancipates itself from childhood through rebellion against authority, so a little bit needs to be allowed, provided it doesn't disrupt the work of other children. If their urge to rebel is suppressed, they don't overcome it in adulthood and keep fighting illusions. If their anti-stance is acknowledged by you, however, they begin losing interest in it and become more cooperative. Their "bad attitude" is also a cry for attention. Once you have established some rapport and understanding, you can approach them for honest discussion.

If you accept their resistance rather than fight it with your own, they rapidly lose interest in it and become more cooperative. Apart from approaching them with compassion, also approach them with the understanding that their "being difficult" is a good thing. It's a cry for attention. Don't approach them while feeling resentment. They sense your energy field and will try to rebel and shut off from really listening. With the right mood and energy what you say is secondary. They will soften up and do some of the talking. Directing their attention to their wants ("What do you want?") is always a good idea because it helps them take some responsibility for their state and to shift their attention from being stuck to goals. It may also be helpful for you to have a firm goal for the conversation as well and to mentally intend that goal for yourself throughout. I don't recommend you spend too much time and energy with these attention-seekers, but the right type of quality time with them can go a long way. Spending too much time with them at the expense of your time with other children with the primary teaching focus of your class only serves to confirm their belief that if they act up they get attention. What they need to learn is to give themselves some attention and to find solutions and goals within themselves.

I worked with difficult teenagers early in my career and I was a difficult student myself. The trick I always use (because it almost always works) to access these kinds of students is to find out what they are madly interested in, and associate the learning material with that. In my twenties I worked with some "difficult children" by teaching them languages. I found it rather easy to gain their respect by the simple method of establishing rapport. I would ask them what they most liked or what their interests were and then talk to them about that. If someone was a fan of some sports team or video game I would have to know enough about that to establish report, so that it didn't come across as fake. As a synchrony of energy was established I would then connect the learning of the language to activities they enjoy. I once taught a teenager windsurfing while also teaching him a language. I played Star Wars figures with a child while teaching him a language. I used a picture book about horses to teach a young girl a language, because she was crazy about horses. I then promised to take her to a horse farm if she would learn a certain amount of vocabulary during that day. The method is simple and effective: "Combine what interests them with what they need to learn". It was so simple that parents were often perplexed at how I had achieved what they had been struggling years to do. What comes into play here however, is that a neutral person can sometimes achieve more than parents and spouses who are involved on a daily basis. The main idea is that if it interests them, they can suddenly concentrate. In fact, if they are enjoying themselves or have some reward to look forward to they can concentrate for many, many hours and will learn anything.

3

HOW TO SKYROCKET YOUR SUCCESS

1. Simple, Simple, Simple

Simplicity – be baggage free. That's one of my top success formulas. When you drop over-thinking and micro-controlling and just **trust** that life will figure most things out for you, you become calm and life becomes simple.

Do you have to read dozens of books on how the stock market works before buying stocks? No, you just need to know whether a company is going **up or down. Simple. Simple!** Do you disagree? Maybe that's because you have had bad experiences in the stock market and now believe you have to control, plan, and prepare everything meticulously so that you aren't burned again, but then you're approaching the whole thing from a fear-mindset, and your fear will attract more losses.

Does the tax form look inscrutable to you? Actually they are just asking what you **made and spent. Simple.** All this complexity surrounding taxation is just smoke and mirrors.

Do you need to learn strange scripts and languages in order to build a website? No. It's only a matter of writing texts and putting up pictures. Simple. Anyone who can write an email can also build a website.

What about marketing for your website? That's simple too. There are thousands of books and sites teaching marketing but you *don't need any of them* if you follow these marketing steps: Step 1: **Offer something people want.** Oh, excuse me…it's only one step! Could it really be that simple? Don't you need to take marketing seminars, special retreats, online courses, get a marketing consultant, etc.? No, not unless you're offering things people **don't** want. That's when you need great marketing. If your product or service is valuable to others, you don't need marketing. It sells itself. Truly, most of the "marketing advice" I have received from people, I rejected because it's too complex, too pretentious, and too obnoxious. Some, for example, have "strongly recommended" that I send out an email newsletter every day or at least every week. How obnoxious would that be? If that kind of "marketing" works at all, it's only to attract people who like being overloaded and brainwashed. I keep my marketing plan simple *"Create products and services that you like and others like".* End of story.

Do you need to process hundreds of traumatic incidents and past lives in order to feel well today? No, all you need is to become present. Simple. I have seen many people stop trying to heal themselves, therapize themselves, process themselves, find themselves, etc. and become better remarkably quickly. Sometimes it's the **search** for healing that makes you sick. Sometimes it's more effective to become simpler, more humble, and more present.

Is it a mystery why there are wars in the world? No. It's just lack of forgiveness. Simple. You could give me volumes of history books and political treatises, but what all conflict comes down to is lack of forgiveness. I don't really need to know the rest of the story. The mind loves making up stories to justify certain realities. But those are just layers over the truth.

Do you need to amass a large quantity of data and material before you can open your own boutique on Main Street? No. You just need a room, a few clothes racks and a credit card reader. Simple.

Do you need a 50-page contract in order to work for someone? No. A handshake or a one or two page agreement will do. Simple. Unless they are for corporate projects, long contracts are for fear-based people who think they have to prepare for every negative possibility. Here in America we have a fear based culture created and perpetuated by lawyers who can and will sue you for selling coffee that's too hot, so if you don't print on every coffee cup "Warning! This coffee cup could be hazardous to your health. Only touch after you're sure it's cooled down!" you could be facing serious fines. Such are the products of a fear-based culture.

What if I work on a handshake, and then they don't pay me? Then quit working for them. Simple.

What about the money lost? It'll come back somewhere else. Simple.

Wouldn't it give me more peace of mind to at least have a little something in writing rather than just a handshake? Sure. Sometimes that will give you more peace of mind. Go ahead and get a contract. Simple.

What will they think of me when I request a contract after we have been working on a handshake for years? Who cares what they think? Let go of the worry. Simple.

As a coach who works with people daily, I frequently see procrastination and mental limitation in my students when they over-complicate things or make them bigger than they are. Sure, there may be more details to doing some of the things mentioned above, but if you're holding all these details in mind, chances are you'll never get started building your dream. Keeping things simple makes them manageable and easier to visualize. If you want a house, visualize a house, not every detail of the "how, when, where". Just keep the end in mind. Once the house is manifested, the details will take care of themselves. No need to worry about them beforehand. You cross the bridge when you come to it.

It's been my experience that exaggerated complexity and truth aren't good partners. Complexity often masks truth. "My relationship is soooooo complicated, I don't even know how to explain it" someone recently told me. After I learned more it turned out that it's not complicated at all. It was just two people who were tired of each other and were creating all these mental constructs around it. Simple.

Some people are actually disappointed when I reveal to them how simple things are. A few months ago I taught someone how to publish a book on Kindle (which is as **simple** as uploading a .pdf file). He replied, "This is so easy I've actually lost interest". I still wonder why he wanted it to be difficult, but it showed me that many of the limitations people have are merely illusion*s* of complexity, illusions about things being more difficult than they are.

For your dreams to come true, know that the laws governing them are **simpler than you assume**. If you want to win Olympic Gold in swimming, you have to swim. You have to swim more than the others swim. It's simple. I didn't say it's easy, I said it's simple. There's a difference between simple and easy. If winning Olympic Gold were easy, anyone could do it. But even though it's not easy, the "how" of it's so very simple.

Any subject you put your attention on can be simplified to become more understandable and to speed up your learning. When I learn a foreign language, the first thing I do is to simplify the whole thing. I drop all superfluous and redundant data and focus on what is really important first. This is the 80-20 rule. Focus on the simple 80% and discard the complicated 20%. So I ask: "What are the 1,000 most used words and phrases of the language?" They are the same in any language. I start with those. Not with grammar, not with the exceptions-to-the-rule, not with difficult words. Simple. **Later** in the game I'll get into the complexities and nuances of the language, but I'll get there because I **started** with simplicity. If I ever get lost in the complexities, I go back to the simple basics, before I return to the complex. When you get lost, simply go back to the basics.

People who know me privately remark what a "hard worker" I'm. I have no idea what they're talking about. I subjectively experience myself as someone fairly lazy who works no more than 1 hour a day. But they don't see it that way. "No Fred, you work all the time. I have never seen anyone work as hard or often as you. You're constantly working, even on weekends, even in the evening". Statements like these (and I've heard them often) puzzled me. Then I realized that I don't even notice that I'm "working" because I'm doing what I really enjoy and really like. It doesn't even feel like "work". Because I do what I love and keep things very simple, my life feels like a perpetual vacation. Recently I did a series of seminars for a company in Italy. Due to poor planning I didn't have a weekend break, and I was in seminars 12 days in a row. After he realized the "mistake", the CEO apologized to me and said, "I'm so sorry. Next time we'll make sure there are breaks in between the seminars". I thanked him. What I didn't mention is that I hadn't even noticed I was working without a break, because I was enjoying myself so much.

This attitude comes from a simple question I asked myself long ago: "Fred, if you were already wealthy and complete, what would you be doing?" The answer was "teach seminars, research and write". The answer wasn't "hang around at the beach for the rest of my life". That would become boring rather quickly. **If you simply do what you would be doing if you were already whole and complete,** you're starting to make life simple, happy and successful.

2. Being Authentic

"Being Authentic" allows you to walk through life and communicate with people without being shy, self-conscious, fearful, groveling, evasive or unkind. When you're your authentic and true self there's an air of confidence, poise, ease and humor about you. Instead of thinking "How do people see me?" and "What do they think of me?" you'll be thinking, **"I'm sexy and I know it"**. Compare those two inner thoughts. Compare "I'm sexy and I know it" with the usual stream of thoughts you have in daily life.

How can you be authentic and feel confident and at ease with others most of the time? There are many, many things I could say about the how-to of this, but you may not remember any of them when you really need them. Being authentic isn't a "technique," it's the absence of any technique.

I can summarize how to attain and maintain the state while communicating with others in one sentence:

Want nothing, resist nothing, externalize your attention and allow yourself to flow a state of gentle Humor.

That's it. That's the whole formula. For some, it can take decades to learn, but sometimes it can also be there in an instant, just by remembering this statement. The instant you want something from another person, you're no longer entirely free, calm and clear. If I want nothing from that person and don't want them to say or do anything in particular, that means I **accept them exactly as they are right now**. That not only allows me to feel at ease, but helps them feel comfortable, too. Not wanting anything from them also has another benefit: I can tell them the truth about anything. If I don't depend on them to like me, give me money, give me love or anything else, **because I'm an Infinite Being and already have all I'll ever need within,** then I'm not shy, awkward, withholding information, seeking approval, etc. On the other side, I resist nothing either. If they are awkward, uncomfortable, in a bad mood, shy, etc. that doesn't bother me, I don't resist it. I either go somewhere else or try to heal their state by sending **waves of appreciation**.

Externalizing your attention makes it easier to be at ease. Too much preoccupation with how others see you and with your inner emotions and mental stories isn't conducive to communication with others (and not conducive to your state in general). Externalizing your attention means to extend interest in their direction rather than only desperately trying to get noticed. You give interest instead of trying to get it. You lend an ear instead of seeking one. You lend a hand instead of needing one. This attitude immediately turns the game board around, making you a source of goodwill and energy instead of a beggar.

Allowing yourself to flow a gentle state of humor quickly dispels negative vibes, social masks and tension. "Flowing gentle Humor" doesn't mean cracking a joke every minute. It's an inner radiance I'm referring to. That radiance can be activated just by remembering to activate it. In a state of lightness (Humor **IS** lightness) it's easy to be authentic. You don't have to hide anything, scheme anything, avoid anything, calculate advantages and disadvantages, imitate someone, or be someone, you're just present with what is, here and now.

If the above statement is too long for you to remember, you could reduce it down to this shortcut: "Don't be anything, just **BE**".

From that basis, authenticity develops. Wearing no masks at all, being vulnerable and open, you also become free from the various social roles and games usually being played. From that basis you can create new ways of being, with the difference that these will be deliberately chosen and guided rather than masks put on to please others or avoid their disapproval. You're then real, honest, straightforward, daring to follow your bliss, daring to speak up, not caught up in any inner story, daring to follow your unique lifestyle, daring to do what is right and true and congruent in your thoughts, words and deeds. **How do you know when you're not being authentic? When you're nervous. Your soul or true self is never ill at ease. Only the Illusory-self is ill at ease.**

A reason why some people suppress showing their true selves is because initially it makes them stand out. Someone who is shining brightly receives an inordinate amount of attention. **Authenticity is a radical deviation from mediocrity**. It may stir people up and you may get not only get positive attention but also negative attention. It's best to add a dash of humility to your overall being and **habitually forgive** those who envy or attack you.

3. If you're not Growing, you're Declining

As a coach I instill certain concepts to move people toward the fulfillment of their dreams. One such concept is:

"If you're not Growing, you're Declining"

This concept has helped thousands of students to *get going*. Don't rely on the status quo. Don't rely on past achievements. Don't rely on past greatness. Stagnation is actually decline. Mass consciousness is moving and if you quit moving with the flow, you decline. This is how success itself can sometimes become an impediment to more success. Life is forever unfolding, evolving, moving. If you say, "I made it" or "now I know", you come to a standstill and stop participating in life. Past achievements mean even less if you have to repeat them over and over. If you've achieved a comfortable position at your job, even that achievement becomes stale if it goes on for years. Continue to learn, grow and explore. The achievements themselves aren't the main point of life. The main point is all the fun you have on your path to those achievements.

Another way to convey a similar principle is **Discipline and Focus lead to Success. Success can lead to a lack of Discipline and Focus.**

By the age of 30 I had "reached the top" (or so I thought). I had all the money I wanted, all the recognition, all the relationships, the looks I wanted, the entrepreneurial success I wanted. I had achieved and created everything I had set out to do. I had even experienced the high spiritual states I had set out to experience - and I was extremely unhappy and restless. I didn't know it back then but my unhappiness was created by the thought that I had "reached the top". My unhappiness lifted when I created new aspirations and goals, new challenges and new opportunities for growth. "If you're not growing, you're declining" was my wake-up call. The soul is programmed for limitless expansion in all directions, just like the Universe is limitlessly expanding in all directions. There are trillions of things to become aware of and to enjoy.

4. The Predictability of Success and Failure

In my work as a success coach I can predict whether someone will fail or succeed with an endeavor 80% of the time. You might think that's very judgmental, but it's based on many years of experience working with thousands of people. 20% might surprise me by having things turn out differently for better or worse. My highest frustration as a success coach is when I can see failure looming and communicate that, but the person I'm coaching doesn't accept it. Many people would rather "be right" than succeed. Admitting mistakes or ineffective approaches seems more painful to them than growing. The reason success is fairly predictable is because it always builds on the same factors – attitude, focus, commitment, passion, energy and unwavering decision. **A true intention creates a vector that is pointing in a certain direction**. If you're open to it, you can see which direction the vector is pointing. If you make a decision in the here and now, you create a vector that points to the future. By looking at where the vector points it's easy to say whether a person will succeed or fail. Half of all people I work with are aligned with success before they even start working with me. Those are my easy students. As someone wise once said, "***every battle is won before it's even fought***".

New success sometimes means shedding the old. Old decisions, old behaviors, old negativity, old things. Letting go of the old requires some sort of **sacrifice**. Could you sacrifice that which no longer serves you? The fear that comes up when I ask people to adopt radically new attitudes and behaviors is quite stunning sometimes. They then see that it's perhaps easier to stay stuck in the old rut than venture out and try something entirely different, to re-invent themselves, to venture where they haven't been before. It's precisely why most people don't actually **succeed** in the true sense of the word. Most people don't want to make those decisions, don't want to disturb their comfortable life, and don't want to create any **turbulence**. If you break down old walls to create new walls there might be some turbulence. Don't pout when things don't go smoothly. If you're truly committed to a new reality, then your plane is going to lift off the ground and that can create turbulence. The feeling of flying may be unfamiliar and some will want to go right back down to the comfortable ground. Really, there's nothing to be afraid of if your trust in life is intact.

A good example of how hard it can be to release negativity is letting go of negative people who are part of our lives. I recently coached a woman whose husband beat her, but she wouldn't leave him. Why? Because of familiarity and comfort. They had spent 10 years together and had some wonderful times. Those wonderful times coupled with cozy closeness made the prospect of leaving him terrifying. I looked at the vector and predicted: "If you continue to accept being beaten and abused by him, you're going to continue to fail in all areas of life. Neither your health nor your finances will improve. Why? Because you indicate that you're of low value by letting someone treat you as if you're of low value". After receiving that email, the good lady immediately cancelled the coaching and said she didn't need my help, that she loved her husband and wasn't leaving him. In fact, she wouldn't even entertain the idea. Nor would she apply any of the other suggestions I made, such as hitting back, confronting him on it or getting outside assistance from family or even the police. She entered the coaching with me to address health and money problems. Like so many others she will probably move on to the next book, next workshop, next coach, looking for someone who will tell her nice-sounding words with which she can remain in her comfort-zone.

The "comfortable life" isn't really all that comfortable in the long run. Short-term it might be more comfortable for that wife to stay with the abusive tyrant at home, but not in the long run. She would have to **accept brief pain for greater gain**. Another example might be an alcoholic: Short term it might feel more comfortable to have a glass of alcohol but it's destructive in the long term. You would have to accept the brief pain of withdrawal for a huge improvement in your life. Quitting a job that leaves you sad and exhausted might cause brief pain, but there will be a greater gain overall. The successful person is willing to take that leap of faith and enter a brief spell of uncertainty and turbulence for that which is good and true.

5. Stretch Yourself

Stretch Yourself. If your dance lessons go for 2 hours, go 3 hours. If your clients expect work done by this evening, deliver it by noon. If your language program was to learn two words a day, make it five. If your friend asked if you could drive her to the train station, drive her all the way home. If your wife asks you to run an errand, run five. If you planned to write two pages of your book a week, write twenty. If a customer requests a refund, give him not only a refund but a gift as well. If you're complaining about a "long day at work", quit complaining and extend your working time to midnight. If you have had difficulty concentrating for one minute, practice until you can concentrate for ten minutes. If running a mile is your record, run one and a half miles.

Stretch Yourself. Why? Because you only live this particular life once. Quit saving your energy for another day, your soul wants to live fully. Stretch yourself because the more you exercise your inner willpower, the easier life gets. You'll hardly notice things that used to overwhelm you. All resistance toward life and action fades. A long day of work seems like a walk in the park. Stretching yourself is the one and only secret of High Performance.

6. Set Higher Standards

Resting on past successes is a block to future success. Assume that reaching level 10 on a 1-10 scale doesn't mean a thing, that the new standard is level 100. In a strange way certain types of success breed laziness and complacency as you rest on your "laurels". If you succeed at something I don't recommend celebrating that, praising yourself for it and using it to brag or boost your self-esteem. Instead see it as a milestone on the road to something more. Say: "You ain't seen nothing yet" or "I haven't REALLY achieved anything yet". This will keep you poised and focused to set your standards higher. You'll notice that the joy is in the path to achievement more than in the achievement itself. Life really takes place on the path, not at the destination. Winning Olympic Gold is over in one hour – what about the thousands of hours you're not winning Gold? Life is really about that time, not about the goal, but you set the goals anyway, because there's a journey you want to take and you need a clear vision of where it leads..

Just because you manifest your dream house doesn't mean life is over. Just because you have the perfect relationship doesn't mean it's time to lay back. Persistence of Drive is what separates Greatness from Mediocrity. Did you know that many people who have achieved heroic greatness or fame for some awesome feat or became self-made Billionaires didn't come from the middle class but from lower classes of society? That's because they had enough pain and desire to drive them to fantastic heights, whereas most of the middle class are simply comfortable, residing in their television-and-internet comfort zone of "everything is alright". You might have noticed that if you get too comfortable, the energy field of life on this planet tends to drag you down. On the other hand, **once you get enough momentum going it takes less effort to succeed. An airplane needs the most energy when it lifts off the ground but much less when it's in the air.** Before you rest on your laurels get into the air first, high into the air. This will take some effort and more effort still. But effort is fun. Get rid of the notion that effort is somehow a bad thing. Let go of needing everything to be convenient and easy. Your soul doesn't want that. You would get incredibly bored if you could manifest a Trillion Dollars without effort. Manifesting a Trillion with special types of skill and effort on the other hand, is pure joy. If you're getting too satisfied with the way things are, set new standards, higher standards.

7. Stop Rewarding Negativity

One of the main reasons people continue negative behavior is because there's a payoff or reward to it. If there were no perceived advantage, they would stop saying or doing harmful things. You wouldn't reward a child that keeps causing trouble, you wouldn't reward a dog that pees on the carpet and yet many are willing to reward adults that display unpleasant behavior. How? Through giving them attention. Giving attention, getting involved, and even getting emotional is a kind of "energy reward". Even getting angry with a negative person gives them energy. Let's say your spouse comes home from work every day and complains. They complain about work, complain about the house, and complain about you. If you continue to participate in their litany of complaints, try to "make it up to them", try to be nice and understanding, try to acknowledge them…this acknowledgement will usually help them calm down and be at ease. Any sort of acknowledgement leads to relaxation. But if that behavior continues, in spite of repeated engagement, it should no longer be acknowledged (rewarded). Why? Because after a certain point, the other person **is using** your attention as a way to get energy. They fall into a pattern of using complaint and negativity as a means of getting acknowledgement because they have failed to acknowledge themselves.

Another example: There's someone in your neighborhood that commits various small crimes. Some theft here and there and occasional acts of violence. What this person lacks is love and acknowledgement. If he happens to come across a person who gives him that love, he might experience a healing and from then on improve his behavior. Love heals, but if his emotional state is below a certain threshold, rather than using the love of others to find self-love, he will subconsciously interpret the bad behavior as a way to get more love and attention. If, after rehabilitation and after providing plenty of support he *continues* his destructive behavior, its time to apply "tough love", which is to quit rewarding him. By making it clear that he will no longer get your attention with bad behavior, he will have to learn to change if he wants to get people's attention.

It's wiser to reward (give attention to) people's upsides, to people's exemplary behavior. I recently sat in a park. I saw one child slap the face of another child. The other child started crying. What did the mother of the first child do? I saw her caressing and calming him down, as if he had been the one who was hit. She was rewarding bad behavior and thereby reinforcing the idea that it's OK to hit another child. One could tell that the child was rather spoiled because only a couple of minutes later he was taking someone's toy away by force. He would go on acting like a brat until his mother quit rewarding that.

When I'm in low energy, I like it when my partner soothes me and gives me some love and attention, but when that bad mood turns into complaints and insults toward her, she won't take it. She'll remove herself from my presence instantly…with zero tolerance. I find this response to my negativity immensely helpful because it reminds me that I have no right to unload garbage on others. It helps me improve my mood by giving myself some love and attention first. Because I know that my negativity is never rewarded, I almost never fall into it. So my state is upbeat and happy most of the time.

It may be new and difficult at first to no longer reward others negativity and no longer seek reward for your own, but ultimately it liberates both you and those around you.

At what point does the attention you send to someone in low energy turn from helpful to unhelpful? At what point does the money you support someone with turn from helpful to unhelpful? The tipping point is when getting healed turns into getting spoiled. It's when you see that they didn't use your money, support, attention, love, forgiveness, or care to improve their situation but instead continue on the very same path over and over. This applies to individuals as well as entire countries. The care and support you give should help people get back on their feet, not perpetuate their negative state. Give unlimited love and care in the beginning, but stop doing it if the undesirable reality persists over long periods of time.

8. Your True Vocation

People only strictly distinguish between free time and work time when they don't enjoy their work. Once you have found the vocation that is "really you", you no longer strictly discern between the two.

The way you behave in one part of your life is likely also the way you behave in the other parts of your life. The only time strict separation or compartmentalization is advisable is when one area happens to be going badly and you don't want it to spill over, but if it continues to go badly in one area it will eventually spill over to the others. If you improve one area, you improve all other areas. There really is no separation between your Job, Health, Relationships, Communication, Spirituality, Friendships, and Hobbies. It's all part of one thing: YOU and your Life.

The Formula "Working at a Job I don't like = Making Money" doesn't work. Bad = Good doesn't work. Good = Good works, so find a vocation you enjoy. The only reason there's a "financial crisis" is because mass-consciousness still believes that doing work you don't like will make you prosperous. This goes along with the false belief that prosperous people are generally evil. Being evil and getting rich is much harder work and usually happens at the expense of ones health. Negative energy and prosperity don't mix well.

People tell me: "I can't just give up my Job. I depend on it for money". If you were actually making real money you'd be liberated from the need to have that job in the first place. Jobs like that never make a money. How could they? You generate no joy, so you generate no energy, so you generate no prosperity. Jobs like that will keep you a slave. Staying at a job you don't like makes no any sense at all. It's good for nothing, and it's only fear keeping you in that job, so your reality remains based in fear.

If, in the end, you still insist you have to keep a bad job, then at least try changing your attitude toward it. Try embracing it.

"Love it or Leave it"

Those are the only spiritually valid options. Staying there and not loving where you are is spiritual suicide. If you're going to stay there and not have the courage to move into the unknown, at least practice embracing everything that happens on the job, embracing its space, its people, its concepts. You thereby transcend it, and it will be easier to leave, because you no longer have sticky resistance energy attached.

9. What Failure Teaches you about Success

One way to succeed is by "Modeling Success", studying what successful people are doing in the areas you want to succeed and following their example. This also works the other way around:

If you want a good life, go to a psychiatric hospital, study the people there, do the opposite of what they are doing, and you'll lead a healthy and successful life! That sounds like a joke, but I actually mean it. Look at what the people suffering the most are saying and doing, and do the opposite. For example, while researching the diet of women in psychiatric wards, scientists found that an above average number were habitual users of alcohol, nicotine, sweets and caffeine. What follows from that? Don't mix alcohol, cigarettes, sweets and coffee. Why? I don't know. I just know that by modeling successful people I become successful and by modeling unsuccessful people I become unsuccessful. Studying how people who suffer and how people who are happy live and behave teaches you everything you need to know about everything.

A technique I sometimes use with my students: can you teach me what I have to think, say and do in order to fail the same way you think you're failing? Can you teach me the method? What are the steps I have to take to incur that much debt? What are the steps I have to take to feel depressed? What look on my face do I have to cultivate? What outlook should I keep focusing on? In the process of re-creating a problem, you become the cause and source of the problem. Once you become the source of the problem, it's easier to release the problem. If you know that the ingredients to a certain issue are X + Y + Z, you can disassemble that procedure.

10. What Sports can Teach you about Success

Athletes and sports teams can teach you everything you need to know about succeeding. All you have to do is watch and study the behavior of the most successful teams and athletes and you have learned *all about it.*

In team sports for example, in order to perform at the very top of your game, **the concept of time needs to be dismissed**. You'll see players getting fouled, bullied, and beaten, but if they ponder that setback one second too long, they will have lost concentration and lost valuable moments while the opponent strikes again. You'll see players scoring, winning a tackle or challenge, achieving, making headway, but if they think about a great play for too long, they'll lose concentration and valuable moments and their opponent will strike while they are daydreaming. A professional athlete doesn't care about what happened a minute ago, he only looks forward, ever forward. If he rests on his past successes he'll soon lose his top position. If he frets over lost chances he will never achieve that position. With focus it's possible to succeed, but it's more difficult to maintain and keep first place, because as #1 you become a target and everyone else wants your place. Defending and confirming your position is accomplished by simply doing more of what you did to achieve it. Watch how quickly successful teams in any sport overcome a loss. They quit talking about it on the same day and focus on the next game. Watch how they celebrate their victories…but not too long. They never lose their focus on winning their league, and one game is just a step toward that goal.

11. In which League do you Play?

Sports leagues offer an ideal metaphor for all of your areas of potential. There are many different *versions* of the job you do. Your career can be played in the First League, the Second League, the Third League, the Fourth League and an infinite number of other minor and major leagues.

You must recognize the league you're playing in. If you're a Third League professional, trying to play too many First League or major league games will exhaust your resources. Playing too many Fourth and Fifth league games will underwhelm you. You need to be clear which league you're in and the boundaries, limits and frontiers of that domain of success. You measure your success in comparison to other players in the same league. If you do fantastically well and perform above and beyond what you have ever done before, you'll finish the season at the top of your league. You'll then rank #1 in the Third League and will be respected within the context of your success domain. In the next season you'll be allowed to progress one league, to enter a new domain of success with wider and more expanded boundaries, limits, rules and frontiers.

If you celebrate your #1 spot too long or rested on your laurels, you won't have the energy to stay in the Second League. You see this with many sports teams who can't maintain the new league and full back into their original league the next season. Some fall even deeper due to awful decision making. And then there are a few who can maintain the new level and make it their new baseline. Do whatever got you to #1 of the Third League and you'll be able to stay in the Second League. But you will notice that your very best players and tools, the superstars of the Third League, don't work quite as well as in this new league. At one place they may have been revered by thousands of people, but in this higher success domain they aren't the top performers. If they're going to thrive in this higher league they'll have to step up their game. What's fun about life is that there's always a higher league, no matter how high you go.

Suppose you shed old habits and re-invent yourself so that you not only survive in the Second League but, over time, reach the top. You rank #1 in the Second League and your success story goes on and one day you rank #1 in First League, but that's not it. The next league is international league. And then interplanetary league. And then inter-galactic league. And then inter-universal league. The Domains of Reality are circles within circles, expanding infinitely in all directions.

To see which league you play in, compare your status, budget, reputation, and number of employees with similar jobs or companies to your own. Who does something similar to you in a lower league? Who does something similar to you in a higher league? What are the uppermost limits of your league and what is required of you to lead your league? And then, what would be required to enter the next higher league?

If you're success-oriented it may be helpful to view life as a game that can be learned and skillfully played. Obstacles and challenges are then seen as opponents that make you better. Reaching the top is a stepping-stone in an even greater domain of experience. Related: *The Leadership Course*

12. Children Try until they find out What Works

At what age do people stop trying new things? What's so striking about children is how they instinctively try new things. They try this, they try that and they learn how things work. I watched a child try to turn on a TV. He tried all kinds of strange things. Tugging the cable. Pushing the screen. Scratching the button. Pushing a button (but not the one that turns it on). The boy didn't get "demotivated". He just kept on, ever curious and playful. He had seen its parents turn on the TV so he knew and believed it was possible. Finally he went over to mommy to get her to turn it on. Asking experts for advice is great. But what then happened was even better: Mommy asked the child to try again. She gave him the remote control and in doing so gave him the understanding that it's possible to achieve the feat with that device. After trying out many more buttons to no avail (and not deeming himself a failure for it and not deeming life "a struggle" because of it) he finally found the magic button. His face lit up with an ecstatic smile and he blissfully giggled.

You can fail a thousand times, but you're not a failure. You're just a human living life, trying things out. Don't be afraid to try things out. Sometimes you'll want to listen to what the experts who have already tried it have to say about something, but not always. Sometimes you'll want to go through the experience yourself. There's no fear of failure, no resignation and no excuses in a child. There's only curiosity to learn.

13. Learn from People who have Already Achieved what you Want

Find people who have already achieved what you want. Spend time with them. Learn about them. See things through their eyes. Be prepared to find that they see and experience things differently than you do. Explore those differences. Talk to them. Ask them questions. With some humility, an open ear and the ability to empathize with that person, you'll soon learn their thoughts, words and actions.

To put it more bluntly:

Don't take advice on money from a "financial analyst" who can't afford his own car. Take it from the guy who owns the dealership.

Don't take health advice from a chain-smoking doctor. Take it from the healthy doctor.

Don't take spiritual advice from a depressed guru. Take it from the one who shines brightly.

Don't take relationship advice from someone who is going through his fourth troubled marriage. Take it from the guy who is already experiencing what you would like.

Don't take advice on how to be calm from the guy that keeps fidgeting. Take it from the one who IS calm.

My key question to students who tell me their goals:

Do you know someone who is already experiencing that?

14. Overcome Procrastination

We tend to more easily remember and feel urged to complete tasks that we have already started. Tasks we have completed are easily forgotten. This knowledge is used by marketing experts to produce "cliffhangers" in movies, books and on the web to compel people to return to see the next episode. The story is incomplete and people can't wait to come back for the next chapter.

You can create this urge to complete a task within yourself if you understand that you're much more likely to remember a task you've started than one you haven't started yet. The technique to end procrastination is to **start somewhere**. If you've started, you're much more likely to return to complete a project or a goal than if you're still fantasizing about it. It doesn't matter where on the map you start out as long as you begin. A major cause of procrastinating is feeling that a task is too big. By knowing that it doesn't matter where you start, you're more likely to start somewhere. You probably remember the sensation of something feeling too big to even start from your life, but when you started it anyway you just decided to start at one point. And already having started somewhere..anywhere!..you made the commitment to the project, task or goal and it was easier to continue the next day. Start now, not later.

15. Your Job as a Work of Art

No matter what your job or profession is, never devalue what you do by talking it down. One of the great mystical secrets of life is "**the way you do one thing, is the way you do everything**". This means that you can learn the lessons of life in **any** job. You can experience **any** job in many different negative or positive **versions**. If you're an ice-cream seller you can do it in a manner that is joyous to yourself and the children buying from you, or you can do it as a grumpy person dissatisfied with their job. The mystical key to work is that **a job isn't about what you get out of it, it's about what you put into it**. Ask not what your job can do for you, ask what you can do for your job.

As a human being you want to create, produce, contribute and elevate your craft to its highest version possible. This means that even as a trash collector you can perform the job with grace and focus or carelessly and frustrated. It's not about the external, it's all about the internal. If you've been waiting to be promoted in your company for years but it hasn't happened and you're frustrated about that, it's time to let go of wanting to be promoted and do the job you have more impeccably. Doing this creates an energy field that makes it much more likely you'll be promoted. By approaching it with care and diligence, any job can be elevated to an art form. It's a joy for people to enter a well-run company or a well-run shoe shop or to visit a well-run website. It provides inspiration to them and they learn from **your example**. The quickest path to success isn't to yearn for another job but to do your present job the best you can. You've then surrendered your resistance and returned to the **stream of life** which carries you to better places more quickly. Be mindful about your work. Your work is co-creation at its best. Badmouthing ones job has become a mass epidemic, but you don't have to participate in that losing strategy. Play the cards you're dealt well and with care, and you'll quickly get better cards.

16. People with Enthusiasm

Losers often complain and rarely deliver results. If they do deliver results, they are frequently unsatisfactory. People with **enthusiasm** are notable for their responsiveness and availability. Rather than being primarily focused on themselves, they are dedicated to serving their customers in the best ways they know. Rather than waiting for people to tell them what to do, they initiate, start, make suggestions, provide ideas, and get balls rolling. They take risks and aren't afraid to fail. Usually they'll tell you "Yes" or "No" frankly, without equivocation. They over-deliver on their promises.

A person without enthusiasm will ponder for a few months whether he should take action or not. In the meantime an enthusiastic person has taken hundreds of actions. Of course, if you have no energy, you have no enthusiasm, and where there's no enthusiasm, there's no success. What comes first, enthusiasm or energy? It's a two way street. If you don't have many life problems bogging you down, you're more enthusiastic, but if you deliberately intend to step up your game more than just one notch, you also accumulate more energy to **rise to the**

occasion. Here are a few things you can do to increase your enthusiasm and thereby your success:

* Don't complain. There are endless things to complain about. The list never ends, so just stop. It doesn't take you anywhere. Communicate what you want to people, not what you don't want.

* Be responsive, communicative and available. Openly state things you agree and disagree with.

* Let go of ego and focus on what you can do for others instead of what you think others should do for you.

* Do the best job you can on any task, even if you don't like it. If you've already agreed to do it, deliver excellence.

* If your customers or colleagues ask for help, help them rapidly and to their satisfaction. This can be very fulfilling for you. Seek to make others successful and you'll be a success. This is the ultimate success formula.

* Start, Initiate, Begin, move forward, **do it now**.

* If you experience difficult times, heed Winston Churchill's advice: "If you're going through hell, keep going".

* Deliver more than people expect or pay for at all times. Exceed their expectations. Under promise and over deliver.

* Put relationships above money, virtue above gain, giving above taking.

* Become more energetic, courageous and active in every aspect.

* Make very clear statements, give very clear responses.

* When you make commitments, keep them. Then make new commitments.

* Don't require reward to give your best – do it for the sake of doing good.

People will be **delighted** to work with you and you'll become an unstoppable success.

17. Techniques to Pass Exams

Many people have contacted me in recent years for help to pass tests or exams for their degrees or to enter universities, graduate schools, etc. My advice to all of them is to apply Reality Creation techniques (Visualize, Feel and Act as-if you have already passed the exam, allow yourself to enter a mental-movie in which you experience the entire exam in a relaxed but focused manner, visualize reacting to problems, blocks and tension in a calm and collected way).

In addition to psycho-emotional alignment, I give the following advice (where applicable):

* While taking the test, chew the same flavor of gum you did when studying - your memory will be improved. Smells, tastes, sights and sounds can serve as memory anchors because they transport you to the state you had last time you smelled or tasted or saw a thing.

* Go online and find a trial version or simulation version of the test you'll be taking, and take it over and over until you get the result you want. Succeeding at the test before you take the test is the best guarantee that the actual test will also go well.

* While it's good to study thoroughly, it's not good to overstrain or overstress. You should be focused and dedicated to your studies and to passing the test, but that shouldn't be your **ONLY** focus over long

periods of time. Open your attention a little, release your attachment a little and remain interested in things other than your studies. Understrain can occur when people get lazy and don't do enough for their exams, but overstrain is more common with success-oriented people, where there's too much attachment, and thus tension, to really succeed. Being fully dependent on only one thing and having no life outside your studies, won't make you happy, and when you lack well being, it negatively affects your ability to think and act. Try to find just the right amount of focus – not too little, not too much, just the right amount of time spent studying. Apathetic people understudy, fear-based people over study. Calm people simply Study – and Learn.

* You can learn data and information more quickly if you can structure, contextualize or categorize it, explain or teach it to others, or fundamentally grasp what something means and how it's applicable in life. Rote memorization of data isn't really "learning" and doesn't serve your memory well. It may be necessary sometimes, but it's not enough. To pass higher exams, you really need to know your material and have a fundamental grasp of its entirety. Put differently, rote memorization is for the conscious mind and will soon be forgotten and have no bearing or consequence. Grasping something fully, and being able to imagine it, imprints the subconscious mind and therefore affects long term memory. (See also: *How to Learn a Language in 5 Days*). You really want to understand in-depth what you're learning and not just copy facts from a book. This will help you deduce some answers to exam-questions you might otherwise miss.

* In the days before the exam, continue to live normally. Don't obsess, simply do the daily routines you always do. On exam day, should you become nervous or tense, simply bring more consciousness to your being…breathe consciously or move consciously…that will calm you down.

Don't apply mind techniques or tools beyond the ones described here; that would define the over-fixation I've already warned against.

Best wishes to anyone out there facing a big exam!

18. The Illusionist

I recently met a Mentalist, Illusionist or Magician. He showed me a number of card tricks. Later he presented some tricks to a whole group. To our untrained eyes he could make objects disappear and appear, use telepathy, remote viewing and other feats, but it was all trickery. Everyone was enthralled by his tricks, because **they expose our lack of awareness and our ignorance** and compel us to become more aware, to see more, to know more.

The Illusionist accomplished this manipulation through **misdirection, sleight of hand, speed and semi-hypnotic suggestion**. Misdirection is a distraction of attention. For example, in one card trick, while he was directing my attention to the cards he was holding by asking me questions about the cards, I didn't see that he was holding one of the cards in his mouth. Had I noticed this, I could have exposed a "mysterious" appearance of that card later in the trick. Because he was emphasizing the cards so much, requiring their careful examination, I would have never looked up at his mouth. With a quick movement of his hand toward his mouth, he could have grabbed the card easily without me noticing. I was unaware because I wouldn't normally expect a card sticking out of someone's mouth.

Semi-hypnotic Suggestion or a "Belief Command" was applied when he told the group of people that they were seeing the cards Ace of Diamonds", King of Clubs and Eight of Hearts, although the Ace of Diamonds was actually an "Ace of Hearts", the Diamond-shape being carefully concealed by two other cards. By convincing us that he was holding the Ace of Diamonds we "saw" an Ace of Diamonds. Had we asked him to slow down, and ask to take a closer look at the cards, or to properly lay them out on the table rather than holding them in his hands, he could not have manipulated us in this way. Of course, in order to make us believe we were seeing the Ace of Diamonds, he had to believe it himself temporarily. If you believe something strongly, at least temporarily, you can make it true for others, even if it's not objectively real.

That's how all manipulation in society and daily life really occurs (not to mention in magic shows). If someone is trying to manipulate or cheat you in a business transaction, they will try to speed things up, make faster gestures, speak more quickly, and urge you to take action or make a commitment more quickly. Slowing things down, taking a closer look at contracts, etc., will prevent you being cheated.

Skeptics of spiritual and paranormal phenomena like to point to Illusions to prove that all spiritual phenomena are the unreal results of trickery and manipulation. Illusionists often fake and pretend that they are "really" practicing telepathy and "really" making objects appear and disappear. So skeptics of spiritual phenomena are actually afraid of being manipulated…that is why they are so skeptical, but I have personally experienced real spiritual phenomena…real remote viewing, real telepathy, and real out of body travel. The challenge is being so aware and knowledgeable that you can discern between reality and tricks, between authenticity and illusion.

What I enjoyed most about meeting this Illusionist is how even at my supposed high level of awareness, he could easily fool me. The only way for me to prevent being fooled is by asking him to slow down so that I could consciously perceive what was happening. Of course I didn't do that, because we enjoy being fooled and being unconscious, only to slowly regain consciousness again. It's why we came to Planet Earth.

4

SUCCESS AND LIFE MASTERY

1. Habits of Mentally Strong People

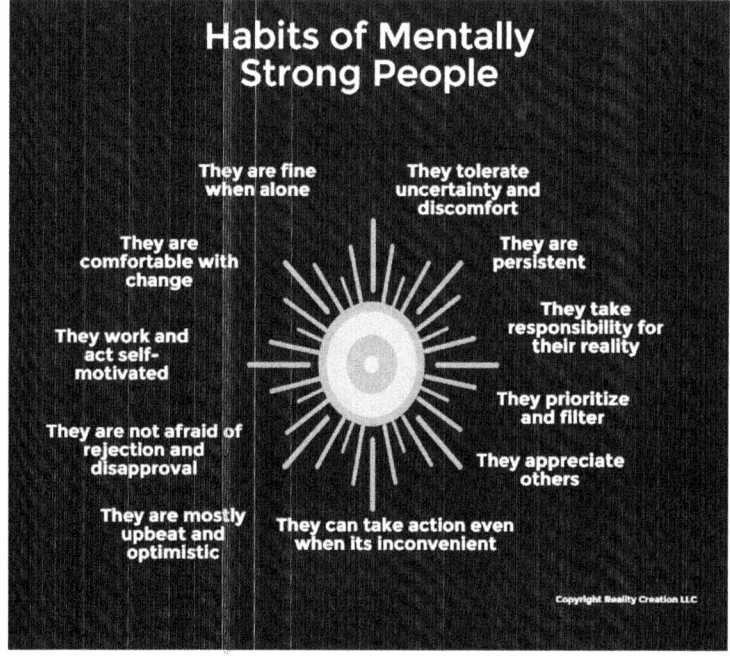

One of my favorite live-seminar exercises: You sit in the middle of a circle of people and have them criticize, insult and doubt you while you stay calm. The exercise teaches that others' bad vibes have more to do with them than with you. Instead of becoming worried, justifying yourself and becoming a slave to others' actions, you develop genuine compassion for the attacker. If you can do that, their anger will only bounce off of you and hurt them. Others' negativity can be a gift…an opportunity for you to grow and transcend the need to push back or lower yourself to their level. In a seminar context it's easier to do this than in real life because you pre-set the intention to stay calm no matter what the other person says.

It's not always easy to see, but it's not really the other that is "making you feel bad". You make yourself feel bad with how you interpret what was said and how you react. When someone delivers negative energy to the doorstep of your heart and you start feeling sorry for yourself, you can catch yourself in that instant, wake up and realize: **others don't define who you're**.

What if you actually made a mistake? Isn't their criticism valid? Sure it is, and you can acknowledge that. But "needing to be perfect" or "always look good in front of someone" indicates mental weakness. You don't need to be perfect, you don't need to pretend to be without fault, without desire, without aversions, etc. You don't need to protect an illusory "clean sheet" at all costs. You can admit to your shortcomings without wallowing in guilt. Being OK with not being OK makes you truly OK. The mentally tough understand that **a calm sea doesn't make a skilled sailor**. It's not the sea that must stay calm, it's the sailor who must remain at ease.

The mentally tough person doesn't mind being verbally attacked. It gives him or her the wonderful opportunity to practice new types of responses, including the important **delayed response**. The delayed response helps you not react on impulse or pure emotion, but in a more reasonable, humorous or kind manner.

When the mentally tough find themselves falling into the role of trying to please others, they will catch themselves and regain perspective. Why? Because trying to please others doesn't actually please others. Being yourself and being good to yourself pleases others, because when you're in a delightful state, you have more energy to give …in the form of admiration, kindness, respect and ideas.

As a mentally tough person, you rarely dwell on the past. You may have had the time of your life with a group of people, but the moment you leave the room you can attend to what's before you and leave the group behind. You may have had the greatest night of your life with a loved one, but the instant you leave the house you return to the here and now and forget about him/her. Does that sound a little harsh? Maybe so. But it's a good exercise in mental toughness. When you were with the loved one, your attention was completely there. And when you were out on the street, your attention shifted completely there. Being present is a sign of mental toughness. You love being with them, but you also love being alone.

The mentally tough are persistent. This can sometimes be seen as stubbornness. When they have committed to a goal, they stick to it despite changing moods and circumstances until it's achieved. Their motto is "I don't quit when I'm tired, I quit when I'm done". Even when inconvenient or uncomfortable, they can take action toward their goal whether the sun shines or it rains. They prioritize and filter their activities according to their main goals. That also means there's no hesitation in cutting ties to people who are harmful. This quality may seem cold to onlookers, but staying with a negative person out of "compassion" is actually a false compassion that serves neither you nor that person.

Mentally strong people are generally upbeat and optimistic and appreciate others. It can require some toughness to stay upbeat in a generally low-to-mid-energy world. The mentally tough are self-motivated. They don't wait for guidance, permission or approval. They don't require weeks or months to overcome negative events, only a few hours or days at most. The mentally tough are comfortable with change. While change makes many people fearful and rigid, the mentally tough feel elated and adventurous when things are moving and transforming.

Mental strength follows from a basic understanding of the nature of reality. The mentally strong understand that they are continually connected to the abundance of the universe but that access to that abundance comes from within and only by their own initiative.

2. Authentic, Aware and Shamelessly Successful

There's no "secret" to success. This section contains all of the shiny golden keys to success. Everyone intuitively knows what success is and how to have it, but few will actually do what it takes.

Surround Yourself with Success

What happens outside is a reflection of what's happening inside. To attract something into your life you first have to feel it. If you can't feel it, you have no experience of it. I like to say "If you want to have it, you first need to have it". As frustrating as that is to some, it's true. You attract more of what you already **are** into your life. That's why, if it's money you lack, you should be carrying around $1,000 in cash in your wallet at all times.

If you can't feel something, then you can try imagining or verbalizing it until you feel it. Often, fantasizing about something isn't really feeling it but rather feeling its lack, as in "well, I fantasize about it because I can't have it". If you fantasize properly, then you can feel it and attract it. But if you have a weak Imagination, then you have to be in the **vicinity** of it, be **close and familiar** with it every day. You literally have to **BECOME** what you want, **BE** what you want. If you want to be pretty and healthy then surround yourself with beauty and health; touch it, smell it, handle it, dress like it, be in its presence. Of course you shouldn't spend more time in a hospital than you have to, especially if you're not that sick…simply because it's the neighborhood of illness, not health. If you're surrounded by negative people all the time, then be sure to put your attention on nice things every day…a nice book, nice movie, nice thoughts, nice people, just to balance things out.

Be Committed as if Nothing Else Matters

If you have a goal that's important to you, dedicate yourself to it as if nothing else mattered. Invest love into what you do, as if it were the last thing you'll ever do. Of course **how** you do a job matters more than what the job is. All human beings go through the same lessons and experiences throughout a lifetime, **nobody can escape the human experience,** which includes ups and downs for **everyone**. Nobody is spared, no matter how things look from the outside. Who you're in response to the events of your life matters more than the events themselves.

The world is, in general, rigged against the success of the common person. Honest people admit they would like **unlimited abundance**, yet, we hear that unlimited abundance is "unsocial", "unchristian", "unfriendly", "immodest", and "unspiritual". In reality, most people do the following with increased abundance: feel more secure and **provide** for their loved ones. Give up your negative definitions and befriend money, study it, build a relationship with it, and drop any victim attitude you have created. **Money comes to people who feel good about themselves.**

Don't settle for just Dreaming

Dreaming is important, but not enough. Become the producer, director, writer and actor in your mind and continually view the movie of your dream, 3D and in color. Just as gravity pulls the apple from the tree, so does the Law of Attraction pull that which you visualize (without attachment) to you. If you do this properly, you can have almost anything. From what you Imagine, you must act. Act from completeness, rather than acting to gain completeness. Act as someone fulfilled rather than acting to become fulfilled. **Reality is a delayed reaction to consciousness.** Every time you realize that, your life gets right back on track. You may forget it often, because the mind isn't rooted in higher spheres, so it's important to remember it just as often.

Be a Trailblazer

A trailblazer lays new tracks through wild country. Trailblazers are rare. The rest of us look for tracks already laid, something to follow. We don't pioneer or break new paths, we take existing paths. We aren't groundbreakers or innovators but stand on ground already broken by trailblazers. We're not masterminds, conceivers or originators, we consume what others have created. To achieve major success, though, some trailblazing is required. **If you only tread ground already trodden you become part of the downtrodden.**

If you can make a kind of music the world has never heard, create a product that has never existed before, or do something that has never been done before, then you're a trailblazer. Laying new ground is rare because it requires a high degree of energy and courage. When I first sent my book "Parallel Universes of Self" to publishers back in 2006, they asked me "Which books can we compare this to?". That was a problem. I didn't know which books to compare it to, because I was trailblazing. In 2006, there was no book that related parallel universes theory to self-improvement practice. Now, nearly a decade later, there are numerous books that do, but there had to be an **initiator** and **initiation** to lay the ground on which other things could be built.

Everyone has something unique about them that they can contribute to the planet so that they can live respected and die regretted. You can increase your own trailblazing abilities, even on a small scale, by asking yourself what your unique contribution to planet earth is.

"Why am I here?"

"What is my unique purpose in life?"

"What do I see about X that nobody else does?"

"What can only I give to this job?"

are particularly useful questions in this regard. A Trailblazer often sees and does things very differently than what "everyone" would recommend. **When you hear the phrase "but, EVERYONE is doing it!" that's often (not always) good advice *not* to do it**. If you do what almost everyone does, you'll end up where almost everyone is. Where are most people? Wallowing in mediocrity. Genuine power is at the small tip of the pyramid and beyond what the majority deems to be right. In the Middle Ages the **majority** thought it was right to burn people at stake. In ancient Rome the majority thought it was entertainment to watch animals eat prisoners. Today the majority thinks that the complete erosion of privacy through the internet is acceptable. I wouldn't give much credence to what the majority thinks.

Trailblazers have a high degree of personal energy to begin with, but their energy is increased after their trailblazing through those that follow them and what those followers build on the tracks they laid. Society doesn't always reward originality. Societal inertia leads to conformity and "fitting in". People are terrified of standing out, being noticed, being different, and being better. Of course there's a big difference between people desperate for public attention that stand out and behave as ostentatiously as possible, and those who quietly stand out through talent and merit – such as trailblazers.

Rise to the Challenge

The sayings "Rise to the Occasion" or "Rise to the Challenge" mean that you meet the challenge of an event, that you **become better with greater responsibility**, which you improve through challenges. Many team sports athletes are at their best when opponents are strong, but tend to play lazily when opponents are weak. If a boss has doubts about your abilities but promotes you in spite of those doubts, and then you suddenly perform really well, you have risen to the challenge.

Without some adversity or challenge, it can become hard to generate energy. Many people tell me they lack energy. When examining their lives, I often see that they lack challenge, opposition and adversity. They have no occasion to rise to. If you sit around at home all day watching TV, you don't really need any energy, so don't expect to have any. If only good or easy things happen to you, you don't have the opportunity to be brave, creative or focused because there's no need to be brave, creative and focused. If, on the other hand, you experience some adversity, you can train your skill. That is why it's good to…

Embrace Conflict

There's no such thing as a relationship without disagreement. You might as well take off your rose-colored glasses and learn to take life as it's. If you insist that relationships must be defined by constant agreement in order to "work" or "be good" or harmonious, you're setting yourself up for a lot of trouble. **By the nature of two people being different, disagreement is certain in *any* relationship.** The idea that peace and harmony must prevail at all times and under any circumstances doesn't allow any room for disagreement; precisely because of that, disharmony will **increase**. It's not about eliminating disagreement but about how it's handled, how you react to it and play with it. You can approach disagreement with playful humor or grim anger.

Everything in life is a relationship. Just as there's no such thing as a relationship without disagreement, there is no such thing as a non-relationship. You exist in relation to everything else. Countries are in relationships with each other. You even have a relationship with the people you don't care about, even if that relationship is to ignore them.

Express Your Unique Gift

In my profession I meet many so-called "Life Coaches", "Therapists" and "Yoga Teachers". Many of them ask me about succeeding professionally. I give them about 10 points of advice. I'll share the most important one here: discover your unique gift to the world. The implication is that **everyone is born with something unique to give to the world**, something nobody else can give.

If you happen to be a "Coach" or "Yoga Teacher" or "Therapist" or "Healer", don't call yourself one. Why? Because too many people already call themselves that. There are thousands of so called "yoga teachers" and "life coaches" and "spiritual coaches" and "success coaches" in every city. When someone searches for "Coach" in Google, there will be millions of results. **Do you want to be one of millions or one of a kind?** Hence, I'm not a "Coach", I'm a **Reality Creation Coach**". That's unique and one of a kind. Furthermore, I'm "Frederick Dodson" – a brand that can't be copied. My most popular book isn't on the Law of Attraction" (there are already thousands of those) but rather on "Parallel Universes of Self" (there's only **one** of those). There are some people who now also call themselves "Reality Creation Coach", but because I was the **first** to call myself that, they will always be considered second. Similarly, Coca Cola will always be more successful than Pepsi Cola, simply because they were the first. So as a "life coach" you must position yourself as someone who has something uniquely interesting to say. If you want to reach the top of your game, develop and create your own unique style, method and vision. The essential question I ask all people who wish to succeed as "Coaches" is

Why should I come to you, out of all of the Coaches available?

Your life should be the answer to that question. 99% of the answers I get to that question are insufficient. "Because I help people" is insufficient. Millions of "Coaches" say that. "Because I'm a good listener" is insufficient. "Because I healed my own cancer"….wow! If that were true, that would be a sufficient reason for me to check you out as a coach. That's just one example. If you can't find any reason why it's absolutely essential for people to listen to you over all of the alternatives, you should find another vocation.

Increase Your Own Value

What kind of customers, clients, partners, and employees do you want to attract professionally? Whatever you define yourself as, you'll attract. As a professional, the price you ask determines the clients and customers you attract. What many people don't understand is that there's a target group for every price range in every field, no matter what price you ask. Whether you ask $10, $100, $1,000, or $10,000 an hour, there are people willing to pay for it. **Asking a little more money than you're accustomed to helps you grow into a bigger version of yourself.** You'll become good enough to be worth that. Regarding pricing it's also important to know that people only want things that aren't that easy to have. If you underprice your service or product, people won't want it. I know that sounds strange, but it's human psychology. Higher paying customers and clients make less trouble and complain less. This isn't only due to being better off financially, but has to do with a subconscious justification – "If I paid so much, it must be good!". So in their minds they will perceive higher quality, which is actually good for the customer-client relationship and business process and really does help them solve the issue for which they came to you. Asking higher prices isn't only good for you, it's also good for others because it allows them to afford more…by which they automatically attract more money into their lives.

Be Shameless and Authentic

Be who you are, without taboos. Release all pretense. You can't fool life, so live with fullness and trust. Be fully conscious all day and life will naturally lead the path. Only if you fully and authentically accept what is, can you transform into what could become. You can't change a reality you deny or try to avoid. Take stock of what is, take responsibility for what is, take care of it, then you can easily move to what you prefer. Everything you experience is a kind of earth-life-training to prepare you for the challenges that lie ahead. And what lies ahead is fascinating.

3. Life in Balance

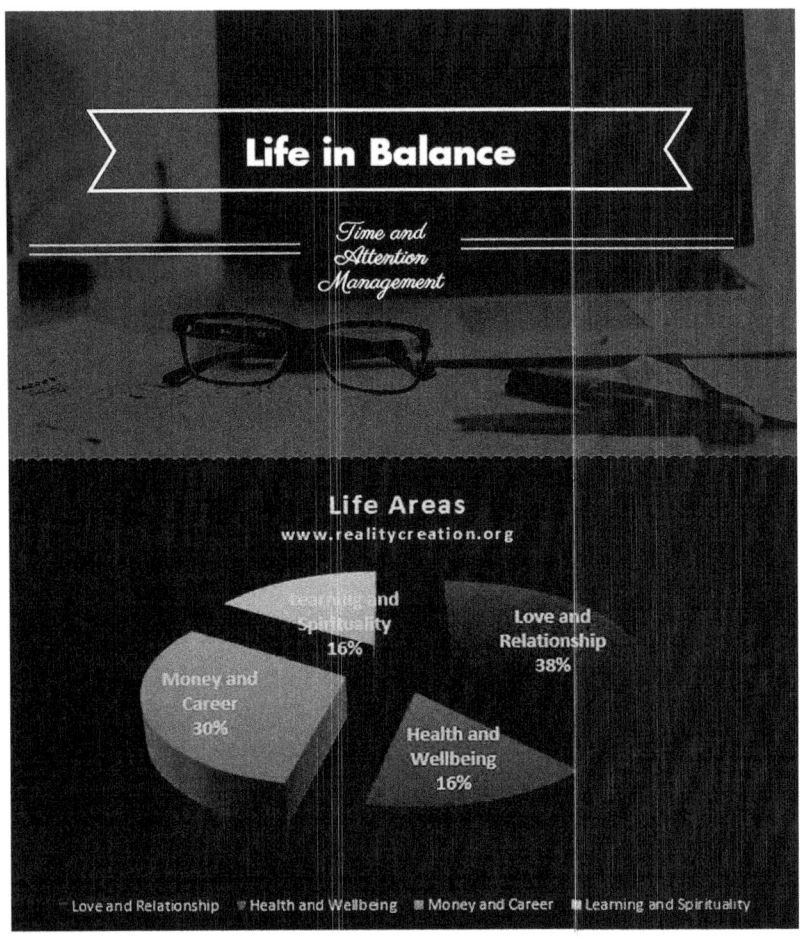

This is an example of a balanced life. This person in average invests 38% of their attention to relationships, 30% to their career and 16% each to Health and Learning. Such balance is rare in society. We tend to become fixated in one area at the expense of others. Consequently, life feels "out of balance". To bring it back into equilibrium, take stock of what you have been investing attention, time and money into.

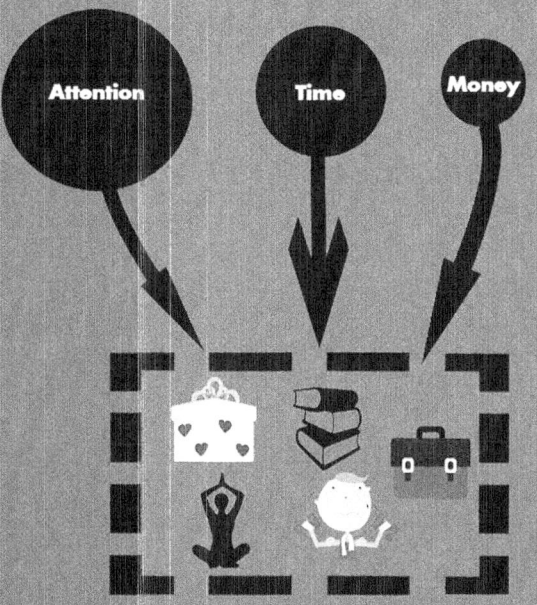

The three basic energies you have for investing are attention (which may include thought and action), time and money. The more you invest of one, the less you have to invest of others. For example if you wish to build a house but have no money, then you'll have to invest your own time and attention in building. But if you have money, you can let others build it and invest less time and attention. Or if you have no time for your partner you can make up for that by investing more attention within the little time you have. Or if you have no attention/energy to learn the guitar, simply spend more time at it.

With most people, attention, time and money are limited. It is therefore vital to prioritize.

Take Stock of your Energy

On a separate piece of paper list

a) five to ten thing you have been doing in the last weeks

b) five to ten other things you have had your thoughts or attention on in the last weeks

c) five to ten things you have spent money for in the last weeks

With the 15 to 30 items you wrote down make the following notes:

* Which Area of Life it belongs to
* How important it is (very important, somewhat important, not important)
* How complete it is (complete, in progress, incomplete)

Based upon your results you are now more clear on what to prioritize and what to let go of (release attention from).

Top Priority:

Things that are very important, incomplete and belonging to a Life Area that is underdeveloped.

Medium Priority:

All other things that are very important, incomplete or in progress.

What you can Let Go of for Now: All other items

Clarity = Power

www.realitycreation.org

4. Stop Trying so Hard

If you try too hard at something, it's because you don't really believe it.

Recently I was in a bike shop purchasing my first e-bike. It looks just like a normal bike, but it's actually an electrically powered model with pedaling optional. I got into a conversation with an elderly guy who examined my new bike and said to me "That's cheating. I believe that you should *suffer hard* to make progress. If I were out bike riding, I'd be concerned about what other cyclists think when I go uphill. It's like I'd be having an unfair advantage. They go through all this struggle, while I'm just cruising up the hill".

The guy's attitude summarized a widespread limiting belief, namely that "trying harder" is the key to success. I have found this philosophy to be true – *if one is unfamiliar with the power of mind & spirit.* At higher awareness levels it's entirely untrue. If you've programmed your subconscious with appropriate beliefs, you no longer need to "try hard" to succeed. The positive inner programming regulates almost everything. Trying hard is merely a compensation for poor inner beliefs. Yes, you'll succeed when you try hard and even harder, but you can also succeed with much less effort if you just adjust your emotions…which are your energy vibrations…which magnetically attract the right circumstances into your life. Case in point: in the bike shop the guy's face looked exhausted. Mine looked fresh. He said he couldn't afford the bike anyway, I could. My own health and wealth has nothing to do with hard work. It's everything to do with consciously adjusting thoughts and emotions. Another limiting belief apparent when he spoke was about the envy of others. Succeeding BIG, without much effort, carries a stigma in society. People get angry that you don't suffer like they do, but deep down inside they would actually love that, so don't worry whether others approve of your success or not. Even if they seem angry with you, it's not really **you** they are angry with. They will learn by your example and eventually improve.

As I enjoyed my new e-bike, I discovered that it didn't make me lazy. I consciously chose to turn off the electronic boost many times and ride it manually. I was able to cover vast distances with this bike…something I wouldn't have done with a normal one. Rather than seeing it as "a bicycle that cheats", I saw it as "a motorbike that allows me to pedal and work out if I *choose* to". The device allows for more *options. Rather than causing me to move less, it will cause me to move more because I'll choose it over a car when I have things to do in the city.*

Accelerating a car up to highway speed requires a lot of horsepower. Maintaining that speed requires a little steering, but much less power. One of the lessons ingrained in the Attention Training program, is that people generally try too hard. The purpose of the program is to achieve results in life with less effort. People generally try too hard at almost everything. That's why they may succeed in what they focus on, but it will take more time than necessary. I observe this "trying too hard" in all areas of people's lives. Trying too hard comes from lack of confidence. If you feel confident about something, you don't try so hard.

For example, if you try really hard to convince someone of something, it's because deep down you don't really believe it. If you try really hard not to make mistakes, it's because deep down you're afraid you won't get it right. If you try really hard to look good, it's because deep down you think you don't. If you try really hard to control your thoughts, it's because you don't. If you try too hard to impress someone, you've made external reality the source of relief. If you try really hard to make money, it's because you believe yourself to be poor – and will remain so, due to your belief. If you trying really hard to lose weight, your weight loss won't be permanent, there will be a relapse. Goals that require little effort, on the other hand, are easy because they feel normal and natural to you.

Where in your life are you trying too hard? If you look a little more deeply, can you sense the negative beliefs behind that? Behind those negative beliefs there are negative emotions. You may not feel the emotions clearly anymore, because they are suppressed. In that case, you no longer feel the fear, shame or guilt; you just feel a vague tension. As you get in touch with and observe your negative thoughts, they may arise again. Where they do, just feel them and relax into them and do some Emotional Clearing.

When I teach this idea, some have a hard time accepting it (they are *trying too hard* to figure it out:-)). They'll say: But then I'll become lazy! That's not true. Laziness is usually just a reaction to trying too hard. Laziness is the opposite polarity. Trying too hard leads to unnecessary exhaustion, the exhaustion leads to laziness, the laziness leads to trying hard again. It's a negative cycle. Consistent, gentle and incremental improvement works better than occasional bursts of unsustainable effort.

5. Life Outside the Comfort Zone

A great life lies beyond the comfort zone. This must be constantly repeated because when someone achieves something great, it's easy to go right back into their comfort zone by resting on their laurels. Those, on the other hand, who are still "hungry" and haven't gotten what they want are often more willing to step out of the comfort zone, to take risks, to show real courage, creativity and visionary action.

I know you're eager to get some relief, satisfaction and achievement, but don't want it too soon. Life is all about the journey, the path. The goal is a carrot to get you on the path, but don't for a minute think that actually achieving that goal is any more fun than the path to it. In fact, when you get a point where you can really have it, most of the time you don't even want it anymore. We only want what we think is out of our reach.

What do you do to stay outside of the comfort zone? You commit to never stop learning. You can make new goals once your old ones are achieved. You improve already existing situations. You trust your dreams more than what others think is doable. Or just choose something you're afraid of and then dive right in.

6. Components of Success

The components of success aren't external things such as titles, status symbols, objects, and certificates. Those are just props. They are side effects of success, not success itself. They lose their sparkle a few weeks after you get them. Real success is the cultivation of inner qualities that you develop on the path to your goal. These experiences can't be taken away from you. They're stored in your energy field forever. They're the core energy from which external symbols arise. Rather than focusing on the achievement of external approval, these are some qualities to develop:

1. Enthusiasm
2. Determination
3. Assertiveness
4. Integrity
5. Toughness
6. Communication
7. Clarity
8. Belief
9. Appearance
10. Competence
11. Technical Skills
12. Compassion
13. Teamwork
14. Awareness
15. Forgiveness
16. Action
17. Calm/Poise
18. Vision
19. Energy
20. Willpower

This list gives you a quick overview of what to improve if you're uncertain where to go or what to do. You can, for example, take one quality a week, write it down on a card and hang it up somewhere you see it every day. Then, in the next week, take a new trait. See if that doesn't fundamentally boost your outlook.

7. How I went from being a "Loser" to being a Success

In my late teenage years I worked for a sports shop, selling sports shoes and snowboards. The boredom I felt on that job was mind numbing. I could explain all the technical details and benefits of a snowboard but it all meant nothing in comparison to just jumping onto a snowboard and riding it. Who cares about the technical details of how a snowboard is built, isn't it just fun to ride the snow? Did the original snowboarders obsess about weight, structure and cost-benefits or did they just get on a piece of wood and ride?

Sometime in autumn of that year I was told that I would be fired because I wasn't selling enough and because I was generally too lazy and aloof. This was my first job, and I was broken hearted. My parents and I thought, "If you can't even succeed in retail sales, what can you succeed at?" At the time I didn't see that I was leaving a job that was a complete mismatch for my talents and interests, I looked at it as a deficiency on my part. My boss was right to fire me. While at that job I spent a lot of time partying and coming to work tired and hung over. Sometimes I partied all night and had to struggle to stay awake in the shop and even in front of customers. If I were the boss I would have fired me, too. It seemed I had failed at my first position of responsibility; instead it was the first crisis I turned into opportunity and then into success. Something awoke in the young me that wanted to prove that "*I can turn this around*".

The boss told me I needed to find a new job by the 1st of January and then said in a harsher tone "*You're no longer welcome here*". In the first weeks after hearing that I tried applying for lesser jobs in the mistaken belief that I wasn't "good enough" for that job. As I went to job interviews and was rejected every time, the whole situation started turning into a real crisis. I was even rejected from working as a cashier at a grocery store. Actually, I had failed at everything I'd done to that point. I had failed at school so I began working. I failed at work so I began applying for lesser jobs, and now I was failing at that too, a very humbling experience for a young man. In one sense I was a "loser" because I hadn't succeeded at *anything* the world thinks is worthwhile. Reality looked grey. While others would be buying Christmas gifts and fancy clothes I'd be unemployed and broke.

I started reducing my party time and taking very long walks alone thinking over life in general. In these walks I thought and thought and thought. Once I was done walking, I was also done failing. I decided that I *can* change my situation. A fighting spirit had awoken in me on these long walks and I started coming to the job I had been fired from and began behaving in a wide awake manner. "*These people are going to beg me to stay*" I said about the managers. Within weeks, my sales skyrocketed. Every hour I consciously intended and decided to be charming and friendly and to sell more than even the senior shop clerks - and I did. I began shaving, dressing well, always arriving on time and never being seriously hung over again. By December I had made it all the way up to becoming the third best salesman of the entire shop and the top salesman in my age group; in a staff of about 30 that was quite remarkable. The boss gave me strange looks of bewilderment (October) that eventually turned into amusement (November) and then into gratitude (December). During Christmas time when the shop was the fullest he came up to me and said: "Have you found another job yet?" I said "No", and he said "We need to talk. Don't sign a contract anywhere else yet". The next day I was up in his office and he said: "Well, Fred, I'm quite surprised with your performance in the last months. What happened to you?" I shrugged my shoulders, pretending that nothing out of the ordinary was going on. He said: "If possible, we'd like to extend your contract".

That moment was exhilarating, because I had turned "You're no longer welcome here" to "If possible, we'd like to extend your contract" within only a few months. It was then and there that I learned a very basic lesson about reality: I can influence external reality by first changing my internal, **attitudinal** reality. In this case I had so radically changed my perspective (and with it my behaviors) that I declined the contract extension because I knew I was seriously working well below my capabilities and not at all challenged by the job. **I had not only ascended to the point where I could keep the job, but even higher, to the point where I wasn't even interested in it**. When you transcend something, become bigger than the situation, you're truly ready to let it go. I had gone from begging for a job to having people beg me to take one. In the three months that passed I evolved from bragging, hyping my performance or trying to look good, to simply doing my job to the very best of my ability.

With my new confidence I applied for a job at a local Television station and got it and stayed there for a while. The job interviewer said he normally only let people with a college degree work there, but that he liked my **attitude** so he gave me a chance. I had made up for my lack of education with a high-energy attitude, describing to the interviewer the many things I could bring to the channel. Every success strengthened my belief and made it easier to generate an even better position and a better one – until I stopped working for others and simply invented my own job and company.

That one instance of turning around a grim reality created a pattern – a pattern for life. The pattern was "I **can** do it if I change my attitude". Another decisive thing I learned isn't to escape the job or the old reality, but to "make it right" before entering a new one. If you don't make the old reality right before moving on, you take the same failure patterns into the new one. It's been my experience, through many coaching sessions with people, that it's best to first "love what you do" before moving on to find something you like and "do what you love". The same goes for relationships: Before leaving a relationship, make it right, so you won't be carrying old baggage into a new relationship. Before moving to another country, make your life in your current country right and you'll be moving to even better times. Reality is holistic and the way you do one thing is the way you do everything.

8. Super Success Week

This is an example of how a typical success week might look. A week in which motion, momentum and energy are generated; focused not on what you reap but on what you sow. You'll want to adjust and change it to correspond to your individual situation. Know that it's not massive action that makes you mentally tired, it's boredom and resistance. Massive action gives you energy.

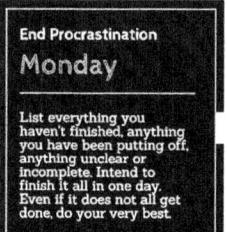

End Procrastination

Monday

List everything you haven't finished, anything you have been putting off, anything unclear or incomplete. Intend to finish it all in one day. Even if it does not all get done, do your very best.

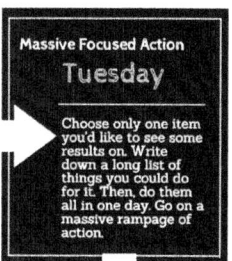

Massive Focused Action

Tuesday

Choose only one item you'd like to see some results on. Write down a long list of things you could do for it. Then, do them all in one day. Go on a massive rampage of action.

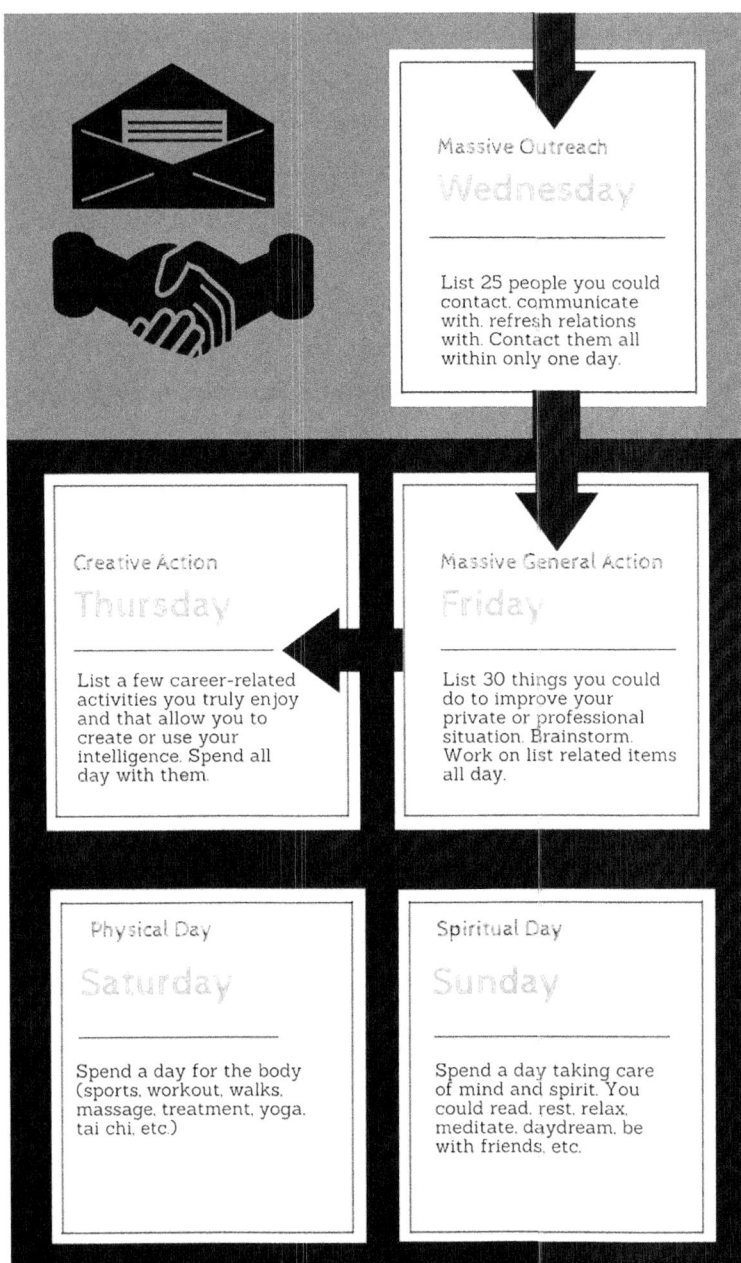

9. 30 Things you can Improve in your Life

It's easy to make small improvements in gradual steps day by day. Small steps don't overwhelm your attention span or your schedule and don't create backlashes or bring up difficult emotions. With that in mind, here are thirty things you can improve. This list will help you to focus:

Health

Income

Relationships

Job

Spirituality

Time

Self-Confidence

Attention Span

Popularity

Well Being

Accomplishments

Mental Toughness

Appearance

Business

Communication Skills

Interests and Hobbies

Skills and Abilities

Enjoyment

Willpower

Physical Fitness

Emotional State

Knowledge

Friends and Family

Creativity

Productivity

Influence

Assertiveness

Sex

Material Possessions

Inner Calm

Since there's no such thing as perfection, there's always room for improvement.

10. A Fork in the Road

"When you come to a fork in the road, take it." – Yogi Berra

There are points in life where you reach a fork in the road where you must decide whether to go left or right, to take one job or another, to choose one relationship or another, one journey or another. These are commonly seen as pivotal points of great importance. From a higher perspective, these **aren't** the most important "crossroads of life".

The really important pivotal points **don't involve doing or having, they involve being or reacting**. Every positive and negative experience is a fork in the road, an important moment of destiny-creating decision making.

Let me explain: Most of the time there's no fork in the road; we are just walking the highway of life. We are in a "normal state". Things are going "fine" or "OK". But when something *good* or *bad* happens, something out of the ordinary, that's what I consider a real fork in the road. These are the points at which you have the chance to recalibrate who you're, where you can redefine your reality more rapidly. A positive event can turn you to a lighter or darker highway, a negative event can turn you to a darker or lighter highway.

My hope is that you see the difference between this perspective and the common definition of a "fork in the road". The common view is that positive events leads to positive roads and negative events lead to negative roads. This **false** way of seeing is a limitation. Whether a positive or negative event changes your life to the better depends on how you react to it, how you handle it!

Sometimes when I teach this, people are initially puzzled or resistant. "What? Why would a positive thing be bad? And why would a bad thing be good?" We've all seen positive events in people's lives make them lazy, complacent, depressed, and arrogant. People say, "success went to his head". We've also seen positive events in people's lives make them resourceful, happy, creative, calm and strong. The success gave them a boost. It all depends on the meaning they attach to the event, and how they choose to react to it.

We've seen **negative** events in someone's life make them suddenly resourceful, calm and strong. They use the negative event as a wake-up call, rise to the occasion and become better than ever before. And we see negative events in people's lives make them depressed, fearful, lazy, tired and angry – just crushed. The event drained their energy. It depends on the meaning they attach to the event, and how they choose to react to it.

Every day has numerous small forks in the road, moments where you can choose to react positively or negatively. At the core, I don't really teach "setting goals" so much as "daily improvement" or "daily choices". Every day offers opportunities to go more into the light or more into darkness. Choosing whether to do one thing or another can be important at times, but even more important than which path you choose is how you deal with and experience the events on your chosen path. If you had to choose between 5 good partners, you may have preferences for one of them, but if you're healthy inside, you could probably find happiness with any of them. If, on the other hand, you're sad inside, choosing the best one won't make much of a difference. What **you make** of an event is where your power lies. What decisions does event X spark? Who would you like to be regarding event X? The soul doesn't have strong preferences regarding the roads you choose. Sure, a nice looking environment with nice people is preferable to somewhere bleak and gray, but the primary consideration should be with your inner state, not with the external world. You could actually "choose the wrong job", but your higher self could still derive plenty of valuable lessons and growth from it. You could "live in the wrong country" but the soul could still thrive there. It's rarely the events that are "wrong". Your inner attitude – that defines right or wrong, not always the circumstances themselves. In my life I've been in poverty-stricken war zones and made the best of the situation by lending a helping hand to the people there. I didn't complain about "first world problems" like "why isn't there any Wi-Fi here?" Instead, I used the situation to free myself of the need for comfort and become more blissful. On the other hand, I've also spent time in completely safe and prosperous circumstances, but never let those times lure me into complacency. **Anything** is an opportunity to go up or down.

11. Ten Things Sports can Teach you about Success

In many respects life is a game. A game with rules, boundaries, wins and losses, good days and bad days…and a game played in many different leagues and domains of experience. I teach the **rules of the game** because school doesn't provide a complete manual.

Because of the game-like nature of life, sports matches are no longer diversions or wastes of time but rather lessons in life itself. Sports matches are about reaching goals, focusing, overcoming fear, performance, courage, training, the dynamics of action and reaction, polarity/duality, and symbolism. **A sports match is a microcosm of life** and watching one good match can change your attitude towards your day. The study of winning teams can teach you all you'll ever need to know about success. Better than studying a winning team, how about playing on a winning team? It's 100% your responsibility what team you're on.

The successful team is well trained physically and mentally and **derives joy from competition**. If there's an adversary, that leads to joy, getting better and concentrating more fully, not giving up and retreating into victimhood. The winning team will play its game regardless of the weather. It will adjust to new situations. **The players won't let up if they win** (this is the main ingredient of long-term success). They will have comprehensive knowledge of the game and the opponent. They will work as a team. The fascinating thing is that, after some time studying sports, you **can begin to predict** who will win a game. You know so much about it that you can start reading a team's energy. From the players' statements before the game, their body language during the game, and their attitude on the field, you can just "feel" a win coming. I can see which team is in the flow, I get a tingling sensation in my forehead and can say "that team's definitely going to win this match". I'm no gambler but if I were I'd be pretty good at sports betting because any metaphysically trained eye can immediately see who will win the game.

All of this can be emulated in your daily life, far away from the playing field. From examining the nature of **games** and **play** you know that practice makes you better. You know that what you tell yourself and envision before your day (game) starts, has a huge effect upon that day. You know that you can "beat" weaker teams without much concentration, but if you fall out of the habit of concentration you may have difficulty summoning it when you really need it. You know that a game, like life, becomes easier and more predictable the longer you play. You realize that with concentration and a little help from your friends (team) you can achieve anything.

Don't be played, be a player. Make sure you know which league you play in and what is required to enter the next higher league in whatever you do.

If your life was a sports match, you would see the "difficulties" of life in a new light…as things that keep you on your toes and train you, not bog you down. In *The Pink Panther* Inspector Clouseau paid a villain to attack him randomly at unexpected times. He said "I pay him to attack me because it keeps me awake!" That's a radically different approach to difficulty than that of fear, worry or apathy. It embraces the game fully, ready to play. It's here that your search for the meaning of life ends, your search for spirituality ends and the playing can begin In summary, these are 10 things sports can teach you about success:

1. There's always a higher league in which you can play. There's always a higher version of your abilities and there's always an even stronger opponent to test your skills. Watch a major league game right after watching a minor league contest in the same sport and notice the difference in levels of excellence and performance.

2. You can ascend more quickly as a team than alone. Having the support and cooperation of good people around you or being part of a group-goal speeds up your ascent to the next higher league.

3. Willpower can be learned and trained. The more you practice, the better you get.

4. Speed, Force and Surprise impact Reality. The team that exerts the most coordinated speed, force and surprise usually wins. Transferred to daily life, this means: wake up and get going!

5. Having fun on your path to the goal is more important than the goal itself. Its important to keep the end in mind, but even more important to enjoy and learn from the process and all the ups and downs on the way to that goal.

6. **Losing can either pull you down or motivate you to get better. You decide.** "Losses" or bad days can't stop you, but your reaction to them can.

7. **Body language is important.** An athlete's body language affects his own and his opponent's psychology. The same applies to your body language, posture and stride in daily life.

8. **When your physical limits are reached, your inner (psycho-spiritual) attitude takes you the rest of the way.** Psycho-spiritual proficiency works best when you have already done the physical part.

9. **Success isn't a snapshot, it's a process.** Sports teams that succeed year after year don't do so overnight, they have been preparing for it, often for years.

10. **Life is meant to be fun.** Life really can be taken as a fun game to play and become better at.

12. Be a Skilled Person

It's a pleasure to meet skilled people. We've all met (sometimes in the mirror) those poor people who spend hours on the internet, when they could actually be learning to

Cook

Dance

Play the piano

Speak a second or third language

Carve wood

Snowboard

Play chess

Read a new book

Write a short story

Write poetry

Fix things in the house

Do card tricks

Design websites

Invest in real estate

Surf waves

Play the guitar

Study law

and do or learn millions of other things.

Every skill you learn is stored in your energy field and aura, radiating as self-confidence, a sense of achievement and purpose. Everyone can feel and sense whether you're a person with skills or an empty pot, deep waters or a shallow pond. Don't waste your life on other people's stories through news feeds, TV shows and Instagram updates, **write your own story**. You won't regret it - but you might later regret it if you spend your life sitting in front of a screen consuming "information".

13. Start Strong, Finish Stronger

Have you ever noticed how people tend to start strong and then quickly lose steam? A boss might employ someone who puts on his very best face at the job interview, excels in the first week of work and then slacks off quickly. In a relationship, two partners might show their very best sides in the first few months but than slowly recede into less interest. Someone might enthusiastically discover the Reality Creation materials, try it out for a few weeks and then fall back into old habits of thinking. Someone might reach a long-held goal but then completely disintegrate thereafter.

Why is that? It's because that person has no inner intention or motivation to keep focus, sustain focus, maintain focus, or persist in focus. That person will only be able to keep his energy high if reminded externally. The employee who slacks off when the boss is no longer watching lacks an internal reason to keep it up. His motivation depends on the external approval/disapproval of the Boss. The motivation is "I hope the Boss likes me" rather than the internal motivation of "I'd like to do this job really well for…myself! Because I enjoy doing a good job!"

Another reason for this is ignorance about how energy and reality work. The common misunderstanding goes something like this: "OK, first impressions count. I'll give a lot of effort in the beginning and then the ball will be rolling and I can relax. This ignores the fact that maintaining effort actually gets easier the longer it's maintained. If it's interrupted while you slack off for a while, it's more difficult to get back into sustained focus and flow. The person putting in small pushes of effort here and there will have to expend significantly more energy than the person who maintains their focus for weeks and months. That person develops momentum, an energy that can move mountains. One of the best places to watch the effects of sustained energy is in sports. Any athlete or team winning big does so because of sustained focus, leading to momentum, leading to being unstoppable.

For a moment, review some situations where you started strong and then slacked off. Examine why you were enthusiastic at the beginning and then quickly lost interest. Examine how you tried to make a good impression on others without really being dedicated, and then examine how you would like to instead start strong and finish stronger, because anything you dedicate yourself to in this manner brings with it the fruits of manifestation.

14. Non-Linear Success Dynamics

To achieve anything you first have to "really want it" (I don't mean "want" in the lacking sense). If you're not already acting to achieve what you say you want, you have to probe yourself on whether you really want it. A key question I often ask as a coach is: "If you **really** wanted that, wouldn't you **already** be doing it?" You see, if someone you love very much is suffering some illness and would require you to travel to the Antarctic to get medicine **you would do it rapidly and without hesitation**. You can tell whether a goal is real and appropriate by how eager you're to act on it. If you're, it's appropriate for you at this particular time and you don't require extra motivation or invitation. It feels effortless to get started, just the most obvious thing to do. This leads us to another subtle truth of everyday life: The things you're already doing every day are the things that you consciously and subconsciously really want! You might say "No, I don't really want this job", but if you keep doing it, on some level you do want it. Maybe you want it because you connect it to survival, but want it you do. Saying "OK, I admit it. I want all of this" is a good step in the direction of taking responsibility for your life. When you take that responsibility, it's easier to change your life.

Once you know what you want, you can add extra energy to your goal by asking yourself whether you're **willing to have** it. You don't just want it, you're also willing to have it, and you develop the feeling of

Willingness, which is a step higher than Wantingness. Everyone wants something, but are they also willing to have it? Are they willing to commit to it, to love it, to decide for it, to embrace it? That's how reality is created. Feel the difference between these three statements:

"I want it…"

"I really, really, really want it…"

"I'm willing and determined to have it".

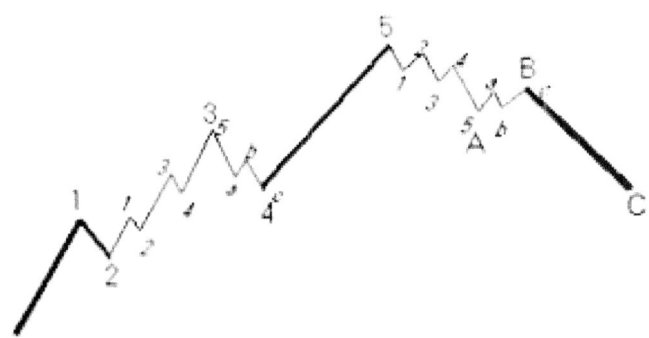

When you set a goal, progress doesn't occur in a straight upward line, but in waves. That's' why it's so important to sustain attention and maintain momentum toward any goal you choose. Point C on this graph represents "half way to achievement". But because it appears as if things have gone downhill, this is where 95% have already given up. It's like a "final test" to see whether you're truly willing to take it all the way. 95% – that number is staggering but its true nonetheless and explains why so many people are heteronomous. The "C point" on this graph just feels like "a good time to give up".

"It didn't work".

"Its just too difficult"

"I cant do it"

"It's just a dream"

Just beyond the C-point things move upwards again – if you have sustained your attention and belief in the goal. It's because things move up and down and up and down like waves that I keep teaching to "maintain focus", "stay aligned", "stay poised", "don't react to evidence contrary to your chosen reality", "don't cave in at the first sign of difficulty", "release doubts". Often it goes all the way upwards in rapid succession from point C. And sometimes it doesn't – sometimes it gets worse before it gets better. And so what, if it does? The "getting worse" is only another test to see whether you're really willing to stay true to your hearts desire. Goal achievement can therefore be summarized into one word: **Commitment**. You're either committed to your chosen goal or you're not. Everything else is just thinking and time.

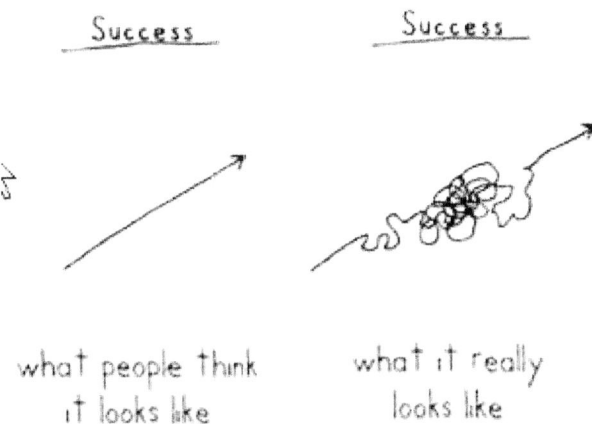

Reality Creation (manifesting reality by thought and intention) is non-linear. It comes from "the field", from "quantum potential". This means that it's not an exact science that can be measured in a laboratory. It doesn't always cause the same effects. 1+1 = 2 isn't how it works.

Instead, when you hold a firm intention in mind, the "field" or "universe" selects your intention out of millions of alternative energy probabilities. Whether your thought manifests or not is contingent on many factors, so strictly speaking you don't "create reality" and can't "manifest your desires". Instead, your intentions, decisions thoughts and visualizations **create probabilities**. Choosing to think, say or do A over B makes it more likely that you move in that direction. Choosing A over B many, many times makes it very probable that things with A-like qualities happen in your life.

When really wanting and really willing are in place and you remain committed to a goal, the particular method of achievement is no longer the primary concern. Methods and Techniques are entirely secondary to inner drive. When you fetch that medicine from the Antarctica to heal your loved one, you're not concerned with methods. There are many methods of accomplishing it. You could send someone to pick it up, you could have it mailed to you, you could book a ship and go there yourself, or you could book a helicopter. At a higher level, you're completely intent on getting that medicine and your resolve is unwavering.

Of course, sometimes this type of resolve has to be developed and built up. Because I'm very happy and comfortable with my life as it's, I don't "really want" anything that strongly (this is why hungry people can often develop more willpower). In my case I would deliberately increase the importance of something mentally and emotionally to amplify the feeling that it's something I really want. I would not, however, increase the importance too much, lest it turn into an obsession. On a scale from 1-10, I'd increase the importance to level 5. Level 10 would turn me into a crazed and unbalanced fanatic for that goal, likely creating more lack/desire than actual achievement. Level 5, however, would motivate me. One way you can increase the importance of something is by associating some pleasure with its achievement and some pain with its non-achievement. We do this subconsciously, but it can also be done deliberately. If I lack motivation to get that medicine from Antarctica, I'd have to think in terms of the pain it will cause if I don't get it (my loved one will die) and the pleasure if I do get it (my loved one will live). Connecting goals to people you love, of course, makes it easier. Love is one of the strongest motives around. The lone wolves among you'll have to put in some imagination to connect the achievement of a goal with emotional motives.

15. Creative Success

This section is for those who have creative jobs (artist, musician, designer, actor, writer, etc.). You can optimize your success as follows:

Stay true to your own ideas, don't take too much advice.

If you're working creatively, others can't really give you advice on what to do, because you're channeling your work from your own higher mind. People's opinions and society's trends are all well and good, but art is meant to create new pathways that aren't always based on what worked in the past or what experts think should be done.

Rely on yourself. "They" don't really care about you.

Don't wait to be discovered, liked, approved, and followed. Success doesn't come from the external. Success is loving what you do and doing it really well. It's OK to network and use others expertise but don't expect people "out there" to promote or discover you. They will, but only after you promote yourself.

Give it Time, Space and Attention

Every project, without exception, flourishes when given time, space and attention. Why not give your field of creative expression many decades or even an entire lifetime of time, space and attention? In this way you'll acquire skill unsurpassed by most people.

Giving is more Powerful than Receiving

Be the source of approval, the source of good works, the source of help, the source of energy, the source of love, the source of beauty instead of a beggar for them. This is the ultimate key to power.

Passive Income

Work to establish a source of passive income so that you have more freedom and time to do what you creatively want to do.

Realize your Unique Impact

What you create as an artist should be recognizably you, typically you. If people say or think, "That's a typical _____" (fill in your name), you have achieved unique branding.

Be Bold

If you want to rise above mediocrity (and don't we all?), courage is required. Be bold enough to put yourself out there, to show up, to become a target, to say things not everyone will approve of, to take risks. You're never going to make your mark unless you get a little crazy.

Enjoy the Path

Have a goal but once you have it, enjoy the path instead of lamenting that you haven't reached the goal. The path is what life is all about. Make small improvements to your creative project every day.

* *Everything has an audience*

Remember that absolutely everything has an audience. There are billions of people and among those billions are those that resonate with what you express. These people (your clients, customers, followers) are actually similar to you.

* *Be the first to do something*

With millions of people competing in your field, you'll have to be the first and only source of something. Find out what that is.

* *Make use of your current resources, be grateful for what you've already achieved.*

Don't project too much of your success into the future. There are resources you already have. Make use of them. There are things you've already achieved. Be grateful for that and do your best with what you have. Play the cards you were dealt well, and you'll stay in the game and get new cards.

16. Simple Success Tools

Please see the Video "Simple Success Tools" at www.realitycreation.org

17. On Having Goals

I first realized the overarching importance of goals in my early twenties when I was asked to assist parents with their difficult teenagers. I realized that once these "difficult teens" had a goal worth striving for, they rapidly straightened out. Without a goal, the mind is prone to wander randomly, getting lost. Even a vague idea of what you want and where you're heading is a start.

18. Let your Subconscious do Most of the Work

The subconscious can be programmed to do most of the work for you; it's an impersonal goal achievement mechanism. If you give it positive goals (through imagined or visualized images and emotions) it will automatically act toward their achievement. The same goes for negative images. Goals you program into your subconscious through visualization (during relaxation) will cause you to "do the right thing" naturally and habitually, without much conscious effort. Conscious effort is only the beginning of Reality Creation. Once you're "in the vibe", it should become near effortless. Hence people who are on a winning streak always win, no matter how lousy they are playing. There are some people who are on such an intense winning streak that they will succeed in whatever they do, whereas those on a "losing streak" will fail in whatever they attempt, regardless of how good their work is. Whatever you program into your subconscious is filtered through your identity (or self-image), so it's good to get that fixed first, to identify "Who would I have to be to attract what I want?" If you have a negative self-image then the positive goals you program for yourself are rejected, deleted or modified.

The subconscious responds to imprinted images, strong emotion, an authoritative voice or source, intensity and repetition. Picture your goal with intensity and authority and as absolute and the subconscious takes it as fact. As you become good at this, you simply show the subconscious an image or thought and it takes care of the rest.

In any case, being goal-oriented is preferable to being problem-oriented. Instead of wasting your time trying to fix the past, build a better future.

19. Something to Look Forward to

The real value of having goals lies in having something to look forward to. If someone lacks something to aspire to, the result is often a kind of apathy in which their mind pollutes their life with negativity and doubt.

Many depressed people originally became depressed because they didn't have any goals. They didn't know what to do and where to go so they sat around and did nothing. Sitting around is only beneficial if you're a good meditator who knows how to release the negativity of the mind. If you haven't learned to release the ego's tendency to express lack, resistance and aversion, it's best to keep the mind occupied with tasks and goals.

When you have something fresh and exciting to look forward to, you're aligned and focused in a different way. You have purpose; with that comes energy. Lack of energy is the consequence of having no purpose that you would need energy to achieve. In this state even small and mundane tasks exhaust you. **When you're looking forward to something, nothing exhausts you**. Remember the first time you were in love as a teenager, how easy it was to get out of bed in the morning and go to school? And remember how difficult it sometimes was when you weren't in love? That's how the mind works. Give it something positive to look forward to – even if it's only a weekend trip – and it will be more energetic and productive.

20. Accepting What Is but being Eager for More

Sometimes I receive correspondence in which people set out to achieve something, didn't achieve it and then tell me they are "OK" with it or have "found peace" with the failure or have "accepted" it.

Acceptance of what is, as it is, is important and a sign of maturity and a path to serenity, but it doesn't have to be practiced at the expense of achievement. *Always* "accepting" is just as pointless as *always* trying to achieve. Therefore:

Accept What Is but be Eager for More

The two concepts aren't contradictions. Being at peace with the present leads to inner peace, eagerness for more leads to growth. Both play an important part in life. Having a little edge of dissatisfaction is a good engine for creating and experiencing more. If your life is in turmoil it can be good to go to that lonely mountain peak until you're at peace, but stay there too long and it can get really boring without new challenges.

Buddha, Krishna and Jesus warned of **Desire** causing suffering, each in their own words, but it's significantly easier to release your desires after you have actually achieved some of them! Letting go of goals you wanted to achieve because you lack the courage to pursue them isn't really "letting go"; suppressing these goals creates tension at a subconscious level.

If you really want to achieve something and then a year later say "Well, I haven't achieved it, but I have found peace, I'm OK with that", it likely indicates you're not being honest with yourself, but making an excuse. If you do this too often you soon replace **Experience** with **Thinking**. If you wanted to have certain relationships but haven't achieved them, if you wanted to have a certain job but haven't achieved it, if you wanted to have a certain body weight but haven't achieved it, if you wanted a certain skill but haven't achieved it, you can either keep on moving toward those goals or you can give up. Sometimes there's merit to giving up, for example if you'd rather reach for something closer to you, but if too many dreams are given up and replaced by "peace", it's not really "peace" you're talking about, it's apathy, which is fake peace. Real peace is the feeling that settles in after you have really achieved a number of things and no longer depend on worldly items for your well being.

21. Should Life Be Easy or Challenging?

Compare the following statements:

"If things go smoothly, you're on the right track"

"Nothing that is easy to get is worth having"

***

"Follow your Bliss"

"Face Your Fears"

***

"Life is meant to be fun! Life is meant to be easy!"

"You can do what's easy, or you can do what's right!"

***

"Follow the path of least resistance"

"We learn and grow through challenge and struggle"

***

"If it feels good to you, it's good"

"Stand up for the truth, even if it's hard"

***

At first glance these ideas seem contradictory. Is life meant to be easy or challenging? What is more beneficial to the development of human consciousness? Lightness or Resilience? Safety or Adventure? Ease or Challenge?

The simple answer is **both**. It's a matter of balance rather than one extreme or the other. When life is fairly easy, you do what feels good, you relax, improve your health, get new ideas, and feel happy and tranquil. Taken to the extreme, this could turn into a selfish attitude that ignores suffering. Taken to the extreme it might create inertia and weakness. When life presents obstacles, it develops your resilience, character, courage and integrity. You become stronger, more confident and perhaps even more compassionate toward suffering. Taken to the extreme, however, this could become a recipe for perpetual struggle and hardship.

The truth, as usual, lies somewhere in the middle. In my view, most people don't have enough fun in life. They seem to subscribe to the belief that "life is a struggle" and that "doing the right thing" usually involves some sort of sacrifice. I'd guess that 80% of all people that I've met should have more FUN. They take themselves, their jobs, their relationships and their bodies, their communications and the world in general, way too seriously. This makes them heavy and they need to **lighten up**.

On the other hand, this doesn't mean to shy away from challenge and suffering. There are times for fun and there are times to be more serious. People who always look for the "easy way" by ignoring and avoiding difficulty generally become too weak to handle challenges. They mistake avoidance with "following one's bliss" or "following the path of least resistance", but avoiding problems isn't the same thing as following one's bliss. Two examples: If bills are piling up in your mailbox, then looking away from them won't make them go away. If someone writes you a complaint email, ignoring that email won't "fix" the problem. A student of mine once said: "I ignore all negative emails because you taught me not to give negativity any attention". That's a misinterpretation of what I teach.

Potential future negative situations shouldn't get your focus. Negativity that is already manifesting in your life should be acknowledged and addressed directly and swiftly. Once completely dealt with, it should be re-thought to a more harmonious state.

In other words, avoidance of already-manifest negativity does nothing to dissolve it. Avoidance of things you fear doesn't dissolve your fear. When I speak of "not focusing on the negative", I'm talking about potential negative situations or events that have not yet manifested. You shouldn't worry about falling ill, losing money, losing your partner, etc. if it hasn't happened, but if these things have already happened, rather than ignoring them and "going out to have fun" instead, you should fix them as fast as possible. It's this mix of confronting the already-manifest negative and then shifting your attention to solutions and the positive that creates a good balance in your life.

A recent discussion with a friend brought up a very subtle variation of this idea. He had told a woman how good she looks. "Does she look good?", I asked. My friend said "No". I asked, "Then why did you tell her she does?" and my friend said "Out of courtesy". And I said "So you lied to her out of courtesy? Wouldn't it be more helpful if you told her the truth?" and my friend said, "It's not a lie, its politeness" and I said "but if she never learns the truth, how can she improve?" My friend said "If I make her happy and she believes it, it will become the truth". And I said, "So you prefer to make people feel good rather than confronting reality?"

We both had valid points, of course. Courtesy is preferable if she is so fragile that she can't handle the truth. It's also preferable in social situations where nothing is at stake. What's the point of going around insulting people for the sake of "truth"? Most people eventually find truth in their own time, without me forcing it upon them. Implanting positive beliefs is often is more beneficial than reminders of a negative here and now reality. If I keep reminding myself and others of a negative "truth", there's too little energy given to a preferred outcome. But for a preferred outcome to manifest, attention must be directed there.

On the other hand, if you sense people can handle it, truth is better than courtesy. And by "handle it" I mean they are able to convert criticism to positive growth. Someone at the right consciousness level will prefer you to be straightforward rather than polite, but there are ways to communicate a hard truth without insult or damage. Authenticity doesn't contradict sending positive thoughts. If I were with the lady and she asked me "Am I good looking?" I'd probably bluntly say to her "You're not good looking to me". But rather than leaving it at that, I'd add "I think you'd look better if you wore less make-up". I call this "confronting the negative, then shifting to the positive". It's essentially how I handle all of reality. If I sensed she couldn't handle my true view of her, I'd buffer it by mixing in some praise: "You're generally attractive, but you use too much make-up for my taste". It really all depends on the context and what feels right at the moment.

I would never recommend that you mask the truth out of fear of repercussions. For example: Your wife asks you whether you can drive her to the shopping mall. You don't really have time and you don't want to. But you say, "Yes, sure honey". This kind of false politeness has consequences. At a subconscious level, you'll be holding it against her and won't enjoy the trip. You might even later blame her: "You know, I have more urgent things to do than to chauffeur you around!". But your blame would be misplaced because you agreed to take her when your authentic preference wasn't to.

Coming back to the unattractive lady: At a higher level, you're not really responsible for her reaction, regardless of what you say. If she feels attractive within, your judgment that "You're not attractive" won't hurt her. It might elicit a smile. Furthermore, if she feels attractive within, you'd have difficulty even coming up with the thought of her unattractiveness while in her presence. Unfortunately, most people aren't aware enough to realize that they don't have to buy into other people's beliefs…and for this reason, we use courtesy.

In my experience, life is delicious in just the right mix of ease and challenge. Paradoxically, life becomes much easier when you no longer shy away from challenge and hardship but rather embrace whatever comes your way. **People feel most satisfied when their day is split up in a mix of work, play and rest**. Challenges and problems make us stronger. Fun and rest help us remember our playful soul and re-energize for new challenges ahead. A life that is only struggle becomes unbearably mind numbing. A life that is only fun and rest becomes boring.

In my seminars I like to demonstrate this subtle balance of lightness and toughness. Lightness reminds us of higher realms, toughness teaches us to deal with earthly matters in effective ways. Some of the seminar activities combine lightness and hardness to convey the two worlds.

While most people probably think I play these seminar games just for fun, to me they are a model of life itself and its duality of lightness and toughness. I've played this particular game in several seminars and some have avoided participating for opposite reasons: "Because self-improvement seminars should be serious" (= Life is painful, not fun!). "Because self-improvement seminars should not be dangerous" (= Life should be fun, not painful!). Some avoid "too much fun" others avoid "potential pain". Their behavior toward the game was reflected in their real-life issues, which I sometimes point out after the game is over. The fun-avoider had the problem of being overworked and tired most of the time. The pain-and-challenge-avoider had the problem of always losing out to competitors. Why? Because whether you're afraid of losing or afraid of pain, your fear attracts its object. Embracing problems, on the other hand, repels them.

To live fully then, embrace everything: Tears and Laughter, Challenge and Fun, Down and Up. Life should not be hard, nor should it be easy. Life is whatever you make of it.

22. Your Bucket List

A question I sometimes use to get in touch with my **true** goals (or another's) is to ask:

What will you do before you die? A good exercise is to make a list with answers to this question. That should re-focus your attention where it belongs.

"It's difficult to understand the sum of a person's life. Some people would tell you it's measured by the ones left behind. Some believe it can be measured in faith. Some say by love. Other folks say life has no meaning at all. Me? I believe you measure yourself by the people who measure themselves by you". – From the opening of the movie The Bucket List"

"Bucket List" is a colloquial term referring to the things you want to do before you kick the bucket, i.e. die. **What do you want to see, do, experience, try, feel and be before you die?** I wrote my first bucket list at the age of 22 and had already achieved the entire list by age 30. I then wrote another bucket list where I have yet to cross off all items. The movie quoted above speaks of things "done for my own joy" and of things "done for the joy of others". This is rather interesting because at the age of 22 my bucket list was all about what would bring me joy and the later, more mature, bucket list also included how I might bring others joy. I won't go into the details here. No matter what your age, your situation or your position in life, you, too, should have a bucket list. If you're not sure what kind of items your list could include, search on the topic on the internet. A bucket list is for anyone interested in conscious and deliberate living. When you're peacefully resting on your deathbed and look back at your life, what are some of the things you would have wanted to do during your stay on earth? What would you like to do just for fun, and what are some of the more serious items on your list? What would you like to do for yourself and what would you like to do for others? I wish you well and hope that creating your bucket list is just as inspiring to you as it was to me.

23. Follow your Goal whether you Feel Like it or Not

I hear self-defeating and conditional statements like these a lot:

"I only write when the muse hits me"

"I'll only love her if she treats me with respect"

"I'll only work out when I feel like it"

"I'll start working properly when I get a pay raise"

"Once I have a relationship I can start following through on my goals"

Such statements make you the servant of feelings rather their master. They put you in the mode of waiting rather than creating. If you only write when the muse hits you, you're not going to be writing much. The truth is that when you just start writing, no matter what your mood is, your muse will follow your initiative. Of course there are good days when you're feeling great, but if you can also write on "bad days" and just move through that resistance, you'll come out stronger on the other side – and with a finished book!

If you only love her and feel good when she loves you first, you've got it the wrong way around. It's not about the energy another is flowing to you (saying, thinking, doing), it's about the energy you're flowing to others. It may sound shocking to you, but nobody owes you any respect. **The world owes you nothing. Focus on giving love, not on getting it.** We all fall into this trap of actually expecting and trying to command respect from others. We say, "You need to show more respect! You need to respect me!". Seen from outside, this is laughable. You can't demand respect. Respect is something that you earn from others. You're respected for who you're, not because you demand it. If you have been demanding respect, see if you can respect yourself first. If you truly respect yourself, you'll soon be respected.

If you're only going to work out when you feel like it, guess how long it's going to take before your body shape changes to one you prefer? If you're only going to visualize a perfect body when you're in the mood for it, guess how often you're going to visualize? Am I saying "force yourself to do it"? Yes, in a way I'm. This goes back to what I said about Willpower and Moving through Resistance. The first initiative is an act of will. It's by that first act of getting-over-yourself and moving through the resistance that you come out on the "other side" at a place that feels elated, high and strong. As you train your will muscle throughout life it becomes stronger and stronger and you become eager to live life rather than to avoid it, eager to face challenges rather than to avoid them, eager to test yourself rather than hiding in your shell.

Don't I also teach that you should follow your bliss and use feelings as your navigation system telling you whether something is good for you or not? YES! When choosing a goal, go within yourself to check whether that goal **feels right** or not. Yes, the idea of life is climbing the scale of emotions, but you don't climb by avoiding bad feelings, by running away from fear, frustration, sadness, resistance and anger. You climb emotionally by embracing and moving through frustrations, not by saying "Oh, I feel fear, so I better not do this". What happens if you say that? The fear will come up again the next time a similar opportunity presents itself. Do one of two things in this case: Release and Clear the fear in meditation and look for a higher feeling or state or take the action you're afraid of several times until the fear subsides. The way out is the way through.

If I go bungee jumping once, my knees are trembling, and I'm terrified. If I go bungee jumping 5 times I'm no longer terrified, just excited. If I go 10 times, it's a pleasant experience. If I go 20 times it's routine. If I go 30 times, I've mastered it. If I go 50 times it's boring. This is how we move through various layers of resistance to a goal.

Decide that I won't only love her if she respects me, I'll love her no matter what. I'll love her because I have made that commitment. I won't only write when I'm in the mood, I'll write even when I'm not in the mood. This is how writing has become a habitual pattern for me, why I'm **always** in the mood to write, because I decided to.

A mind that can create reality can also create long lists of excuses not to create that reality. Let go of excuses and follow through. When you set a goal that feels good to you, make its achievement unconditional. As you move through the resistance it may not feel as good as it did when you set the goal. That's alright. That doesn't mean it's not the right goal, it just means you've hit on some resistance to move through. And move through. And move through and move through, all the way up to the top, up to the climax.

24. How to get Yourself to Write a Book

Out of 100 people who say "I'd like to write a book", one, at best, actually ends up writing one. This section was written for that one person who will actually go ahead and do it.

I've written about 50 books and I've had 25 of them published. Some of them are with traditional publishers, some are self-published. Bottom line: **You can only write a good and complete book if you're really interested in what you're writing about.** If you're writing for others or considering what others might like to read or what the market wants to hear or believe, or what an audience will accept, you're cutting your energy short. If you write primarily about what brings you joy, your writing will be effortless and you'll get a whole book done. Sure, you might get a book done based on what others like, but it won't be a joy to read. What you feel while writing jumps out at the reader, as if by telepathic transmission. If you were enthusiastic writing a book, the reader will feel better reading it. If you felt bored, the reader will feel bored.

The basis of all working motivation is joy in its many gradients – desire, interest, fascination and passion. I recently talked to a guy who couldn't get himself to go to the gym regularly. I knew the gym he was referring to and recommended he go to another gym. The difference? The one he was avoiding was populated by big, muscle-packed guys, the one I recommended to him was populated mostly by pretty women. Immediately his morale went up and he started going to the gym regularly – just because of one small change, that made the task pleasant.

It's the same with writing or any other discipline. If you can't associate beneficial, beautiful, interesting, nice, fascinating, sexy, desirable, prosperous, awesome things with the discipline, you're not going to do it (unless you were raised to be a discipline fanatic).

Writing is easy when something really touches me or when there's something really interesting to explore. In that case, doing the research is enthralling and I eagerly look for every piece of data I can get my hands on. Later in the process, when editing, adding other viewpoints, re-writing some parts, willpower and discipline enter the mix. To not be "in the mood", but go ahead and write anyway…that's discipline, but that only works long term, if there's some heartfelt passion for the topic.

To be clear, you need not and should not wait until "the muse strikes". Once you have found something that really interests you and that you understand from your own experience, apply willpower to get started. Don't wait. Give yourself that **nudge to just start**. The longer you wait and think about it, the more you procrastinate. Procrastination expresses itself in these terms:

"I don't feel like it now"

"I`ll do it later"

"I don't have to do it"

"It's not really that important"

"What difference does it make?"

"Who needs my writing anyway?"

Etc.

Procrastination can be mastered by **just getting started**. In this case, I actually teach the opposite of what so many pop-psychology and self-help new-agers teach, namely that its best to "follow your Bliss and only work when you feel like it". The "follow your Bliss" part has already been established by choosing a topic that fascinates you. But from that initial point forward, if you don't start writing **whether you feel like it or not**, your book isn't going to get done. I completed 50 books because I wrote whether I was in the mood or not, whether I felt like it or not. You might object: "But if you don't feel like it, then you'll feel bad while writing and you'll transmit that bad feeling to the reader". That's not at all what happens. If I have chosen a writing topic that is blissful to me, then after only a few minutes of writing I get into it and start enjoying it. **Only the initial resistance must be overcome**. Only the first nudge is needed. Sometimes it takes a few minutes to get into a flow that wasn't there before. You don't allow resistance to dominate your Consciousness and move ahead in spite of the resistance. You break through the resistance, then you get into flow.

If you want to write, read as many books as possible, and not only in your field. I've read thousands of books in my life. I've been blessed with the time to read that many. Even today, I probably read around 20 books a year on my Kindle e-reader. My rule of thumb is "for every book you write, you should have read a hundred". I often read books that have nothing at all to do with my line of work. Why? Because it introduces a new, broader perspective into my consciousness. Even if you don't write about it, the information is "stored" in your overall energy field and enhances your aura as an author. You can sense whether an author has deeper knowledge or is only superficially educated. For example, I write "Law of Attraction" books and have noticed that many other authors writing in this field know very little about any field other than their own. It makes their author's aura shallow, and their work less relevant to readers.

To summarize the three ingredients of getting yourself to write a book:

a) Be highly fascinated by something

b) Have the willpower to start writing regularly

c) Read as many books as possible

Many will object and say, "I can't get myself to write regularly, what advice can you give me?" I'll answer "No advice. That's the nature of things. 1 person out of 100 will make it. In writing books it may even be 1 out of 1,000 or 1 out of 10,000. It's that way in every line of work. If anyone could write books, it would become boring. Writing a book means you're able to focus for long stretches of time. Not everyone can do that in every kind of situation and with every job. Simply accept that you're not in the 1% of authors. Release wanting to write a book, find the field where you're part of the 1%.

Read as many books as possible – that really means books, not the internet, not magazines or newspapers. Topically focused books allow for more immersion than the Internet (not to mention that the internet is full of bad journalism and poor writing). Have the willpower to start writing regularly – that doesn't mean every day. If you intend to do something every day you're setting yourself up for disappointment, because "every day" isn't sustainable over long periods of time. Be highly fascinated by something – and unless you're writing fiction, perhaps also combine it with something that is useful to others, too. Writing what's interesting to you'll give you the energy to write a book, but making it valuable to others, will bring in the money.

I'm not giving instructions here on finding a publisher or marketing your book. Why? You shouldn't be writing books if you're primarily interested in publishing. Don't get me wrong. Publication and marketing are very important parts of the package, but the primary motivation should be to enjoy getting an important message or story onto paper. If the content is good, the rest will almost take care of itself, and if it doesn't, I'm available to coach you to become successful with your book.

25. Going for the Win

Recently I was coaching someone who wanted to win a contest. This person brought up a common phenomenon: Initially he said he didn't want to win the contest but just participate in it, because going for the win seemed "too big" and could lead to disappointment, whereas saying "I just want to do my best" would protect him from that disappointment. After all, the competition was tough. I argued that he should go for the win whether he won or lost the contest. Why? Because

going for the win is the courageous thing to do. Going for the win is the **risky** thing to do. Going for the win is a victory in itself because you set the bar higher and step into a realm of excitement and challenge. And what if he loses? That's alright. All winners lose many times - but they play! Those who don't go for the win often don't even play in the first place. Every big winner in history had to accept many losses along with their wins.

Going for first place in the contest is a fun exercise that will help them grow no matter if they ultimately win or not, and make future victories more likely.

26. Spheres of Fantastic Success

Some people ask me why my coaching services and products cost so much. The simple answer is because they lead so many people to spheres of super success that dwarf the amounts I ask for my coaching. Consider, for example, the long term student of mine who will soon host a TV comedy show for tens of *millions* of viewers although he was penniless and ready to give up his career two years ago. The principles and techniques I teach are geared for long-term success in life (not short-term quick fixes) and anyone who properly follows them over the years ascends similar ladders. I'm not at liberty to disclose the identity of most of my students but there have been those who have gone on to become famous bestselling authors (surpassing my own book sales a thousand fold), become established movie actors (I had one student who was famous in the 80s, disappeared in the 90s and has recently regained fame as an older man), well-known business consultants and even life coaches like myself. Ironically many have become significantly more successful than me. As a coach I delight in others' breakthroughs even more than my own.

A common thread links all of my students that have achieved high levels of success: they all had the patience and persistence to stick to their vision over years, through many trials and errors, many of them being on the brink of bankruptcy, some of them having lost it all. "Losing it all" leaves one with "nothing to lose" which in turn gives the freedom to meet life **fearlessly**. When you meet life fearlessly, you succeed. With some of these students I share all the pains and problems over years of coaching, witness their sleepless nights, the dark nights of the soul, the initial mini-breakthroughs and finally rejoice when these accumulate to major breakthroughs. There's nothing more inspiring to me than a human being who has achieved huge success against all odds.

Not all of my students have risen to those levels of success. I'm quite certain that 90% of them are better off than before, but most people are actually satisfied with less than they can truly have or achieve, and that's fine. That's OK, but some aren't aware that they're satisfied with less. Their pattern is to achieve some progress in various areas and then rest upon those laurels. If you want to ascend to levels of fantastic success, you never rest on your laurels. Instead you continually look for an even higher version of yourself, a higher version of your experience. My guiding statement for writing websites, articles and my books is always: "You can do better than this, Fred". It's not: "You did a great job", it's "you can do better than this".

In the last two decades there have also been many faces I have seen for only one day or even one hour and then never again. I always wonder what became of them all and include them in my nightly meditations and prayers.

Reaching fantastic spheres of success also requires knowing your purpose in life, that is, what type of plan, profession, mission, vision and values are allotted to you in this life. It's as if there's a certain amount of success allotted to you for one lifetime and if you know what this is, you can access it. Your allotted amount is limited. That is, you probably won't be a famous basketball star or U.S. President. Those positions are allotted to others. But there's one field of work or area of life in which you can **shine** and experience fantastic success. Be willing to give up your relative success in another field if you sense that your purpose in life is actually something else entirely.

Last but not least, the best thing about your own success is that it inspires others to elevate themselves from difficult and unpleasant conditions. That's why I frequently ask for your success stories and miracle stories for publication on my website, to inspire and uplift those who haven't yet experienced success, to act as a guiding light leading them in the right direction. I give great thanks to everyone who has ever sent in their success stories, to everyone who has ever done this work in consciousness, to all who have shared my articles, and to all who have "liked" and commented on them on Facebook. You're all part of a movement to improve, to ascend, to do even better than before.

27. Let Go of Past Success

Attachment to past success can inhibit future success. This is one of the most overlooked inner obstacles. We consider past achievements meaningful and valuable and are unwilling to let go of the strategies, attitudes and beliefs that seem to have attracted those high-points. We fear that by letting go of those old methods, success will leave us. However, the past doesn't equal the present, much less the future. Attachment and clinging are a primary cause of failure in general, even if the clinging is to success. By letting go of your past, new doorways open to your future. Even the greatest success of your past can become stale and boring. There's no need to rest on your laurels, those laurels can be enjoyed and let go. What happens when you let them go? They don't just disappear, but your hands are no longer desperately clinging to them and you're now free to do other work, create even greater achievements. When you let go of an object by dropping it on the floor, it's still there but no more energy is wasted gripping it.

A typical place you see this "clinging to past successes" phenomenon is in sports where an athlete or team may have won a big trophy, medal or championship and then suddenly experience a dip in performance and vigor when the next season begins. Their mind is still on previous accomplishments and they are trying to re-create or ride on a reputation that is already fading out of memory. Getting to the top is one thing, staying there's more challenging.

We also see this in the "one hit wonder" phenomenon. A new pop star becomes so enamored with their sudden success, money and fame that they forget to keep creating it. Because narcissism isn't conducive to success, they soon lose it again and become what is known as "one-hit-wonders" who generated energy once, experienced success, found it to be lacking (external success is never fulfilling if you don't have inner spiritual fulfillment) and then failed to generate that energy again (subconsciously thinking "what's the point of re-creating it, its nothing special").

Sometimes, in order to achieve great success, you must surrender minor successes. A simple example: in my twenties I was invited to teach English to a very famous person. This job would have been a real success for me and built my reputation. I would have been able to appear on talk shows and give magazine interviews, and from there I probably would have become an English teacher to many other superstars. The only problem was *I didn't want to be an English teacher!* I had already taught English for many years and was thoroughly fed-up with the job, so I sacrificed this minor success opportunity, for another path - being a Reality Creation coach. I wasn't clinging to a minor success. The soul's integrity is always more important than success, and by advancing my career as an English teacher I would have "sold my soul". This is a really important point that every person needs to watch out for. It's very easy to become tempted by the glittery lure of fortune, but not all that glitters is inner gold.

You can let go of your attachment to past successes the way you let go of anything: By viewing it in your mind, without judgment, detecting the stuck emotions behind the thought form, letting those emotions run out and un-stack on their own and deliberately deciding to release attention from that mental image and emotion. With this technique you can release out of date success memories, success habits, and success beliefs. You remember times you were praised and applauded by others and let go of them. Times you achieved a goal and let go of it. Times you won a competition and let go of it. Times you were in a good flow and let go of it. Methods you believe lead to your success and let go of them. Something difficult you went through and conquered and let go of it. Support you got from someone and let go of it. A good feeling or state you had and let go of it, etc.

That will leave you with a clear mind that doesn't need to exert energy to maintain past data. A clear mind is creative and allows new ideas and pathways for your overall career. You may still choose to call upon some of the methods from your past, but now it will be from a state of freedom rather than attachment. Many of the beliefs that used to work at one time, don't necessarily work today. You're a different person, living a different life and have different attitudes than 10 years ago, and the things that led to some success yesterday may not lead to success tomorrow.

Have you ever noticed how some people seem to be stuck in another decade? Their fashion sense could be from the 70s, 80s or 90s, along with their taste in movies and music, their mannerisms, their hobbies, their business philosophy, their politics or their beliefs. A flexible mind isn't stuck in any decade or time. There are universal values that transcend time – they were valid 10,000 years ago and are still valid today. The striving for Love, Peace, Compassion, Strength, Freedom, and Unity are examples of such values. Everything else is just temporary, including fashion quirks and opinions. What the people stuck in another decade show us is that humans generally have a difficult time letting go and moving on, flowing with the ever-changing river of life. Flowing with that river however, puts you on the leading edge of human consciousness, where you're not stuck in the past, and can even sense what the next decades will bring and make use of that perception. The leading edge is a fresh and exciting place. It's full of surprises. *Surprise* can't happen if you hold on to the past and project numerous conscious and subconscious **expectations** of "what's going to happen", "what should happen", "what might happen", "what must happen" etc. Ask yourself: what inner expectations are you walking around with? Let go of them and allow life to surprise you with its many precious gifts. Today is a **brand new** day in which you can reinvent who you're.

28. Do what you Love and Love what you Do

I teach people to **do what they love** but also to **love what they do**. Both aspects are crucial because they guarantee a life full of love all around. If you never do what you love, your energy will deplete over time. Do what you love to find flow, ease, grace and a more rapid manifestation of your dreams. But what about all the things that come up in life that you don't love? That's where "love what you do" comes in. You're on planet earth, which is a place of great contrast and polarity where you can't and should not **always** do what you love. If you were to only do what you love, nobody would take out the trash, build train tracks or raise children – basic requirements of modern civilization. So with the things you "must" and "should" do, learn to love doing them. As you learn to embrace them you no longer allow external "musts" and "shoulds" to dictate your state. You transcend difficulty and ascend to the place where you can more often do what you love. If you resist and deny the "musts" and "shoulds" you descend in levels of consciousness. If you embrace and love them, you ascend. Find a vocation you really enjoy (do what you love), but don't give up when difficulty arises on the job (love what you do). Find a partner that is right for you (do what you love), but don't leave at the first hint of difficulty (love what you do). Look for something you would really like learning (do what you love), and then stick to that until you have mastered it (love what you do). The balance of doing what you love and loving what you do makes for perfect life success.

30. Success Attracts Success Audio Series

You can Download the "Success Attracts Success" Audio series from the Membership section of my website www.realitycreation.org

5

WILLPOWER AND SELF-CONTROL

1. Homeostasis and the Law of Attraction

Homeostasis is the tendency for self-correcting biological systems (like your body) to create and maintain stability. In physics a similar state is called Equilibrium. In everyday language it's also called "inertia". Related concepts are entropy and momentum.

This is why, when you endeavor to change something in your life or to create a new habit, a new success, or a new pathway, you'll typically encounter **resistance**. This is **normal**. Why? Because things tend to stay the way they already are, and they tend to return to their beginning state when you try to change them. If you focus your willpower to stretch a rubber band, you'll be able to change its shape, but the moment you stop monitoring yourself and stop applying conscious willpower what happens? The rubber band snaps right back to its original state. **This can be incredibly frustrating** for people who wish to create a business or lose weight or release limitations or find a partner – for anyone who would like to create new habits and a new reality. You invested all this effort and the rubber band just snaps right back to its original state! You tried to change the rubber band, the rubber band resisted, but with enough willpower you changed it and changed it and changed it….but then you briefly removed your focus, and you're right back where you started. Nothing has really changed.

Isn't this terrible news?

No, not really. Without homeostasis reality couldn't work. No reality could stabilize, no reality could manifest for more than a few minutes, seconds or days. This has disadvantages for people who want to change their reality but **very strong advantages for people who have already changed their reality.** When you've already changed your reality and formed a new habit and lifestyle, that becomes your new static-state, your new **setpoint**, your new stability, and then it becomes very difficult to leave your new paradise. When you try to change your new setpoint you again encounter resistance: Inner resistance from your own psyche and outer resistance from other people's doubts. Why do people resist when you change? Because you're threatening their comfort zone, their sense of equilibrium. They subconsciously take comfort in the fact that you remain the same. If you don't change, they don't have to change. "Nobody else is changing, so it's fine that I don't change, even if I'm unhappy with the way things are," they subconsciously tell themselves. Most people aren't even aware of the fact that they loathe your success and will try to bring you down. They are simply afraid of change because it de-stabilizes their world.

This is why for over 20 years I've continually emphasized Resistance, Momentum, Attractor Fields, forming new Habits, Changing Reality, Persistence, Perseverance, Focus, Dedication, Discipline, etc.

How can you deal with the normal Inertia that's part of how reality works? It's helpful to understand that this is normal and expected. Resistance to change is completely natural. It's the way it's supposed to be. When you start a new project, you may get external resistance (people telling you that you won't make it) and internal resistance (thoughts such as "this is too hard" or "I doubt this will work"). You might lose weight on a diet and then gradually creep back up to your old weight after a few months. **Releasing false teachings telling you that this inertia doesn't exist, and instead accepting and embracing this inevitable resistance is the first step to conquering it.** If you know this is normal and actually part of how reality works, it ceases to be a problem.

The second step is to gently and humorously move on in spite of inertia. When people encounter resistance they think "something is wrong" or "this goal isn't right for me". **If you keep stretching the rubber band, instead of snapping back to its original state, it will weaken and break. The old reality will disappear**, and a new reality, a new rubber band will be created. What makes change so painful is resisting the resistance, resisting the stretching of the rubber band, resisting the change. Most people would rather live with the comfortable discomfort of the old reality than to continue feeling the pain they must experience before reality shifts.

The way out is the way through. Once you really practice your new reality and you stabilize there, it's fairly easy to maintain the new position. When you set a new goal, know in advance that you'll encounter situations that run counter to the goal. These situations test you. They are asking: "Do you really, really, really want this change?" By maintaining your new reality, you keep communicating: "Yes! I really, really, really do want this change". And so it shall be.

When you fully understand this, you realize that focused willpower is one factor but it's not the only one. Releasing inner resistance and relaxing deeply and letting go is the other factor. Used together, the Tension of Focus and Relaxation of Focus will let you achieve what you want in life. Another thing you learn from this is the following: **If things tend to remain as they already are, you can act as if they are already the way you would prefer and you'll see quicker results.**

What does any of this have to do with the Law of Attraction? Well, that law states that you always attract more of what you already radiate. This metaphysical concept is, as we have just seen, compatible with the laws of physics and biology.

2. Developing Mental Toughness

The Threshold of Overwhelm

I attribute some of my accomplishments to mental toughness or to having a high threshold of overwhelm or a high AQ (Adversity Quotient), which is much more significant than IQ in my experience. The overwhelm threshold is the point at which you begin feeling stressed, anxious, frustrated, and tired about things and people.

Having a low AQ can lead to failure because you don't have the energy to move on in the face of unexpected roadblocks. Even an unwanted phone call can make someone with a low AQ !SNAP! An invoice in the mailbox can make them lose their composure. Just talking to someone who doesn't approve of them can make them question their very existence. In contrast, those who keep their poise and focus and move forward regardless of what comes up, those who aren't overwhelmed by adversity, **become unstoppable.**

An extremely low AQ, where even joyful events seem challenging, may be a sign of depression and should be addressed as such. A high AQ and resilience are characteristics of psychological maturity. If you're offended or hurt by the slightest events it's time to "grow some skin", "grow some balls", and "toughen up".

In 25 years of coaching I've seen everything from people afraid to write an invoice for a job done well to going into existential self-doubt just because they had a cold. Your dreams can come true if you don't let difficult circumstances, criticism or negativity reduce your determination, so toughen the fuck up.

Believe it or not, some people have such a low threshold that my use of the word "fuck" will offend them. "Fred, a spiritual person shouldn't be using that word". "Fred, I'm very sensitive to words, and I feel that you using such a word creates a wall between you and me and doesn't facilitate my growth". I'm not making this up. So I say: "Well fuck it. If you're that easy to overwhelm, maybe my coaching isn't right for you. How about some therapy instead?" There's a children's rhyme that goes "Sticks and stones may break my bones, but words will never hurt me".

If you decide you're going to attain your goal no matter what, you're not going to let a cold, a bill or disapproval stop you. You're even going to stay calm when storms of emotion rage around you. The eye of a hurricane is always the most quiet. In this way you'll navigate your ship out of the storm even if everyone around you is in panic.

Ideally nothing at all overwhelms you because you know you're not a body/mind but Infinite Awareness. The key to this is to resist nothing. Push against nothing. Don't be "anti-" anything. When you resist nothing, attacks don't hit you, they go right through you. They can only hit you when you put up a wall.

No Pain, No Gain vs. Follow Your Bliss

On a related note, some perceive a conflict between the philosophies of "no pain, no gain" and "follow your bliss". One appears to ask us to go through trials, obstacles, hurdles and challenges in order to achieve a goal. The other appears to say that the quickest way to happiness is by following what feels good.

Both philosophies are valid depending on the Level of Energy from which you're viewing life, and the two can be easily combined. Any time you set a goal or an intention it will always bring up its opposite, always bring up what stands in its way. That means that if you want to be perpetually happy, don't have any goals or intentions :-) Without goals or intentions nothing adverse will be stirred up. **Following your Bliss** means that you choose goals and intentions that feel good, feel right, feel like your **truest heart's path**. Choosing your true bliss is the **fastest** way to your soul, to your real self. **No pain, no gain** refers to the contrariness, roadblocks and problems that need to be overcome before your goal manifests as reality.

The only reason these feel like pain and struggle is because of your resistance. Give up your resistance and they pass right through you and there's no pain. It's a matter of practice to invite, embrace, and enjoy the trouble that comes your way rather than attempting to push it away or avoid it. Being in avoidance is the cause of pain. Embracing life, seeing everything that comes up as being an integral part of your path and the way to your goal is the cause of much joy, so when a an obstacle or challenge comes up, don't cave in that easily. Take the bull by its horns and ride it to greener pastures.

When you set an intention or a goal, be prepared for all the difficulties that come up, **because** you're setting the goal. Setting a goal in this plane of duality creates that which you label as "problems". The reason you enjoy those problems to the fullest is because you know they are springboards to the manifestation of your dreams.

More on Adversity Quotient and Low Frustration Tolerance

"I can't stand it anymore!"

"I just can't take this!"

"This is unacceptable!"

"This is too much for me!"

Have you ever said these things? I sure have, in the past. When I was younger, sentiments like this prevented me from moving to a higher professional level.

Increase your TO (Threshold of Overwhelm) and AQ (Adversity Quotient) and overcome LFT (Low Frustration Tolerance).

At what point do you become overwhelmed? What does it take to make you angry, whiny, exhausted, enraged, livid, resigned, or tired? How many hours of hiking up a mountain will make you grow fatigued? How many job rejections until you resign yourself to unemployment? How many complaints from your spouse until you shout at him or her? With a higher AQ it takes much more to exhaust you. We only get angry when exhausted and drained of energy. As long as you have sufficient energy, nothing and nobody can make you lose your calm or grow tired.

The primary secret to a higher AQ is to **embrace instead of resist**. Let's say, for example, that you don't enjoy the company of a group of people. Their conversation and their topics bore you. Hours tick away on the clock and you say "I can't stand being with these people anymore. They drain my energy". The weather is hot and everyone's had too much beer. The people get rowdy and their conversation level goes down another few notches. A good way of handling this would be to retreat and be by yourself. You enter a cool room and meditate or read a good book for a while. A sense of relief and well being returns. What you're doing here is managing your energy state. That's fine and it's certainly a better option than running aground emotionally, but by choosing this option you're not increasing your AQ or FT. To increase your AQ you would deliberately choose to stay with that group and try to raise your energy despite their unpleasant conversation, despite the hot weather, despite their inebriation. You would embrace them, start looking at them, start being with them, start breathing in and embracing the temperature, start enjoying their company. Taking it to a higher level you'd even offer to fix one guy's car, help babysit one woman's child for a day, lend another guy some money – the exact opposite of resistance or retreat. In doing so, you have just increased your AQ and transcended your resistance. A person with low AQ shows no interest, no support, has no thought of supporting others.

Another example: You might be sitting at home and notice that you need to clean up your living room, but just the thought of that overwhelms. The more you postpone cleaning, the more difficult it gets as junk keeps piling up. If you get up and do it anyway…regardless of how you feel about it at the moment…you're increasing your AQ. The messy living room is the adversity in this case, and you're tackling it. And you feel better afterwards because you didn't allow your subjective state to dominate your actions.

A general rule of thumb: my life is fairly effortless because I don't try to avoid effort but rather seek it out. What seems like a paradox at first makes perfect sense when you understand that "what you resist will persist". I would prefer to carry my own suitcases rather than have them carried for me, but ever since I have embraced carrying my suitcases, there's always someone standing by who would like to carry them for me. It's as if the reality of "carrying heavy suitcases" disappeared once I started embracing it.

The feeling of overwhelm is essentially a narrowing of attention. You're fixating on something that you see as "too much" in the mistaken belief that you "can't do it", but once you actually go ahead and do it, it loses its power over you. Drug addiction is actually the result of a low AQ. You think, "well, I just can't stand the state I'm in when I stop taking this drug. I won't make it. It's horrible". The truth is that nicotine withdrawal, alcohol withdrawal or even heroin withdrawal are no more "horrible" than having the flu. That's a controversial statement, I know. If you go through withdrawal you'll realize that it wasn't as bad as you imagined. When you have a flu you simply stay in bed for a few days, read, watch movies, and lay around. The same can be done with drug withdrawal. You accept that the state of withdrawal depletes your energy so you don't make any plans to go out for a week or so. Overcoming drug or alcohol addiction increases your AQ.

You never experience anything that's "too much" for you. If it were too much, you wouldn't be experiencing it. Anything life sends you it sends you because you can handle it.

Increasing AQ Exercise

1. What is something that overwhelms you? Something where you say "It's so boring", "It's so annoying", "I can't stand it", "It's too much", "It exhausts me", "It's overwhelming", "I need more time to process this", "It's too much of a struggle", etc.

2. How long could you endure it? (State a specific length of time you could "take" or "stand" it).

3. What would be the long-term reward for enduring it? Realize that if there were a reward such as health, money, love, enlightenment, you could endure much, much more than you think. The trick is to mentally associate enduring it with later reward.

4. Purposefully and **deliberately experience** the overwhelming item (stated in Step 1) for the amount of time specified in Step 2 or longer.

5. Reward yourself for having taken it, for having overcome that resistance and stuck energy. Notice that you feel stronger and more able now. Repeat until it no longer bothers you and you have transcended it! Next time the item (stated in Step 1) happens, embrace it. Seek it out.

While experiencing it (Step 4) allow your emotions to flow through and be the observer. Notice how the Ego is resisting the experience and do your best to reduce the resistance. The following three items reduce your AQ:

a) Not enough sleep

b) Not enough nutritious food

c) High temperatures

Make sure to have enough sleep, be well fed and in normal temperatures while experiencing it (Step 4).

This exercise isn't meant to be applied to things you're not experiencing. Don't go looking for adversity, don't go looking for a fight. It's used with things and people and activities **that are already in your life** that seem to be overwhelming or obnoxious. Errands and jobs you don't like, people you avoid, activities that seem to drain you.

Get out of your comfort-zone. If you think life needs to be easy at all times, it won't be. Life is a mix of ups and downs that come in waves. The downs allow us to appreciate the ups. It's not the waves we need to be concerned about, but who we are BEING when the waves are either up or down. "You can best judge a person's character by their patience when they have nothing and their attitude when they have everything". The idea that "I shouldn't have to put up with this" is disempowering. This princess-like attitude will keep attracting difficult circumstances into your life. A better stance is: "Throw me to the wolves and I'll come back leading the pack".

What are some times in the past where you could just **be with** unpleasantness, discomfort, and awkwardness? Contemplate this for a while. You overcome these phases in life not by running away from them but by fully experiencing them and coming out on the other side feeling reborn.

3. Breaking Negative Momentum

Have you found yourself trying to make changes but falling back into old habits? That's because all energy has Momentum. It's a life of its own, and even after you change, it can take a while before the underlying energy changes. Imagine a huge ship sailing in one direction. You turn the rudder in a new direction but for a while the ship still goes straight although you have changed direction! That's because of momentum. Momentum isn't bad, unless the energy is habitually going in a direction you don't like. The ship will change direction soon enough. Before it does, though, it will continue straight for a short distance, and then it will shift to the new Course you have programmed by turning the rudder. The same principles apply to the mind and its relation to experiential reality. Once you change your thoughts you have steered your life in a new direction. At first, your life will stay the same, depending on how much momentum the old energy has. If you're an amateur instead of the Captain of your Life, you'll take the unchanging direction to mean that "nothing has changed". When concluding that nothing has changed, you steer back in the old direction, and indeed nothing will change.

You can break negative momentum by a) knowing that it exists and b) knowing that new thoughts can be created immediately but that it takes the physical Universe – your life and reality – a little longer to adapt to your knew thoughts. Matter is more inert and exists within time. Thoughts are quick and exist outside of time.

As you continue to practice your new thoughts, these new thoughts and mental images become Beliefs. As you continue to practice these Beliefs they become Actions and Experiences. As you continue to live these Experiences, they become your daily life and habitual reality. At that point you're in the positive momentum called Flow.

Know and understand that unwanted habits have an energy field and drive of their own, one that you originally created without realizing the implications and then put on automatic. Don't beat yourself up if you can't immediately change your bad habits. Changing them is a process. Just keep working it and working it to the positive side and eventually you'll break them and find yourself, once again, in a brand new reality.

4. What will it take to Make You Lose your Calmness?

I began developing an inner sea of silence and inner center of power and awareness early on. I wasn't easily swayed by the winds of change. This inner calm has helped me tremendously in many situations. If you know that you're not the world and its events, but instead unbreakable and invulnerable infinite awareness, if you know that you're an eternal soul, then you don't really need that much strength and courage to practice calm and fortitude.

If I take $1,000 away from you, will you lose your equanimity?

If I give you $1,000, will you lose your equanimity?

If so, you're unaware of the illusory nature of the world. If not, then how much would I have to give you or take away for you to lose your center and balance? What would it take? I know someone who is currently practicing remaining poised, calm and strong at $28,000 debt. They are ready to close her accounts and take her belongings. Will she remain the calm eye at the center of the hurricane? If not, she will be swept away by the winds of change, but if she can stay calm, she will turn this event around to her favor and her long term empowerment. It's not only negativity that shifts us off balance and creates worry. Positivity will have the same effect, if it's "too much". If I gave that woman $28, 000 to pay her debts she would feel uneasy about it. If I gave her $28 Million she might go into shock. How much would you have to lose or receive to lose your center? What is your Threshold of Overwhelm?

Some people think I'm cold, dissociated or crazy because I don't react emotionally to various events. In a car accident I calmly get back up, wipe off my shirt and lend a hand to people stuck in the car. When I win the lottery I calmly announce it to my friends, flip the ticket aside and continue whatever I was doing before. I'm not bragging – this type of behavior is the result of 25 years of meditation. I've deliberately cultivated a state of emotional detachment. I'm able to feel great love and humor but it's very difficult for me to get worked up and worried about things. "Don't you understand??? You just won the lottery!!! Now you don't have to work anymore!!! Why are you still sitting there working???" someone might ask. I respond: "Because I'm already doing what I always wanted to do if I were rich, which is to be a writer and a coach. I don't want to do anything else". People assume that a lottery win will enable them to do something they couldn't already do before, but that kind of thinking is flawed. It's widespread, but it doesn't work. If you weren't doing what you love before winning the lottery, you won't be doing what you love after winning the lottery. All power comes from within, not from outside events. Yes, winning the lottery is nice. But it's even nicer to feel a sense of love and joy practicing ones profession. To create remarkable things is more fun than buying several cars.

How much does it take before you lose your calmness? What would others have to say? What negative or positive statement would someone have to make for you to forget your entire path and go haywire? Test it out. See what makes you go overboard and why, and then try to raise your threshold.

5. Mindfulness and Refraining

"Refraining…is the quality of not grabbing for entertainment the minute we feel a slight edge of boredom coming on. It's the practice of not immediately filling up space just because there's a gap. An interesting practice that combines mindfulness and refraining is just to notice your physical movements when you feel uncomfortable. When we feel like we're losing ground, we make all kinds of jumpy, jittery movements. You might notice that when you feel uncomfortable you do things like pull your ear, scratch something even though it doesn't itch, or straighten your collar. When you notice what you do, don't try to change it. Don't criticize yourself for doing whatever it's you're doing. Just notice what is. Refraining – not habitually acting out impulsively – has something to do with giving up the entertainment mentality. Through refraining, we see that there's something between the arising of the craving – or the aggression, or the loneliness, or whatever might be – and whatever action we take as a result. There's something there in us that we don't want to experience, and we never do experience because we're so quick to act. The practice of mindfulness and refraining is a way to get in touch with basic groundlessness – by noticing how we try to avoid it."

By Pema Chodron, from "Comfortable with Uncertainty".

6. Discipline and the Law of Entropy

List a few ways you could completely ruin your life today:

*

*

*

*

*

List a few ways you could completely improve your life today:

*

*

*

*

*

If you're in a "normal" state, you'll find it easier to list ways you could ruin your life than ways you could improve it. From a certain level of energy it seems easier to go into the negative than the positive. All you'd have to do to ruin your life is to go rob a gas station.

The Law of Entropy says that it's easier to gain weight than to lose it. It's easier to take drugs than to practice restraint. It's easier to leave your relationship than to work on it. However, once you have overcome the negative tendency of this planet's sphere, this law reverses and it's easier to maintain positive momentum.

An analogy: An airplane needs the most energy when it's taking off, once it's climbed to cruising altitude it requires much less energy. It requires less energy to maintain flight than to land again. Applied to your daily life that means it takes some amount of focus and discipline to get going, but once you're in the flow, nothing can stop you. The more focus you invest, the easier it gets. Tasks that seemed overwhelming are suddenly easy.

It's because of the "law of entropy", which is never mentioned in the numerous new age books out there, that I create as many articles, books and audios as I do. The consistent focus on what is good, beautiful and true helps you to maintain flow in a world that thrives on negativity.

7. Ten Ways to Increase your Willpower

The more energy you have, the higher your influence on circumstances. Energy and Willpower are directly related. When you're exhausted, you have no willpower. Energy creates willpower, but exercising willpower also increases your overall state of energy. Ten ways you can increase your energy and willpower:

1. Do one thing at a time instead of scattering your attention.

2. See difficulties not as an interruption of your way to a goal but as stepping stones on the path.

3. Don't suppress or express emotions, instead allow them to come up and pass through.

4. When energy is depleted, meditate or take a short nap.

5. Limit the intake of sugar, caffeine, nicotine, alcohol and carbs (after 6 o'clock) by eating or doing other things instead.

6. Keep relaxation and work in Balance. If you work productively, you can relax well. If you relax well, you can work productively.

7. Willpower is like a muscle that can be trained if you stretch yourself and go the extra mile.

8. Delay the gratification of impulses and desires for later, but don't delay important works for later.

9. Focus on what is important and what you can control rather than what is unimportant or you can't control.

10. First control yourself, then guide others.

8. Break on Through to the Other Side

You can deliberately **develop** willpower. The secret to this is to define a goal and then be willing to go through obstacles and resistance on the path to that goal. This is very clearly laid out in my book *The Reality Creation Technique*. This method isn't for marshmallows who cave in at any sort of challenge or difficulty. It's for people who know that resistance, obstacles and problems are an integral part of achieving the goal, not obstacles to the goal.

A good example of how this works is sports or working out. Working out demonstrates perfectly how willpower achieves results and how you must go through various levels of resistance to break through to a feeling of natural high and achievement. You might lift weights for 15 repetitions. At around the 13th repetition things start getting painful, but if you push on, through the resistance and make it…not to 15…but one higher…to 16…you have broken through a barrier and will feel elated afterwards. Over longer periods of time my persistence helps you lose weight, gain better physical health, release and overcome resistance, feel more alive. Sports is one of the best ways to train willpower.

You can read and hear people say that you can't achieve things through willpower alone. "Obesity is genetic. You can't get rid of it through willpower". "Smoking is a strong addiction. You can't get rid of it through willpower". "I have never really had money, no matter what I try". "I'm too old to find a fulfilling relationship" – all of these statements and a few million more are utter nonsense, no matter how often they are repeated in your mind, in the media and even by supposed "authorities". Throughout my 15 years of coaching I have seen almost every issue either resolved or strongly improved by the application of awareness and willpower. I concede that not everything is achievable through willpower, e.g. you'll most likely not become a famous basketball star, President of your country or a master of Telekinesis, but much more is achievable than many think. Willpower is a mixture of:

Willingness (being willing to go for something)

Decisiveness (commitment "no matter what") and

Concentration /persisting in something until it's achieved)

Attention is directed by Will. Will is a property of Awareness. Awareness is a property of Consciousness. Consciousness is a property of Infinity. Almost any problem imaginable is due to a lack of will, i.e. a lack of **energy**. Almost any human achievement happens through the will of a person or a group of people. Don't let "them" tell you that willpower isn't enough to make progress in most areas of life. I have healed illnesses through relentless visualization and affirmation over many months. I have written 50 books through raw willpower alone. I quit smoking through raw willpower alone. It works when you're willing to fail, to embrace failure. Thomas Edison and Nikola Tesla failed thousands of times before they reached their goals and invented something brilliant. If you're not willing to **embrace failure as an integral part of your road to success**, you'll never develop this supercharged willpower. When you finally understand that you must go through resistance to emerge at the other end, at the goal, you'll love those resistance points because you no longer see them as stumbling blocks but as springboards and signposts that you're making progress on your path.

9. Emotional Releasing increases Willpower

I once read a scientific study (I don't recall where) structured as follows: the scientists gathered three groups of people (A, B, C) and showed each of them a very sad movie scene involving the death of animals due to some environmental contamination. Group A was asked to suppress their Emotions, not to show any emotional reaction at all. Group B was asked to express their Emotions and if they wanted, exaggerate them a little too, so that anyone could see how sad they were. Group C received no instructions. The groups weren't told that they would be observed and they weren't told what the experiment was about. Watching the three groups, group A remained stoically unimpressed, group B saw some tears, and in Group C some looked sad and somber and some not.

Immediately after the viewing each participant was asked to use a hand-trainer for as long as their muscle strength would allow. After a series of repetitions of the experiment it was found and concluded that both Group A and Group B had significantly less strength and willpower left than Group C. Group C had plenty of energy left.

As I read this article I was **delighted** to say the least, because I have been teaching for 15 years that neither the Suppression nor the Expression of mis-emotion leads to a surplus in energy. Hence I teach Emotional Releasing (rather than Suppressing or Expressing), which is merely feeling what you feel when you feel it, and not feeling what you don't feel when you don't feel it. It's **the natural acceptance of what is** that allows emotions to transform and leave a surplus of energy.

In the above example, the willpower (attention, energy) of Group A and B were depleted by suppressing or expressing emotions, whereas the group that wasn't asked to do either naturally felt what they felt when they felt it, with no specific intention or exercise behind it. The above experiment (and as I learned later, many other experiments) also shows that energy and willpower can be depleted. It follows that all problems, whether with your spouse, at work, or anything else, are caused by lack of energy or attention exhaustion when willpower has been overstrained. It follows that the two most important modes of life are relax/refresh and train your willpower!

10. Other Factors that Increase Willpower

Here are some more methods with which you can increase your energy and willpower:

1. Limit sugar and carbs

Foods that are high on the Glycemic Index can lower your overall energy and willpower by giving you a quick boost at the expense of your overall state. Sugar is best used at times when you really do need an extra boost, such as when you're trying to quit smoking or going through post menstrual challenges. Carbs are best limited after 6 p.m. because that is the time your body is winding down and doesn't really require the surplus energy. You'll lose weight if you limit carbs to the morning and afternoon. I normally don't give any chemical advice, but these are time-proven: sugar, carbs, caffeine, alcohol and nicotine are best taken in in limited quantities, when a boost is really needed. By adhering to this advice you'll **certainly** experience a boost in energy.

2. Take naps.

The reason you get tired is so that you go to sleep and regenerate. If you ignore tiredness and keep on pushing yourself, you overstrain and deplete willpower and energy. Even a very short nap of a few minutes can reawaken your sense of alertness and freshness. If your lifestyle allows it, try to distribute your sleep through the day rather than taking it all in one chunk at night. This also applies if you're a teenager or in your twenties.

3. Do One Thing at a Time.

Many people claim that they can "Multi-Task" or that multi-tasking is somehow an indicator of superior willpower. I disagree because I know how split attention can subtly lessen willpower and energy in both men and women. See if your power increases if you focus on one goal at a time. While willpower can be recharged it's finite in the moment. If you're trying to quit smoking, build a new company, save your relationship, take care of your kids and get an athletic body at the same time, you may be overstraining your willpower. By preserving power, focusing it on one thing and doing that **properly**, you achieve more overall.

11. The Self-Control of Human Statues

If you've gone walking in any European city, you have seen "human statues", people dressed up in a costume who don't move for hours (unless someone puts a coin in their hat, after which they make one movement). No matter what happens or who ridicules them, no matter if a bird sits on their head or a drunkard tries to get them out of their pose, no matter how many attractions and interesting things are happening in their surroundings, they remain poised. Some human statues report that they would love to turn around sometimes to check out something interesting going on behind them, or to take a break or to respond to rude passersby, but that goes against their self-imposed discipline.

Human statues have always fascinated me because they exemplify what I try to teach in my coaching: maintain poise, no matter what is going on around you. I hear from students "But my wife said X, and I just had to respond!", "But my Boss did this, and I just had to respond!", "But reality delivered this and I can't possibly stay relaxed!" . Human statues prove that it's possible to remain poised and calm, no matter what's going on, and they gather the awe and applause of passersby, many of whom wouldn't even have enough self-control to focus their attention for 60 seconds.

From interviews conducted with human statues we can glean an important principle of willpower. Most of them report that the job **is utterly exhausting at first, but becomes natural and easy over time**. This is why I teach that effort is a good thing. Whatever you're investing your effort into, really does become easier over time. I also teach that if you wish to control your circumstances, you must control yourself first. Poise lies at the core of Reality Creation. Once you set an intention, simply refuse to respond to circumstances that could shift you away from your intention. If someone speaks harshly to you, just remain silent, or say "OK" and leave it at that. It's a matter of willpower. It may be difficult at first but becomes easier with practice.

12. Free Your Mind from Unfinished Tasks

The mind doesn't like unfinished tasks. It keeps nagging at you compelling you to run them in your mind over and over again. The only ways to free yourself from this are to

a) Complete the task b) Decide to abort the task c) Delegate the task d) Decide what you'll do with it and when

Any of these four frees your mind from the unfinished task. The mind also treats goals and problems (desires and resistance) as unfinished tasks. The more goals and problems as well as unfinished tasks you carry around with you, the more your energy and willpower are scattered instead of focused, depleted instead of stored. You'll experience a marked increase in well being and power by writing down all unfinished tasks, errands, emails, phone calls, projects, problems, goals, desires, hopes and fears and then applying one of the four decisions to them.

If you finish **everything** on your list you reach a place I call **"free attention" or "zero point" or "freedom of mind"**. I recommend that you stay close to zero for the rest of your life, but first you have to get to zero. Once you have gotten to zero physically, you can get to zero mentally, having a completely clear mind. For instance, if you have a tray at your desk where you put all unfinished tasks and letters and you completely take care of everything in there, you'll have reached a physical zero point in that context. From there it will be easier to take an inventory of unresolved inner issues and reach zero point there too.

Am I saying that the peace of mind so many meditators seek can be found by clearing off your desk? Yes, that's what I'm saying! The unfinished and unresolved saps attention (energy) from your overall condition. It's very subtle and not much energy is sapped by any one thing, but it accumulates and makes a difference.

Have you ever had a piece of music you just can't get out of your mind? You usually get these ear-worms because you turned the song off before it was finished. That may sound strange, but test it out for yourself. Unfinished songs are repeated in the mind again and again, whereas songs that have reached completion, are forgotten. That's why many of the ear-worms are often songs you don't even like. You turned them off. An ear-worm can be stopped by replaying the song to the end and then playing another song you prefer. The same approach applies to your thoughts.

The cause of *too much thinking* is a lifetime of accumulating unfinished tasks and issues. Incomplete relationships that were aborted. Incomplete jobs. Incomplete plans. Incomplete goals, they torture you and make you tense. That's why it's good to leave people in a state of peace. If you break off your relationship with your parents or partner, do so in peace. If you do so in a negative atmosphere, you'll think about them for years to come... and when you get tired of thinking of them, you suppress them into the subconscious, but they don't leave, they are just suppressed, depleting your energy even more.

In rare cases you won't be able or willing to finish the task yourself at this time. In this case you can still finish it "in your mind" by applying one of the other three decisions: Abort, Delegate or Decide/Write down how you'll handle it. You abort a task when you realize it's not for you, it's not good for you or productive for your goals, or it doesn't interest you. At that point you decide to no longer invest time, energy, and attention in that direction. This is easier when you list all unfinished tasks and prioritize them in order of necessity and then realize which ones aren't really important. There's always the option to delegate. Being overwhelmed saps willpower, prioritization and delegation saves willpower. If cleaning the apartment starts getting really tedious and you don't use cleaning as a meditation exercise or while listening to your favorite audios, then delegate it to a cleaning person who is happy to do the job for money. If there's some disturbance in your life that you can't get rid of, then delegate it to God or the Universe. Say: "Please take care of this for me. I delegate this issue to you". The third option is to simply write down what you'll do about the thing and the deadline when you'll do it. Some tasks can't be taken care of today, they await you at a later date. If you can put them on some schedule or calendar, your mind won't have to preoccupy itself with them until that date. More energy is saved.

What will you do with all the energy you save by coming to zero point? Well, those ideas will come to you much more easily when your mind is clear. **Free your mind.**

13. Decisions

One of the traits of will is the ability to make decisions. Life offers numerous options from which you choose where to focus. Deciding is the process of choosing to focus on one thing and not another. If you don't like deciding, it means you're reluctant to sacrifice one option for another. Decision reluctance also comes from knowing that too much deciding can lead to fatigue (exhausted attention, exhausted willpower). This type of fatigue is well known to everyone. Have you ever felt exhausted after shopping for clothes, where you tried on several dozen skirts or were asked to choose between dozens of shirts? Candy and gossip magazines fill the checkout areas of supermarkets because advertisers know that your impulse control is most fatigued after you've walked through the Supermarket and made dozens of decisions. Did you know that, according to scientific studies, prisoners that get parole are usually (65% of the time) the ones that are presented to parole boards early in the morning after breakfast, before they have become fatigued by making decisions all day? Have you ever gone to a restaurant, been too tired to decide, and asked the waiter "Can you recommend something?"

Lack of energy causes people to say "I want someone else to decide for me", generally people perceived as authorities. Sometimes that's the most relaxing thing to do, but if you do it too often you give away your power. That's the opposite of Reality Creation. You can exercise both your energy muscle and your willpower muscle by becoming used to making more decisions pro-actively, by letting go of things that aren't good for you (which requires a decision), by being less concerned with how you look in front of others, by prioritizing and by intending to stay fresh and awake despite the many decisions to make.

14. Divine Will & Personal Will

In *The Reality Creation Technique* I differentiate between Personal Will and Divine Will, saying that when one has reached the limits of Personal Will, one should surrender to Divine Will.

Recognizing only personal will without the larger context of Divine Will leads to arrogance and ultimately to humiliation once you realize you're powerful but not all-powerful. One of the people who gave willpower a really bad name in the 20th Century was Adolf Hitler along with Fascism in general. The Nazis' most famous propaganda movie was called "Triumph of the Will". Nazis and other Fascists were aware of the power of will and they displayed it in grandiose architecture, military machinery and athletic superiority. The Nazis strove for a superhuman state, a kind of yogic purity, which included supposedly "cultural, ethnic and racial purity". Fascism results when personal will and the will of "the State" is aggrandized and put above Divine Will. Divine Source is then replaced with a political figure to worship, such as Adolf Hitler. Hitler's arrogance was further fueled by drug abuse as well as the influence of negative-vibration discarnate entities, in my opinion. Similar outcomes occurred in totalitarian communist regimes where the political leader was worshiped instead of divinity. Rather than developing will, individual subjects of these regimes were taught to release all their will to the leader. When this happens, a country is in for trouble, as evidenced by Stalin, Pol Pot and other genocidal dictators.

Because of the horrifying disasters that human willpower has caused throughout History, from the destruction of Atlantis to World War II, humans have become afraid of their power because of the harm it can cause. This is why hundreds of textbooks throughout History contain reference to "thy will be done" rather than "my will be done". Once the Ego-Self discovers that it can create its own reality, it doesn't take long before it discovers that it create mass reality through willpower. If that Ego-Self isn't grounded in love, humility and kindness, its raw willpower is often destructive instead of creative.

Practicing this material gradually increases your powers over time. Your personal will is capable of much more than most people realize, but this personal will also has limits and can have adverse effects if not balanced with the idea of a higher context. Train your will to its limits, use it for the good, and don't forget to request higher guidance in all your endeavors, and to only act for the highest good.

15. The Proactive Mindset

Having or lacking energy can be observed in how proactive people are. The fact that most people lack a sense of self-determination can be witnessed in **any** scenario:

Example 1: Learning a Language

In language courses 80% of language learners prefer that the teacher gives examples of using new vocabulary, to *make* sentences with new vocabulary and to *put* them to use. Only around 20% try to **create their own** phrases, sentences and examples of newly learned words. Doing that requires energy, of course. Once students are prompted by the teacher to create their own examples, at least 60% start proactively making sentences with 40% still "waiting for something to happen". If they have a teacher that has too much Ego and exerts too much of his own will (a teacher that does too much of the talking), this may further reduce the students' efforts. It's not really possible to learn a full language without your **own** speaking and sentence-making efforts, yet many want to do just that. They hope a language can be learned without any effort at all. While there are methods to reduce effort, such as deep relaxation, picture learning and intuitive learning, you can't really learn a language without exerting some energy yourself.

Example 2: Maintaining Relationships

It's easy to be kind and friendly when your partner is also kind and friendly. On the other hand, it can require willpower or at least a deliberate intention to stay kind and friendly when your partner is in a really bad mood, and it could require a little more deliberate awareness to stay kind and friendly when your partner is openly criticizing you. **Most relationships break up due to energy exhaustion** of the two partners. Most fights happen when one or both of the partners are tired. If you have the energy and have built positive momentum, you can literally maintain a relationship forever. If you have been in a relationship for a long time, it may take some effort not to take the other person for granted and instead perceive them with fresh eyes, be there for them, and generate some interest. Once you have invested just a little proactive effort, however, your relationship can go on effortlessly for years. Here's the point: every time things begin to slide downwards, its time to regain some self-determination and control over your life again, before going back to the effortlessness of auto-pilot. I`ll share a secret: **any** relationship, with anyone at all, can be positively maintained with your loving attention to it and them and yourself. If you're clear and cleaned-up within yourself, almost any partner is the right one and **any** relationship carries the potential for mutual growth.

Example 3: Professional Life

Anytime you find yourself waiting for something to happen, for better times to come, or for an offer or a customer or money, you're in reactive mode. Self-determination, fueled by personal will, **doesn't wait** for something better to happen. It goes into focused and inspired action today, making dozens of **decisions** in a day, overcoming dozens of instances of procrastination, initiating new ideas and approaches. Life is on hold as long as you're on hold. Life starts moving again, once you start moving. Nothing happens **to** you, everything happens **through** you. Once you get into the habit of decision making, it no longer depletes willpower, instead it gives you energy. You're then in a state of Flow to make decisions and take action. If things seem to be on hold in your life, I recommend you go on a **Rampage of Action** by getting more done in one day than you got done the entire previous month. After this Rampage you'll be tired when going to bed, but it will be the kind of tiredness that feels really, really good and creates a deep and restful sleep.

Seen from a higher vantage point, the idea that if you invest energy into something it's energy (time, money or attention) *spent,* may seem accurate, but from a metaphysical standpoint it's flawed. Everything you give actually comes back to you and usually manyfold.

16. Free Will vs. Destiny

Is your life pre-destined or created by free-will? Twenty years of psycho-spiritual counseling, intense research and dedication have led me to believe that much of your life can be created by yourself, while some of it's pre-destined. Some think everything is created through exercise of free will, and some think everything is pre-destined and some think everything is random. My own research agrees with none of these stances. There's so much ongoing debate and controversy around the subject because each view is true to some extent, though not completely. I have summarized my own view of the influence of Destiny, Free Will and Randomness on a conscious person in this pie chart:

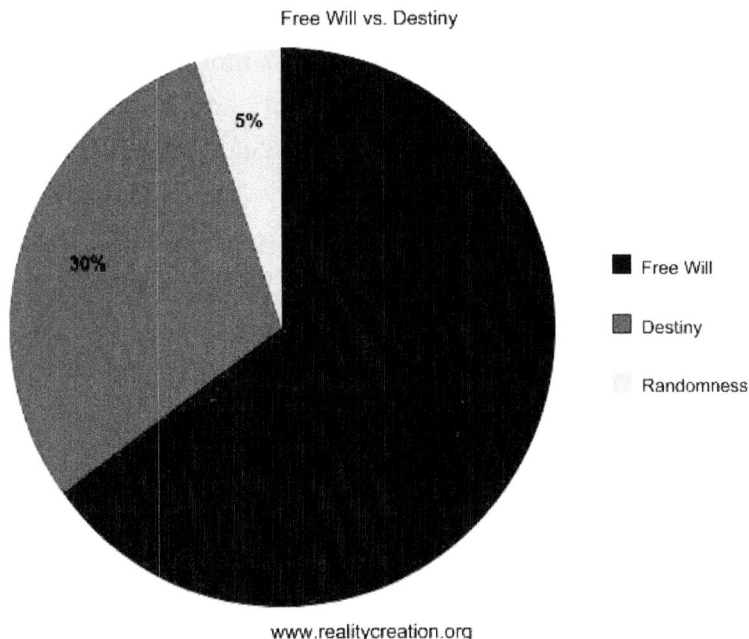

I believe you can shape at least 65% of your reality through the choices you make and what you focus on in thought, word and deed. However, this is merely your **potential** to shape your reality. Realistically, most people use their free will for around 10% of their reality and leave the rest up to destiny, karma and randomness. About 30% of life on earth seems not to be in your power but influenced by higher forces. Perhaps these 30% are your karma at work (positive or negative past life karma that you have accumulated). Maybe it's your soul/higher self at work that has pre-defined a certain path in life that you can't stray from. These pre-defined soul paths are usually very general though. They pre-define that you won't become a famous basketball player because your body is simply too short, or that you'll grow up in a well-off household, etc. What you make of the pre-defined path is up to your free will, if you choose to exercise it. The remaining 30% may also be due to pre-programming by Source/Creator/God, as if to say "OK, the purpose of this soul is X, what this soul makes of it's their free choice". About 5%

of events in ones reality appear to be random or of unknown causes. This is as if the creative intelligence behind reality introduced some randomness "just for fun".

This is reflected in many of the games (board games, sports games, computer games) we play on earth. The results of those games are pre-determined in part (such as the game rules, the field size, the skills), a small part is random (through a roll of the dice or drawing cards) and the largest part is determined by your own choices, moves, imagination and willpower.

I may be wrong about the ratio of the three factors, and many bright minds will disagree with me one way or the other. There are scientists out there trying to prove that we have zero free will. There are also metaphysicians out there trying to prove that everything is 100% created by you. I publish this pie chart so that you can start thinking about the ratio yourself and check for yourself what is true.

I believe that using your own power, you can change around 65% of all issues in your life. For the remaining 35% it's not certain whether they can be changed or not. In this case you either accept them (play the cards you were dealt) or request higher-source (divine will) support.

17. Changing Patterns

One way to increase your overall willpower (and thereby state of energy and vitality) is by deliberately changing your habits and behavioral patterns. The following examples of altering behavior may have no direct relevance to your goals, but any of them can benefit your goal achievement because **as you change one thing in your life, that change spills over to other areas in your life**. The popular view that if you take one positive step forward you're more likely to take a negative step back because, for example working out makes you think you deserve some chocolate isn't true in my coaching experience. On the contrary, one positive step makes you more likely to take other positive steps. Like attracts like.

Reverting to old negative patterns only happens if you lose momentum. A student of mine who is a professional national-team basketball player told me that if she fails to exercise for a few weeks, that attracts other negative habits, such as not cleaning up her place or eating more sweets. (As mentioned previously sweets do nothing for your willpower. They give you a quick high and then flatten you soon afterwards.). If, however, she maintains her regular exercise, this facilitates other positive behaviors, such as being patient with her children or maintaining. I can confirm that this is the way it works. Here are some examples of ways to change patterns, habits and routines:

Walking Backwards

In my early twenties I walked the same path to work every day. I used this time to make several deliberate changes in my thinking and acting. One of the things I would do is walk backwards to work. This changed my habitual morning thinking, which in turn made my day more creative.

Brushing your Teeth with the other Hand

Why not switch the hands with which you brush your teeth? This quick behavioral shift demonstrates to your mind that you're not running your life on automatic but are deliberately creating your experience.

Changing your Posture

Try changing your body posture several times throughout the day. It will immediately transport you into the here and now, making you more aware and awake. Every deliberate act you do trains your willpower.

Enjoy Something you Normally don't Enjoy

Take something you resist, and try to enjoy it instead. It's pointless to resist standing in a grocery store line. Why not focus on thoroughly enjoying it next time? Don't be a victim of circumstance.

Change your Speech Patterns

If you always used fillers such as "like" or "actually", why not do without them for a week? Small changes can create big things. Such a simple tool can turn your whole world upside down because you're actually beginning to pay deliberate attention to how you create your life.

These were only five examples; you could come up with hundreds of other ways to exercise willpower and awareness - the primary keys to success in life.

18. The Value of Repetition and Practice

It's said that "repetition is the mother of skill", and that "practice makes perfect". These are universal truths that apply for anyone anywhere. What you focus on becomes more and more real. One of the primary ways to focus attention is through repetition. Your reality isn't shaped by what you do sometimes. It's not shaped by what you do now and then. It's shaped by what you do **consistently**, on a regular basis. If you have low energy and willpower, you'll find it tedious or impossible to repeat various skills, but if you do have the energy, you'll enjoy any sort of drill. On the other hand, by repetition and practice, whatever you place your focus on, becomes easier and begins taking less energy and less willpower to sustain. This goes for anything at all – playing the piano, playing tennis, visualization, dream exploration, wine tasting, writing, physical exercise, life success, health, romance, communication, playing poker, attending school – anything at all. Often, you go through the following phases as you repeat a skill:

Phase 1: Initial resistance. Having to overcome and discipline yourself to "go there" or "do that". In Phase 1 you'll have to overcome impulses to just give up. Most people never move beyond this phase..

Phase 2: You can do it, but there's still significant conscious effort required and you're not as skilled as others who have been doing it longer.

Phase 3: Sometimes you enjoy it, sometimes you don't.

Phase 4: You have fully embraced the change and made it a habit, a part of yourself. You look forward to doing it and miss it when you don't.

Phase 5: Doing it's become an effortless and natural part of your life.

Whatever you can dream of learning, you can learn through repetition. Time and attention will break through almost any limitation you apply them to.

6

TAKING ACTION AND PEAK PERFORMANCE

1. How to Change your Behavior

Good intentions alone won't change your behavior. You have to add awareness and repeated new actions to the mix if you want to permanently change your old automatic responses. If you find yourself behaving in ways you don't want, it's because some responses are subconscious and automatic. Examples of behaviors one might want to change:

- Shyness every time you're on stage

- Smoking every time you're bored

- Getting angry every time you're criticized

- Getting lazy every time you succeed

- Falling in love every time someone likes you

and thousands more. Instead, you might like to implement new behaviors that you haven't had yet, such as:

- Meditating in the morning
- Being calm in meetings
- Working on your professional passion
- Eating more vegetables
- Being attentive with your partner

and thousands more. **Your daily behaviors shape your destiny.**

Changing your behavior begins with the conscious intention to do so. It should be a strong and firm decision. Once the decision is made to change, you might find yourself falling back into the old behavior now and then. Each time you do, re-state the original intention or visualize it more deeply. To reinforce the new intention, it's helpful if you write it down and say it out loud. It's also helpful if you post it in a place you'll see every day or as the background of your smartphone screen.

The new intention must then be demonstrated through action. You must deliberately notice the old behavior when it occurs and replace it with the new behavior. This becomes easier if you constantly think about your intention to change. You remember it more easily by visualizing the new behavior. Can you imagine it? If you can imagine it in a state of deep relaxation, the probability of remembering it when needed increases greatly. It's a matter of commitment. Some old behaviors are so stubborn, it's helpful to visualize both the old and the new behavior back and forth several times. Try it:

Think about the old behavior

Think about the new behavior

Think about the old behavior

Think about the new behavior

Think about the old behavior

Think about the new behavior

Think about the old behavior

Think about the new behavior

Think about the old behavior

Think about the new behavior

Think about the old behavior

Think about the new behavior

Chances are, you feel much different now because you have taught your subconscious the difference between the old and the new behavior. You have brought up the old behavior from the subconscious and made it very conscious. This means you're now unable to behave the old way unconsciously.

Next time you find yourself about to do the old behavior or already doing it, you can more easily interrupt your pattern and replace it with the new behavior. If you want to magnify your ability to do the new behavior, write down different instances in which the new behavior could be chosen:

I could demonstrate the new behavior when…

I could demonstrate the new behavior at…

I could demonstrate the new behavior with…

I could demonstrate the new behavior like…

I could demonstrate the new behavior when…

I could demonstrate the new behavior at…

I could demonstrate the new behavior with…

I could demonstrate the new behavior like…

If you can consciously maintain the new behavior for a couple of weeks, you've permanently replaced it. The likelihood of the old behavior coming up again is minimal.

This should be more than enough to change any specific behavior. If you'd like to change another behavior, simply repeat the process.

If this was still not enough and the old behavior stubbornly persists, do the following:

- List several disadvantages of the old behavior. Think about them for a few minutes.
- List several advantages of the new behavior. Think about them for a few minutes.

Repeat the steps above a few more times in the following weeks. The idea is to begin associating pain to the old behavior and pleasure or reward to the new behavior. Old behaviors that don't disappear remain because of a subconscious or semi-conscious payoff or benefit you derive from them. If your old behavior still persists, find out what benefit you get from it. Once you become aware of it, repeat the entire process again. In Summary:

1. Define a new behavior that should replace the old one. Decide for it. Visualize it repeatedly. If that's not enough then…

2. Contrast the old behavior and the new behavior mentally several times. Then once again decide for the new behavior. If that's not enough…

3. Demonstrate the new behavior over several weeks, especially before, during or after incidents of the old behavior arising. If that's not enough, then…

4. List disadvantages of the old behavior and advantages of the new behavior and focus on them a few times throughout the next weeks, followed by a repetition of the previous steps. If that's not enough, then…

5. Find out what (possibly hidden) benefit you get from the old behavior. Then repeat the previous steps. If that's not enough, then…

6. Get coaching.

2. Sustained Action makes you a Different Person

"The only thing you're going to do today is: what you do today. Therefore, the only thing there is to do today is: what you do today. That's all there was to do when you started no matter what you thought or think. Most people go around thinking that what there is to do today is all that stuff that there is to do, that is to say, everything that isn't done. This is a lie. This lie leads to stupidity. This stupidity leads to ineffectiveness. The ineffectiveness leads to fewer results being produced, leaving, apparently, more to be done. And there you have the downward spiral which is unworkability. The only thing there is to do today is: what you actually do today! There is nothing else to do today! You get it? There isn't anything to do today except what you actually do. That's all there's to do today. Do you get it? If you do actually get it, you should feel the muscles in your body begin to relax. A sense of freedom and power begins to well up within you. Now, you want to go to work, get to it,

get at it, get it done. And here you have the upward spiral which is workability". – Werner Erhard

What good old Werner Erhard is talking about is what so many "motivational coaches" fail to grasp: Feeling guilty or ashamed for non-doing, procrastinating, being inert and lazy, being relaxed and chilled out won't help you get into sustained action. Motivation through pain (fear, shame, guilt, anger) is very common, but it only creates temporary spurts of action. If you use it long-term you do so at the expense of your health and sanity. When desire for action comes from a place of **relaxation and optimism**, it's so much easier to sustain over long periods of time. Over-thinking "doing & action" doesn't help you to do, it makes you *think* more than *do*. Over-thinkers are typically low achievers. Procrastinators are always thinking about what they "should" do and "must do" and "should have done" and "shouldn't have done". Under the weight of such heavy thoughts it's no wonder they feel too tired to act.

You'll find that any new **sustained action** you implement into your life makes you become a different person. Sustained action forms new grooves in consciousness, facilitating a shift in energy, identity, memory and ability. You form new habits. I have taught chronic procrastinators, the lazy and inert, the excuse-makers and the distracted for many years, and I have compassion for their journey. I was once in their shoes. Laziness comes from subconsciously and strongly resisting laziness. The strong resistance acts like a magnet toward laziness. Procrastination comes from subconsciously hating procrastination. Resistance acts like a magnet attracting whatever you're resisting. Therefore, when you intend to "go work out" but you don't go work out and then you think guilty thoughts about it, those guilty thoughts don't help, because they sustain the belief that you'll keep making the same mistake. If you were sure you won't make that mistake often or again, guilt would be greatly reduced.

If you're in this loop, its good to first learn to embrace laziness and procrastination, to implement "lazy days" where you do nothing productive…but without all the guilt and "should" and "must".

This month I wrote 250 pages of my new book. In order to research this book properly, as it's on a topic I have never written about, I had to read a dozen books and about a hundred websites on the subject this month. People look at my work-pace and say, "That's admirable. You must have a lot of willpower!" But it's not merely a matter of willpower. That's only a part of the whole equation. I'm able to work with intensity because I never put myself down, never guilt-trip myself over not doing, over not working on the project. There were days this month where I just dropped the entire project and went "deliberately lazy" all day or even all weekend…but without guilt, fear, or regret. I might just lie in bed all day and watch movies on Amazon, browse the internet, eat, go for extended walks and bike rides, etc. I'll "non-work" until the point when the urge to return to the project returns or until I intentionally decide to return. The urge returns on its own. You know this from vacations you have taken where, after one or two weeks, there's just a **burning urge to get into action** on some vision that you have. That's because you're thoroughly relaxed and open and in that state you get wonderful ideas flowing to you. This is how laziness and creativity go hand in hand.

However, sometimes that urge doesn't show up. What I do in those cases is what differentiates the 1% who get things done from the rest. I use willed intention to "act anyway". That means my will overrides the emotional inclination to laziness. It's not my emotions that run me, I run my emotions. In those cases, it requires some willed effort to get back into the flow of things where new momentum is created. One form of sustained-action comes from an inner urge and passion, the other from a willed decision. Neither form requires guilt tripping.

Sustained action on something new is wonderful because it's like re-awakening dormant facets of your soul. Long forgotten skills and knowledge return. New talents and qualities are discovered. Long buried memories are newly accessed. New information is attracted and life feels fresh and new, like it did when you were a child.

3. Weekly Awareness Page

Weekly Awareness Page

A tool for energy, intention and clarity

1. Things my attention has been on last week:

Rate each item of your list whether it is important or unimportant and whether it is urgent or not. After that, define whether the item is ongoing or whether you would like to finish it, abandon it or delegate it.

2. Things I'd also like to give attention to this week:

List positive things, thoughts, people, outcomes or actions you'd like to focus on

3. Things I'd like the Universe to take care of for me this week:

👉

👉

👉

List as if there is some "universal manager" who takes care of things for you with no effort required on your part.

4. Things I'll do myself this week:

👉

👉

👉

List the three most important actions you intend to take this week.

5. Who I want to be this week

👉

👉

👉

List emotional states or "I am..." statements. Your "state of being" is even more important than your "doing".

6. Wouldn't it be nice if the following things happened this week:

☞

☞

☞

☞

☞

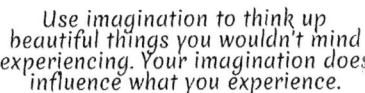
Use imagination to think up beautiful things you wouldn't mind experiencing. Your imagination does influence what you experience.

 7. What I am grateful for right now in my life:

☞

☞

☞

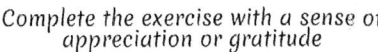
Complete the exercise with a sense of appreciation or gratitude

© Reality Creation LLC

4. Peak Performance

To reach peak performance as a singer, actor, golfer, pianist, tennis player, executive or teacher or in any other area of life, you require at least 3 things:

1. Sustained Focus

This is another way of saying practice and repetition. The more repetitions you take of an action , the more you dig a groove in your mind. The groove can become a limitation, of course, making it difficult to shift focus to other aspects and paths, so it's advisable to dig several grooves for your skill, but also dig some outside of your expertise.

It almost doesn't matter which field you focus on, the art of focusing is itself a valuable skill and also a rather pleasant state of mind. Whether you're focusing on a pebble in the Zen garden or focusing on remaking your website, the pleasant state that arises is the same. It's the choosing and zooming on one thing that allows you to step out of time and space concerns and experience the deep satisfaction of bringing about a new reality by your sustained focus and effort.

2. A Vision Bigger than Yourself

The inner will of a person never acts without a vision or belief in something. If you believe you can't reach the stars, you won't start moving in that direction. Children, on the other hand, will stretch their arms toward something they'd like to achieve because they aren't impeded by limiting beliefs. The child may not reach the object of its desire and you may not reach the stars, but you'll have begun moving in the right direction. **Disbelief or lack of vision is like driving with the parking brake on**.

To achieve peak performance it's advisable to operate from a context bigger than yourself and possibly even bigger than is reasonably achievable. This is why so much of my coaching work involves a **spiritual context.** Without the belief in higher values, higher aims and even a higher world there's not only a lack of essential motivation but also a lack of a bigger picture from which even your loftiest goals look small in comparison. Because I believe that I'm living within an infinite and abundant field of energy, I'm not daunted by any tasks or goals which all seem tiny in comparison. Through meditation, contemplation, energy work, visualization, prayer, lucid dreaming and similar techniques, I get in touch with the infinite aspect of myself. That allows me to emerge from tough situations relatively unscathed.

3. Coaching and Mentoring

You can achieve high performance without outside help, but **peak** performance is usually best achieved with the assistance of experts, mentors and plenty of external feedback. An outside perspective can see things you may be missing (because you have been digging your grooves so deeply), and can provide the few extra bits of energy when you have reached the limits of your own energy reserves. Of course a coach is no substitute for your own power. I always recommend people move forward on their own energy for as long as they can and only book a consultant or coach when they have done everything within the range of their own capabilities. That's the moment a coach is the most empowering, providing extra lubricant and fuel to the engine of your passion.

The three paths to peak performance are really work (sustained focus), belief (vision) and support (coaching), and in that order. Start with the work required to become a top _____ (fill in the blank). When you've reached the limits of what you're able to do, refill your passion with fresh belief and vision. When you've reached the limits of what you're able to believe, refill your passion with coaching. You'll perform in your field at peak level and "be all that you can be", and you'll look back on your life and say, "that was a life lived to the fullest".

5. A Rapid Change of State

If you want to change how you feel, act differently. The idea that emotions follow actions is immediately empowering. Acting as if you're confident overcomes fear. Fear is trying to paralyze you, so *movement and action are natural fear-dissolvers.*

If you struggle with anger, make your body movements and gestures slower and more deliberate. Your emotions will soon follow suit. If you're feeling unhappy, smile at people. As you force yourself to smile at others it will feel unnatural at first, but soon lead to real joy (unless you're covering up deeper-seated emotions, then the smile will only look forced and strained). This principle is where the "fake it till you make it!" idea comes from. It asks us to faithfully move forward, despite fear or a bad mood.

By acting contrary to how you feel, you don't allow any whim or thought to control and dominate your attention and reality. If you're feeling smaller than the situation, you become unmoving and pessimistic. Staying small and contracted over time makes you become small-minded, petty and chronically unhappy.

Moving in your mind is another way to become bigger than emotions. If you keep labeling and seeing things the same way, you keep seeing the things you're labeling the same way. Here's an experiment: Think of someone who was annoyed with you. See their annoyed face and what they say. Notice your emotional reaction. Your emotional reaction actually comes from the label you attribute to the situation. If you have attributed the same label to a certain situation hundreds of times throughout your life, you feel that as an emotion. So if someone is annoyed at you and you take that to mean, "I'm no good, I'm small", then you'll feel that way every time someone is annoyed at you. In reality, someone being annoyed could mean dozens, hundreds, even thousands of different things, but you chose to believe that it means "I'm no good, I'm small".

Think again of someone who was annoyed with you. Notice your reaction. And notice the meaning you *attribute* to that event. Release the meaning for a moment and see the event without any label or meaning whatsoever. It doesn't mean a thing. See it objectively. Objective reality is merely aware of the person's face and body, color, shape, location – purely factual aspects. Then, just for fun, attribute a new meaning to the event. "This person is afraid and insecure and is therefore attacking me". Now see the annoyed person with that new label. Notice how your reaction/emotion changes. If you previously felt small, now you might feel that they are small. Self-pity evolves into compassion for others. Now release that label and see the situation as it's once more. When you see only what is there's no negative emotion. When there's no attributed/default meaning, then the true meaning reveals itself.

Now experiment with a more positive meaning/label. Think: "This means they want to improve themselves". You can actually train yourself that, every time someone gets annoyed with you, you attribute the meaning "This means they want to improve themselves" to the situation. Doing so can be hilarious. Instead of a serious and somber event, annoyance then becomes a cause of humor and laughter for both people involved (other people feel what you vibrate towards them). The meaning and labels game can be done with many different things. This is an exercise straight from my live courses where we do it for many hours, until one's own prejudice is shifted. (Note: This doesn't mean that everything is "meaningless", it just means that a thing's true meaning and level can be revealed by removing one's own attribution of meaning).

This technique is seriously empowering because it helps you liberate yourself from the tyranny of default negative emotions. Grasp it. Understand it. Apply it... and share this technique as far and wide as possible with friends, family and acquaintances.

6. It's not About what you Own, it's About what you're Able to Do

In a recent coaching session I was working with a student who "has everything". She had about 100 pairs of expensive shoes and even more handbags. She had several cars. Her husband had a yacht. And she kept collecting more. Yet she was miserable. Movies like "The Secret" proclaim "you can HAVE everything you want effortlessly" and she indeed had everything she "wanted". So why was she miserable? Because "owning everything you want effortlessly" isn't what life or even prosperity is all about.

Prosperity and joy come from what you're **able to do, who you're, what you know, what you have accomplished**. She hadn't accomplished much of anything because everything she owned was given to her. Her whole purpose in life was to be a "society girl", and she suffered from states of depression she didn't understand.

There's a big difference between prosperity that you create and achieve yourself through your own efforts, and prosperity that's just given to you from birth. People who grow up getting everything for free often face other challenges – emotional and life-purpose challenges that are sometimes almost as daunting as the challenges poor people face. Because she never needed skills, she never developed any. The questions that moved her from depression to living a fulfilling life were

"What would you like to learn?"

"What skills would you like to have?"

"What would you like to contribute to others?"

"What would you like to be able to do?"

Ability is true prosperity. Her type of prosperity wasn't true prosperity because if her money ran out, she felt she couldn't create it again. It could be gone tomorrow and because she lacks any skills, she couldn't provide services to people to bring money back to her. Her constant fear was losing her money. "If I lose my money, I'm nothing". **Skills can't be taken away from you**. Once you've learned something, nobody can take that away, and you'll always have it at your disposal as an asset.

Fundamentally then, it's not about what you "own" but about what you're able to do. If you listed all the things you "have" anyone would get bored pretty quickly. "I have this car, I have that car and I have that car". So what? But start talking about what you can do and people get interested. "I can teach you Chinese". "I can build you a garden", "I can set up your website", "I can do your accounting", "I mix great drinks", "I have a lot of experience with difficult teenagers", "I play guitar in a live band". With your skills, you can attract more "having", but then that "having" will be real "having"…because you created it and you can re-create it anytime you like.

7. Healing Workaholism

Workaholism means to obsess over work at the expense of other aspects and areas of life (health, relationships, friends, leisure, relaxation, smarter moneymaking). Prolonged hard work will often lead to success in a certain area (especially when the work is productive), but it's not the only way to success and not the healthiest or most enjoyable, and it often leads to less success in other areas. It's run by tension and fear rather than creative expression. As with every chronic addiction there's a positive intent behind it, which ought to be recognized so that it's more easily released. That positive intent is achievement, acknowledgment, money.

There's one basic law of reality I tell every workaholic:

The more power you have, the less effort is required to get things moving

As long as your power and influence are small, effort is required and even helpful. But as you age you gain more experience and with it more expertise, so new knowledge and situations require progressively less effort to understand, process and sustain. A person of power just needs to *look* at one of his employees, without even moving a finger or saying a word, and that employee will get moving. Working smarter means to understand how the most results can be achieved with the least effort. Mass consciousness is moving in a direction in which things that took great effort hundreds of years ago take almost none today. For instance to publish an article read by thousands all I have to do is write and then click "publish" on my computer screen. Hundreds of years ago, to get one publication to thousands I'd have to use ink, travel long distances to a printer, pay for printing and then have the material distributed by hand.

Workaholism is therefore lack of leverage and lack of power, and creates more of the same. If you want to have more power, **reduce your work time without reducing your results**. If you think that's impossible, think again. If you're a workaholic you haven't given yourself any time to think. A rubber band is pulled to achieve maximum stretch, but if you pull it too hard, it snaps or becomes worn. Have you ever seen a worn-out rubber band? That's what a workaholic will look like in due time.

Many workaholics claim that they enjoy working from six in the morning to midnight but that's usually a statement of denial. They're afraid that activities other than work might be boring, and so we arrive at the core of all addiction: Boredom. Boredom is a creation of the mind. You can take the same path to work every day for many years and still find something new to see or notice every day. When I used to have a regular job I made it a point to discover something new on the "same old walk" every day. And I did. There are trillions of things going on if you notice them. From a non-apathetic level of consciousness, they are highly fascinating. If you take some time to look and re-discover your surroundings and the rest of the world and let go of your idea of non-work-related things being "boring" you have a good chance of overcoming workaholism. If you enjoy the work you're doing more, you'll also work when it's appropriate and stop work when inspiration runs dry. A life lived in balance between work and rest/play will actually get you far better results. There's only one way workaholism (too much effort) can be healed: Effortlessly.

8. You Don't need a Crisis to Awaken

I've wondered why so many people require a real crisis, terminal illness (their own or a loved one), accidents and disasters to become awake, clear in purpose and focused. I know a lady who lived unconsciously for years. When her husband became very ill, she suddenly kickstarted back to life and did everything possible and impossible to help him recover. She studied hundreds of books on healing (she hadn't read any previously), visited dozens of experts, and tried out countless remedies - and recover he did.

Why wait for the wake up call – which is what a crisis is – before waking up? I'm focused in this manner several days a week, even if there's no crisis. In fact, you'll find that you have no crisis if you require no wake-up calls because you're already awake.

A man I recently coached wanted to become a more successful dentist. I asked him who the most successful dentists in his area were and what their websites were like. He didn't know. A week later I asked him if he had checked out the most successful dentists or at least browsed their websites. He hadn't. He first needed to be told by me to do so. This lack of initiative and drive is a mystery to me. If he wants to be a successful dentist, why doesn't he do his research? I bet if his life were dependent on it, he would wake up and take action. The following ancient legend illustrates how, when your life is at stake, anything can be achieved. I hope to remind you that you don't need to be facing death in order to become committed to your goals. You can simply decide to be awake - without the prospects of having your head chopped off...

"About 260 years ago, in the early Ching Dynasty in China, there lived an emperor called Young Cheng who was very powerful and a devotee of Buddhism. The emperor sent for a Ch'an priest named Tien Huei (meaning "Celestial Wisdom"), who had received the transmission of the Chou Dung Sect, to discuss the Dharma with him. Upon speaking about the High Dharma with this high priest, the emperor at once realized that the monk didn't seem to know the Essentials of the Dharma and had not yet experienced enlightenment. Because he took the Dharma very seriously, the emperor became exceedingly angry with the monk and said, "I'll give you seven days to tell me what the Essentials of the Dharma are. No one can decipher the essentials of the Dharma unless he is enlightened. I'm going to send a guard to keep you under surveillance, and if you can't tell me the Essentials of the Dharma in seven days, the guard will chop your head off!"

In olden times, if a monk was enlightened, he would not be afraid of anything and even emperors would prostrate themselves before him and honor him as Master of the State. But, of course, this monk in question wasn't yet enlightened, so he could not but go into strict retreat in order to get the answer and save his head. Later on, the emperor softened his position and told the monk that he would allow him twenty one days to describe the Essentials of the Dharma.

In the first seven days of his retreat, the monk didn't sleep at all — he could not! Instead, he vigorously meditated to pursue Enlightenment for his life was at stake! He practiced extremely hard for he knew that the emperor meant what he said.

In the second seven days, again he didn't dare to sleep, but practiced even more strenuously. By the fourteenth day, due to lack of sleep, he began to feel dull and drowsy and fell asleep for awhile. In no time he started up as from a nightmare, and he began to walk around the room in order to drive away sleep. During all of this time, guards took turns standing at the door to his hut — the guards who would behead him if he failed in his quest for enlightenment.

On the fifteenth day, the monk walked on in order to drive away sleepiness so that he could continue with his meditation. On the sixteenth day, Tien Huei — who was now extremely anxious — began to walk more quickly. On the seventeenth day, he walked even faster — gradually the walk grew to be a slow run. By the twentieth day the monk still had not attained anything

On the twenty-first day, still anxiously striving for Enlightenment, the monk ran quicker and quicker and the more anxious he grew, the faster he ran, until, suddenly, he ran into a wall. His head was bruised and cut and bleeding, and he fell down onto the floor. At that very moment, all of a sudden, he said, "Oh, I see!" Tien Huei then tranquilly told the guard that he wished to speak to the emperor. The emperor, hearing this, realized that Tien Huei had achieved enlightenment and become a real Master.

This legend demonstrates that, when a person's life is at stake, he will practice very hard, no doubt. It also shows that enlightenment can come unexpectedly, and yet not without much painstaking effort. The monk, now enlightened, eventually became a Patriarch, and the practice of walking-running *meditation (which is called Pao-Hsiang or "Running Incense" in Chinese) became a tradition with Ch'an meditation practitioners. This legend is also the origin of the "Incense Board." The Incense Board is in the shape of a sword — the sword that threatens to chop your head off if you don't try hard to achieve enlightenment! And the sword also symbolizes the Sword of Diamond Wisdom which would cut off the cobwebs of timeless Ignorance and Illusions".*

— *Reverend Cheng Kuan, The Sweet Drew of Ch'an, 1989*

9. How to Form New Habits

As a passionate coach I often receive passionate emails from students that sound something like this:

"I intend to learn a new language, learn to play the piano, learn kung fu and tai chi, study architecture, start to work out at the gym, develop psychic abilities, meditate regularly, learn photography, and practice mindful cooking and eating".

This was a goal list for one month of coaching. Do you notice anything wrong with it?

It's way too much!

Unless you're Superman, developing all of these habits at once is more than 99% of people could handle. I'm not being pessimistic, I'm being pragmatic and results oriented. In my 20-plus years as a coach I've seen thousands of lists like these and also thousands of people who failed in creating new habits. On paper, creating a new habit's easy: Just start, and repeat your practice. In real life it's a little different, especially in modern life where time, energy and attention are occupied by job, family and sleep. The 16 hours of the waking day being occupied, where do these new habits fit in?

The list above is too long. By having too many priorities, you have no priorities. The word "priority" means to choose a few things to focus on while disregarding the rest for the time being. When you put too much pressure on yourself and set the standards way too high, rather than attaining results, resistance and disappointment are created.

It would be better to choose **ONE** thing at a time and **to do that ONE thing correctly, lovingly and consistently**. So for the physical part, that person might choose whether to go to the gym or learn tai chi or learn kung fu. For the mind/spirit that person might choose whether to learn the piano, learn photography, learn gourmet cooking, study architecture, learn meditation or learn a new language.

Then, you take that **ONE** thing you have chosen and firmly intend and decide to dedicate yourself to it until you have mastered it. You don't split and disperse attention and energy but focus them like a laser on one item. By dispersing it on too many subjects you deplete energy and do none of those things properly. Only once the new habit is firmly established and a regular part of your life is it time to go for the next new habit.

I'm a great fan of slow and incremental change, of speeding up slowly. As a coach I have observed that people are typically either a) complacent and lethargic on the one hand or b) seeking dramatic and instant change at super-speed on the other hand. That's an elevator that will go up and down. You may rapidly lose 10 pounds in a week, but you're likely to gain them again. You may radically change your attitude and practice gratitude every day but may only sustain that attitude for a month. The body/mind isn't equipped to handle radical change that easily and it's not equipped to handle ten new habits at once. Creating one new habit that's sustainable for months and even years is very good progress. Otherwise it will just be a bunch of "lets try this" and "lets try that" none of which will be sustained for more than a few days or weeks.

Creating new, beneficial habits isn't about what you do **sometimes**, it's about what you do consistently over **long periods of time**.

10. A Disciple of Discipline

I told a student that he would have to dedicate at least 15 minutes a day to Awareness Practice or Meditation in order for our Coaching to succeed. He wrote back: *"I don't know if I have the discipline to follow through with that. My day is pretty full. Isn't there something easier I could do?"*

This struck me as amusing because 15 minutes is a bare-minimum requirement I have defined for any kind of psycho-energetic progress. My method to get this student to regard 15 minutes of focus as easy was to **contrast** it with the other extreme – people who are disciplined 24 hours a day and the kind of people they become because of that.

I told him of the Japanese Buddhist "Marathon Monks" who practice an art called "Kaihogyo". This is a method of attaining spiritual enlightenment through physical endurance. In order to be admitted to their order, the petitioner has to **run for 1,000 days straight (!),** up to 84 kilometers a day. The petitioner is allowed to withdraw from the training in the first 100 days, but after that he is no longer permitted to give up – he must either complete the 1,000 days or take his own life. Most of the running takes place across the Japanese mountain ranges where these particular sects of Buddhism reside, and the runners' paths are marked with the graves of those who have perished before them. If you thought winning an Olympic Gold Medal requires discipline, you've never heard of these running monks!

Since the 15th Century, only 46 men have completed the 1,000 days, and only three have completed it twice (the last one in 1987). Once the 1,000 day training is completed, the initiate goes on running 40 to 84 kilometers a day **for the next 7 years**. The rest of the time he spends training in meditation and calligraphy.

For the modern westerner, this amount of running would appear to be insane and actually prove deadly for all but professional athletes. The secret is that it's only possible if the initiate transcends the body and becomes spiritually very light. That is the only way one could survive it.

After describing this practice to the student, I ended my email with: *"Do you still think 15 minutes of meditation a day is too much to handle?"*

I'm not asking anyone to become a superhuman, but just a little daily discipline can make it easier for the "impossible" to suddenly look more doable. 15 daily minutes of awareness practice (mind techniques, meditation, Reality Creation, journaling, conscious writing, planning, prayer, yoga, breathing techniques, visualization training, etc.) sets the tone for the rest of the day. It allows you to experience and perceive nuances of mind, body and consciousness that you would not perceive had you not meditated. These nuances make all the difference between a successful day and a wasted one. If you adjust your compass very slightly, your ship will end up somewhere very different in a few years than if you left it untouched.

11. Using Negative Motivation to Reach Goals

Goal achievement is often thought of as being driven by positive thinking and positive emotions, but negative motivation also works. You don't just have the carrot, you also have the stick. I've applied this method with myself and my students every now and then. It often begins as a way I test the resolve and belief of someone stating a goal. Someone might say:

"I'm going to graduate"

"I'm going to double my income"

"I'm going to learn dancing"

"I'm going to quit smoking"

"I'm going to ask this person out on a date"

or any other goal, and I'll say "Alright. Do you really believe that?" and they'll usually say "Yes". And then I'll say:

"Well, if you really believe that, then you'd be willing to be severely punished by me if it doesn't happen?"

I'll generally get an odd look from them. Some might say "Well, I don't need that kind of motivation, I can achieve it without threats of punishment". And I respond:

"Yes, but if you're 100% sure it will happen, there's nothing to worry about"

With those willing to try it, I make a **Commitment Contract** where they write down the punishment they will accept if they don't achieve the goal in a pre-defined period of time. The punishment has to be strong enough to provide motivation. All human action is driven by pain or pleasure. Reaching the goal is linked with pleasure, failing to reach it is linked with pain. Some recent examples:

"If I don't reach my goal by this time…

…send you $500.

…you'll send a nude video of me to all my colleagues, families and friends (email addresses are supplied beforehand and the video is shot the same day)

…I'll spend the night alone in the woods

…I, not my spouse, will wash all the dishes for one year

…I'll give away my best suit

…I'll give up the Internet for 1 month

The stronger the punishment, the more likely it's that you'll actually reach the goal you set out to achieve. This is actually an ideal tool to measure whether someone really believes in his goals. **If they really believe, then they'll have no problem committing**. If on the other hand they hesitate, you're dealing with someone who only pretends to believe but isn't really dedicated to the creation of a new reality. The success rate of this method has been 80% of goals reached.

12. Actions, Expectations and Consequences

Let's say you send out an email to 5000 people, advertising your new product. 100 people end up buying it after you sent it out. Every action has a consequence,

but what if most of the hundred people who bought your product weren't even on your mailing list?

This is where it gets metaphysical: Your action of sending out 5,000 emails had a consequence even if, in this case, the relationship between cause and effect isn't apparent. If you hadn't sent out those 5,000 emails, you wouldn't have gotten those 100 buyers, even if the buyers come from an entirely different place.

Another example: Let's say you make phone calls to 100 yoga teachers, inviting them to your upcoming lecture in which you intend to present your product. Lecture day comes around and there are 30 people present, but only 2 yoga teachers. Does that mean your action of calling 100 yoga-teachers was misplaced? No, not according to higher cause-and-effect rules. Had you not made those calls, you would likely have many fewer participants at your lecture.

When you put out a certain amount of effort or energy, you get back a certain result or consequence. The connection between the effort and the result isn't always clear. This can be difficult for the rational mind to understand. At play here are the invisible energies of **intention** and **expectation**. By engaging in the action of calling 100 yoga teachers or sending out 5,000 emails, you build a certain **expectation** that you **deserve** to experience certain **results**. Those results are delivered, but not necessarily the way you thought they would be.

That's why it makes sense to focus more on sowing than reaping. I've been noticing this phenomenon my whole life: It doesn't really matter what aspect of my company I happen to be improving as long as I'm improving them. As I improve one small aspect in corner D of my company, I might get results in corner A. Put differently: If you expect or **believe** that an action will get you results, then it will, in **some form or another**. Put another way, no thought, word or deed is ever wasted.

The emotions of anger and frustration often lead to making efforts, but without any actual expectation that they'll yield results – and then they don't. So check your intentions and expectations before taking action.

A lady recently lamented: "I have worked so hard all of my life and have NOTHING to show for it!" We were sitting in her garden at the lake, at her three story mansion. I looked around and asked "What about this place? Is that something you originally wanted?" "Yes it's" she said "but this came true for my husband, not for me". "You're living in a house at the lake…who cares through which medium it manifested?" Clearly something within her felt more comfortable with things manifesting through others. She could change that or simply accept that the house she lived in is *her* house.

The woman was seeing things in the linear way, the way the mind sees them. The soul or higher self sees things in a non-linear way. What she wanted had manifested, "but not the way she thought it would". I had news for her - nothing ever manifests "the way you think it will". It does manifest, but in mysterious ways.

Recently I congratulated another woman on getting married. It was a goal we had worked on five years before in a seminar. Her intention had come true. She wrote back thanking me. In her message she was also implying that this manifestation "had nothing to do" with our work back then, it had more to do with an online dating service. She is mistaken; she had put out a strong **intention** some time ago, and it manifested – in this case, **through** an online dating service. Does it really matter which medium brings a desired manifestation? Because of linear thinking, her mistake was to see the online dating service as the cause and marriage as the effect. In truth, her intention was the cause and marriage was the effect. Intention and Expectation are the primary causes. Actions and Events are **the vehicles** or **means** through which the intentions manifest into physical form.

Whatever it's you want: do you **expect** it and feel you **deserve** it? If so, take **action** on it. Act in good faith. But **let go of expecting** it to arrive in a certain form or at a certain time. Your **expectation** should refer to the end result itself, not to the path. The path is up to the Universe, which orchestrates events from a much broader vantage point.

In short, let go of the "how, when and where" and simply **keep the end result in your heart**.

7

TRUE POWER

1. Maintain Your Momentum

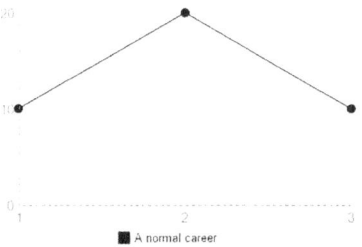

If you follow a career - any career - you will get better in it over time as enough expertise and skill are accumulated. Unless you give up beforehand, you eventually reach a pinnacle or high-point and then recede back into mediocrity due to loss of interest, resting on your laurels or due to your beliefs about age. In your field, you'll be a "one hit wonder"

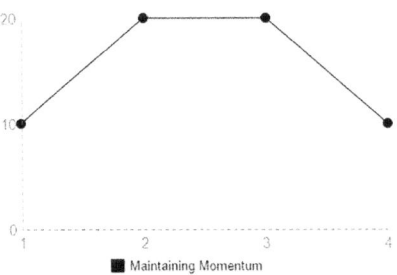

With high energy and focus, some are able to maintain the high-point for an extended length of time. They maintain their momentum because they take success not as a cause to sit back but keep on going. If they however, do not make any changes, the "same old" cannot be maintained forever.

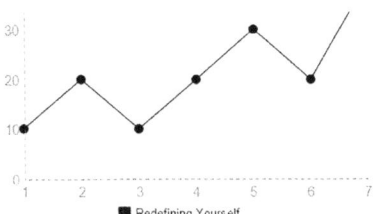

With a little more flexibility and willingness to redefine and reinvent oneself at least once every decade (trying something new) one can keep the inner fire burning for an entire life. A person of passion will have plenty of ups and downs but the overall direction will always be up.

Infographic on how to Maintain your Momentum

2. Personal Power

If you look up "Power" in a Dictionary you'll find these two basic definitions:

1. The ability to control people or things, have influence over them; political and organizational authority over others.

2. Ability to act or produce an effect; efficacy, the capability to cause effects.

The first is the **Authoritarian** or **Controlling** definition of Power, the second is the **Causative** or **Creative** definition of power. In one definition the more you **control**, the more power you have. In the other, the more you **can create**, the more power you have.

These two Definitions can be somewhat contradictory. I usually use the word "power" when referring to creative or causative energy, but people may think I'm using the word to refer to having authority over others. They sometimes object to the word in the second context. They might even reject personal power altogether because they feel uncomfortable with having "authority over others".

"My life's work is to help you have more power!" I often say. What I mean by that is for the individual to have more creative energy, not control of others.

Another example of the contradiction in definition: Authoritarian political rule might attempt to *suppress* individual creativity (power). Creative Power often refers to the Individual; Authoritarian Power often refers to the State, Institution or Organization. ("Anti-Authoritarian Politics" is an oxymoron). The power I teach has more to do with control of self and one's immediate surroundings than collective control of others.

Creative power is the ability to focus, initiate, decide, act, and persist. This creative power may or may not, in time, turn into actual controlling power or authority or societal power. Whether it turns into that kind of power is up to numerous internal factors (behavior, beliefs, emotions, consciousness) and external factors (education, circle of friends, perceived status, expertise, networks, media-status). This is my life's work because people are mostly **powerless** and "working at jobs they don't like so that they can buy things they don't need". I believe it's in the interest of the whole that the individual is given more power, at least enough to sustain himself and his loved ones.

To determine the extent of your Personal Power all you then have to ask is this:

What can I start, stop, change, control, or cause? What can't I start, stop, change, control or cause?

Contemplation along those lines will reveal that you don't have quite as much power as self-empowerment books say you do. But it also reveals that you can expand your sphere of power by expanding on what you *can stop, start, change and cause.*

You could, for example, exert more control over your schedule or timetable. It astonishes me how easily people give away their precious time. They lock up their money in a safe, but when it comes to *time*, they just waste it away. You could exert more control over your eating habits. You could exert more control over yourself. In fact you can never "control" or influence others if you don't control yourself first. *Trying, wanting and needing* to control *others* are, by the way, a fast track to feeling out-of-control. I`ll let you to figure out why. You could *cause and create* new conversations, new images, new words, new ideas, new behavioral patterns…and the more causative or initiative you're, the greater your sense of personal power. So…contemplate this amazing question:

What can't I start, stop, change, control or cause? What can I start, stop, change, control or cause?

I began teaching self-empowerment because there are no schools teaching Power. "Power" is a broad and delicious topic and yet there are no official studies on it. We have entire encyclopedias on the various flora and fauna, on trucks, hunting equipment, extinct languages, kittens, and moons of the solar system. We have college classes on physics, math, biology, chemistry, on the soft skills of psychiatry, communication and even parapsychology. Absent are textbooks explaining Power as it relates to society, economy, awareness, relationships, finances, health, influence, confidence, intuition, spirit, perception, etc.

Not a single class in school teaches the most important of all subjects: **Awareness**. Awareness is the basis of Personal Power. I'm lucky – I was able to make teaching this my career because "official institutions" don't teach it. In society there's great demand for instruction in Personal Power.

When thinking about your personal Sphere of Influence and Authority, it's important to also consider these topics in general. Why are there hardly any "official" (non-esoteric, non-fringe, non-spiritual) books on the subject? Why are there no university classes taught on Power?

Two reasons:

1. **We hide power from ourselves**
2. **"They" hide power from us.**

We hide it from ourselves because we are afraid of it. We subconsciously believe that we are undeserving of power, that disasters will be unleashed like so many times in the past. The subconscious mind has recorded and perhaps even genetically stored our destructive past and said "OK, no more power. Power is bad and shameful". Of course power as such isn't bad, but what you do with it can be good or bad. You can use a knife to kill, or to cut ropes and free yourself, to put butter on bread, to carve a wooden toy. The knife itself isn't good or bad.

"They" also hide power from us. Who are "they"? Those **already** in power. Why do they try to prevent us from learning about power? Because there's a common belief that says:

"In order to maintain our own power, our power must be limited to very few, and we must stay hidden".

By staying hidden as well as hiding the means (and even the fact) of power, their power can't be taken away because you **can't attack something that is unseen**. This phenomenon is played out at a small scale (in families, communities and companies) and on a grander scale (in politics, nations, global corporations and international organizations). According to this mindset, there must be a pyramid structure with a very sharp top and a very broad base **and the cap of the pyramid needs to be out of sight**. This is different from normal, healthy hierarchies where the cap is in clear view and not quite as pointed. This theory, btw, isn't necessarily true or even effective - I can be in my full power while others are, too, without contradiction or conflict as in spiritual realms.

Manipulative power must remain hidden in order to maintain its status. Consider your own private experience: If you're manipulating someone, the manipulation works best if the other person doesn't know you're manipulating them, right? Hence, you can only maintain this sort of manipulative power in secret.

The prevalent **false** paradigm is that "one's gain is another's loss." The "Elite" believe that in order for them to stay in power, others must remain powerless. Even if this paradigm isn't universally true, it's the one that's been believed and played out on this planet. The belief is that if I become rich, someone else must be impoverished.

Universal truth is just the opposite: If I have power, others automatically get more power too, because on an energetic/spiritual level we are all ONE. If I get rich, that enriches others. And this isn't only true spiritually or metaphorically, it's true on very practical levels: For instance, for me to build a yacht, *many* would have to be employed. My building a yacht doesn't make others poorer, it puts food on the employees' tables. Many gadgets would have to be invented. That's a bunch of designers and researchers making money off my building a yacht. Many would be inspired by my yacht. Many would be invited to travel on it. So me getting one yacht can benefit a hundred people. If I don't build a yacht, I benefit no one.

The old prevailing paradigm is that my power must disadvantage others and that in order to keep it, power must be limited to a few and remain unseen. If you remain secret and unseen, you can't be targeted. If you can't be identified and targeted, you can't be removed from your throne. Fortunately, the ego doesn't enjoy power without being seen, so the ego will display and parade power publicly, but it will never quite have as much power as those who can control their egos and remain unseen. This is why the successful seek publicity but the **very** successful avoid it.

It's easy to maintain power structures for thousands of years in this manner. It's easy because **people primarily focus on the visible, not on the invisible**. They focus on manifestations, not what caused those manifestations. They focus on effect, not cause; on content, not context. Even researchers of Power are often more focused on the building (the structure of the pyramid), than what exactly powers the building.

An ancient strategy the powerful use to **obfuscate sources** of authoritarian power is to present **nameless and faceless entities** who are supposedly "in charge" and "have power". So we have

"the media",

"the military",

"the government",

"the powers that be",

"the multinational corporations",

"the men behind the curtain",

"the bankers",

"the secret intelligence agencies", etc.

These are all nameless and faceless "somethings" that you can't really pinpoint. Referring to these when talking of "who has power" is useless. There's no such thing as "the" media for example. The media is a wide array of millions of different TV and radio stations, cable channels, newspapers, magazines, advertising agencies, journals, websites, blogs and news agencies with many different agendas, contexts and goals. I always find it funny when a news outlet complains about "the media", being part of "the media" themselves. Likewise there really is no such thing as "the powers that be", because there are many groups that have power and many of them are in fierce competition with each other. Maintaining unclear or misleading responsibility for various events is one of the methods used to keep the general populace disempowered and ensure that those with power keep it. Edward Snowden revealed to the mass public that the NSA spies on the emails, phone calls and communications of almost everyone and everything, however, this revelation left most people overwhelmed rather than empowered, because it's unclear **who** exactly has been in charge of this mass surveillance The leaders of various countries and even the U.S. President himself claimed ignorance of many of these activities . If not even the President is aware (a questionable claim) then who is? Who exactly is "the NSA"? Who do they take their orders from? Who is whistleblower Edward Snowden? Why did he choose to seek refuge in the only superpower (Russia) that might be even worse in spying on its citizens? There numerous factors here that are **entirely unclear.**

The lesson here is that **Clarity is Power**. If you know **what caused what, who is who, and how things work…exactly how they work…you have more power.** Questioning things is one way to gain more clarity. Children are better at this. They ask questions all the time, until they have fully grasped something. People who have fallen into Apathy and given up on personal growth and personal power have stopped asking questions, stopped learning, and succumbed to the status quo.

Forbes Magazine annually publishes a list of "the most powerful people in the world". At this writing, number one on the list is Barack Obama, number two is Angela Merkel, the Chancellor of Germany. I submit that anyone who has made even a superficial study of Power will find this and similar lists to be **grossly inaccurate**. The people on that list are **representatives** of those in power and not the people with actual power. The temporary nature of their jobs guarantees that. Sure, Obama has the power to make a few decisions that could affect the long term destiny of the U.S. and even the world, but what will his actual power be in 2017? Meanwhile there are certain…."figures"….that had power 50 years ago and still have power today. True power lasts longer than just a decade.

Whenever you encounter a family, company or institution that has retained influence for a thousand years, you're encountering real power.

The more personal power you gain for yourself, the more clearly you'll perceive those who were in power long before you came on the scene. As the earth's level of consciousness shifts to a higher octave, power and wealth are actually no longer hereditary, they are becoming behavioral…which means that anyone can now attain more power for themselves. You do so by learning to think for yourself rather than blindly accept what you're told. I recommend that you read and learn as much as you can, but don't let all that reading and learning pollute your own ideas and intuitions about yourself and the world. To increase your sphere of influence, connect with everyone at all times, don't waste time being shy, don't waste time with people of ill will (remove yourself from them physically), make friends with older people because older people have seen it all and have a lot to teach, orient yourself to people who are more successful and powerful than you. Give up being a consumer and become a creator instead. Status isn't gained through objects; it's gained through experience and the ability to create. Focus your career efforts on one thing you love until you become a master at that.

My personal definition of power is "the ability to succeed" or "the ability to deliver results". "Success" means to intend A and then have A happen. A popular delusion is that there's some kind of mysterious "secret" to power or worldly success. But there's no secret. The clues on how success is attained are everywhere and all around you every single day. The successful have been behaving in a certain predictable manner for thousands of years as have those without success. **Success always follows the same rules, unaltered for generations past and generations to come.**

The amount of communications that posit success as a "secret" is staggering. Type "success" into Google and the articles, books and products on the "secret" to success are endless. Many believe that one only has to finally discover the "secret" used by the successful or their hidden techniques or mysterious networks to achieve their own "success". Positioning success as some kind of "secret" is, in my view, an attempt by "them", to keep it out of the view of the masses.

In reality, success is no secret at all. Success is to choose something you'd prefer to experience, and to then experience it. That's all there's to it. This is a matter of **self-discipline, nothing more**. Will I allow myself to be distracted by phone calls, outside pressures, "advice" contrary to my vision, threats, difficulties and setbacks, or will I stay focused and committed to what I have chosen to experience? The **succession** of many individual successes culminates in personal power.

3. True Power

For those in power to stay in power they must spread false information on how power is gained and maintained. The masses must be kept in darkness about how to increase their scope of influence and command in the world. They believe power is gained by money, greed, persuasion, domination and force – all of which are actually symptoms of powerlessness. A few rules of true power are shared in this section. In extrapolating these principles you'll discover others on your own.

…………

Self-Importance vs. making Others Important

………

People are addicted to feeling important, special, better. You gain power not by Self-Importance, which makes you inert and manipulable, but by making others important. You're a unique individual, but by emphasizing this too much and making yourself appear better than others, you'll attract envy. People will want to put you down. By making them important, valuing their talents, beauty and achievements – you disarm their insecurity and wanting to be better. Don't outshine your boss. You're not important, your customers are. You're not important, your superiors are. You're not important, your colleagues are. You're not important, others are. As you give people what they long for, your own power increases.

....

Control over Others vs. Self-Control

....

If you think that controlling others equals power you have been misinformed. Before seeking command over others, take command of yourself. You're all you truly have. The world and what you experience are a reflection of you. Control yourself and you control the world. In any situation where you want to change others, have others think or feel something or manipulate others, you're in a state of lack. You can't change others directly. If you attempt to do so, they'll notice and resist the change you seek in them even more. Wanting control equals not having control. If however, you're an example of poise and clarity, you'll lead by that example. People will change in your presence not because you told them to change or tried to exert dominance over them, but because people always imitate the people who have the most energy. Others are a mirror. If you smile, the image in the mirror will smile in reflection, but you can't expect the image in the mirror to smile first.

Chatter vs. Silence

....

Energy is wasted in mindless chatter, gossip, lying, not keeping your word and verbal focus on the unwanted and the unimportant. In contrast, energy and power are accumulated in Silence. Insecure people can't stand silence and so they talk for the sake of talking – without purpose, reason or focus. Talking is creative, and when you're finished talking you have created a world from your words, so be thoughtful before you speak. Energy diffuses when talking is pointless and unfocused. "Where were you just now?" asks the wife. "I was taking the garbage out," answers the husband. The point of this conversation? There isn't one.

....

Observe those who spend hours talking about the most mundane and unimportant things. Observe how they exhaust their energy (not to mention yours) constantly focusing on issues that have nothing to do with their goals and desires. Lying and deception is another certain way to lose your power. How much creative power do you think your WORD has if that WORD is untrue? Who will follow your command? Nobody. If you have said many things that didn't come to fruition, your inner-self will take this is a signal that your word doesn't mean anything. Talking too much also overwhelms other people's attention spans with things that are irrelevant to them. When you speak to a group of people, it matters what you say but also what you don't say. Too much information will quickly bore them. Giving less information will keep them attentive. Say less than necessary. Never criticize someone behind his back. Bad-mouthing others subtly reflects more poorly on you than on the person you're trashing.

Fixed Identity vs. Formlessness

Water resists nothing and nothing resists it. It's formless and easily passes through all situations. Having a fixed identity, fixed opinion, fixed lifestyle, fixed habits makes you predictable and easy to attack and break. Wood is easy to break. Water and Air are impossible to Break. Change is the only constant. If you're always on the move or in a state of transformation, you can't be located and fixed as a target. Don't fall into the roles and identities society tries to assign you. Be able and ready to adapt to different realities, countries, people and situations. Not being fixed in one position also allows you take on other people's viewpoints – which, ultimately equals being able to lead them.

Reveal vs. Conceal

Don't reveal your goals, intentions, or plans. Doing so will open them up to doubt and attack from others, but they can't attack something they don't know about. They can't doubt something they're unaware of. Revealing your goals before they're achieved can also stifle their accomplishment. Never brag. Don't discuss your weaknesses in public or with people you're not very close to. Remain elusive to the world. You don't need to justify every move you make. You don't need to report your location, whereabouts, past, present and future to the world. Retaining an aspect of mystery enhances your appeal.

Work vs. Productivity

Don't exhaust yourself with work you don't enjoy. If there's an important errand that must be done, don't procrastinate or postpone it, do it quickly. Spend the rest of your time doing things you enjoy. Allow your work to be creative and productive. Delegate the work you don't enjoy to others or to "the Universe". Money isn't important. Approval from society isn't important. Success isn't important. These are superficial things. What's important is that you have joy in being productive and creative. By focusing purely on creating value for yourself and others while ignoring all superficial desires, your power will increase. You won't catch many butterflies by running through the field after them. Instead, use a bait that smells wonderful to butterflies and they will come to you without much effort. True Power does more with less effort.

Take vs. Give

Judge the day's success not by what you reap but by what you sow. Don't ask what you're getting, but what you can give. The beggar always seeks to receive, the wealthy man is always in a position to give. Instead of asking what a customer or a company or a group or society can do for you, ask what you can do for them.

Dishonesty vs. Integrity

The original meaning of "Integrity" is "Being part of the whole". This means treating the world as you would like to be treated. If you manipulate others, you open yourself to being manipulated. Your inner power can create anything and everything without lying, stealing or cheating, so remain clean. Maintain the highest standards of reputation and ethics and you won't have to pretend to be in good standing (which costs energy). Keeping transgressions and lies secret sucks life energy out of you. It makes you vulnerable to attack. It makes you a target for blackmail. By obeying the ethics of your society and community you become someone who can't be attacked or hurt. If someone does decide to attack you or blame you for a wrong, it will reflect back on them – as no evidence of your wrong doing can be found. Also note, however, that people who appear to be "too perfect" or "too clean" usually have something to hide or coverup, which they attempt to do through an exaggerated focus on a "clean" public image. **Work more on the integrity of your character than on your public reputation.**

Reactive vs. Proactive vs. Non-Reactive

At the heart of powerlessness lies reactivity. Reacting to perceived enemies. Reacting to problems. Reacting to attacks. When you react to something, you assign it importance and validity, thereby giving it power over you. When something you dislike happens: Either don't react to it at all, or become proactive in mitigating it.

4. How to Rapidly Empower Yourself

....

To overcome mental limitations, use the following technique.

1. Make a list of sentences beginning with "I can't…". Examples:

I can't just quit my job and still make good money. I can't be in a great state after what I have been through. I can't stop thinking about him. I can't ask for a promotion now. I can't call off that meeting. I can't learn all of this material before the exam. I just can't meet someone who is right for me.

2. Convert all of those statements into "I don't want" statements. With this step you take become the creator, you take responsibility for your creations. "I don't want" is closer to the truth. With most things in life, you **could** do them if you really wanted to. It's just that you don't want to and you have your reasons for that. Examples:

I don't want to just quit my job and still make good money.

I don't want to be in a great state after what I have been through.

I don't want to stop thinking about him.

I don't want to ask for a promotion now.

I don't want to call off that meeting.

I don't want to learn all of this material before the exam.

I don't want to meet someone who is right for me.

………

3. Assuming that you truly don't want to, determine what reasons, fears and frustrations lie behind that. Why don't you want to? Apply some emotional clearing to those fears and frustrations. Just let them come up and release them as you relax.

………

4. Convert all "I don't wants" into "I cans". Write those statements out. Say each of them out loud, emphasizing the "I can!" followed by a deep breath. Examples:

………

I **can** just quit my job and still make good money.

I **can** be in a great state after what I have been through.

I **can** stop thinking about him.

I **can** ask for a promotion now.

I **can** call off that meeting.

I **can** learn all of this material before the exam.

I **can** meet someone who is right for me.

………

Voice these statements with some enthusiasm or by adding some extra words or qualifications such as "I can just quit my job if I really want to and make good money because I'm an expert in my field and because I'm passionate about better work!"

………

Repeat Steps 1-4 until you really feel that you CAN because you **say** you CAN.

....

5. Demonstrate those new realities

....

"I can" doesn't mean you have to take action. However, if you've identified "I can" items you would like to take action on, do so now. Taking action locks the new belief and new energy into physical reality, meaning the item won't be a big problem from now on.

....

Use this process on items that are realistic, and ethical, clearing limitations you really do have, things you really have been telling yourself

....

5. Confront the Bully

Aggression isn't a positive emotion, but it's a higher vibration than fear. If you're coming from higher levels, anger is destructive, but if you're coming from lower levels of emotion, anger is constructive. This axiom is described in *Levels of Energy*. If you're being harassed, mobbed, bullied, threatened, or oppressed you must lift *yourself* out of it by "confronting the bully".

In my childhood doing so was an emotional turning point in my life. At around the age of 12 there was a group of schoolyard bullies who mocked and harassed anyone who crossed their path. They were the cruelest boys around. They had never beaten me up as they had others, but they threatened me when I walked past and sometimes called me names. One day I decided that I'd had enough of looking shyly at the ground when walking past them and I stepped up to their group in full courage. I was ready and willing to have a fight if they attacked me and I was ready and willing to get beaten up. Getting beat up one time seemed less painful than having to shrink from their presence both in and outside of school. Confronting them was less painful than trying to avoid them everywhere I went in town. All of a sudden I found myself standing in their midst. One of them seemed furious that I dare invade their space and he immediately stood up, clenched his fists and got ready to hit me, but his friend held him back and said "Wait for it, wait for it". The leader of the gang said: "What do you want?" Not knowing what to say I just casually said: "Just checking you guys out". They all had a good laugh at my casualness and relaxed. "That's Fred. He's alright," one of them said. I wasn't attacked as expected. I left their circle with a nod of acknowledgement. From that day on they never bothered me again. I became invisible to them.

When you no longer radiate resistance or fear, you become **invisible** to a bully. Like dogs that smell fear they attack others who radiate it. Once you raise yourself above fear and are willing to stand up for yourself, the bully goes away. The truth about bullies is that **they're actually the ones who are afraid**. That's why they put on their bully-act. When you radiate courage, love or humor, you can't possibly be attacked by a force that radiates in lower energy. The same principle applies to anything else you feel oppressed by in life. The final aim is to transcend fear.

6. The Right Dose of Adversity

Do you realize that someone who fires you from a job, is actually doing you a favor? They're giving you the chance to find something better. If you embrace the adversity, you can transcend it. What if you get fired again, and again and again and again? You might be overdosing on adversity and lose hope.

Whether something is good or bad often depends on the **dose** in which it's prescribed. In the right dose a drug can be healing medicine, too much of it can become a poison. If I donate money to you it might help you out of hard times. But if I continually donate money to you, it might keep you in hard times by stifling your initiative.

Adversity is perceived by most as undesirable. That's not true, of course. Without some adversity, without anyone ever criticizing you, without any stumbling blocks on the way, you'd neither learn nor grow.

Did you know that babies born by C-section (less adversity) are statistically not as healthy through their lives as babies born by natural delivery (more adversity)?

Difficulty isn't, in and of itself a bad thing, it's a natural part of life. The opposite would be getting everything too easily and being pampered all your life. How satisfying would that be? Life experience shows us that things obtained too easily are less appreciated. You can demonstrate the truth of this with the following experiment: Give one child a toy only if he/she works for it or sacrifices/trades something for it and give another child the toy for free. What you'll notice 9 times out of 10 is that the child who got the toy for free will soon be bored with it, discard it or ask for a new toy, whereas the child who had to invest some effort, some **energy of its own** will cherish the toy for weeks, maybe months. As an adult you may be familiar with this phenomenon on the internet – a source of limitless free material that you can download with no effort at all. That makes life easier to some extent, but it doesn't breed the wonderful sense of satisfaction of being able to afford something special or having earned something through the investment of time, attention and effort. The overabundance of information on the internet tends to devalue it to a degree.

Someone who inherits all of his money can become just as depressed as someone who never had the opportunity to make a living, but someone who had *nothing* and then, through their own efforts, created something will truly cherish the achievement.

The other extreme is too much adversity. *Underwhelm* leads to a chronic state of boredom and *Overwhelm* leads to tension and pain. An example of too much adversity would be someone holding your face to the ground with a jackboot while slashing your body with a knife and shouting at you. That kind of adversity doesn't cause growth and learning but rather shock and dissociation. Nietzsche's saying "What doesn't kill you makes you stronger" is somewhat, but not absolutely, true. There's such a thing as overdosing on adversity. When the limits of adversity have been reached it's good to shift your attention to the nice, calming, beautiful, relaxing and harmonious things in life. When full regeneration has been reached, it's nice to return to the game and dive into the challenge. Finding this balance will enable you to maintain a high energy state throughout your life.

7. From Victim to Victor

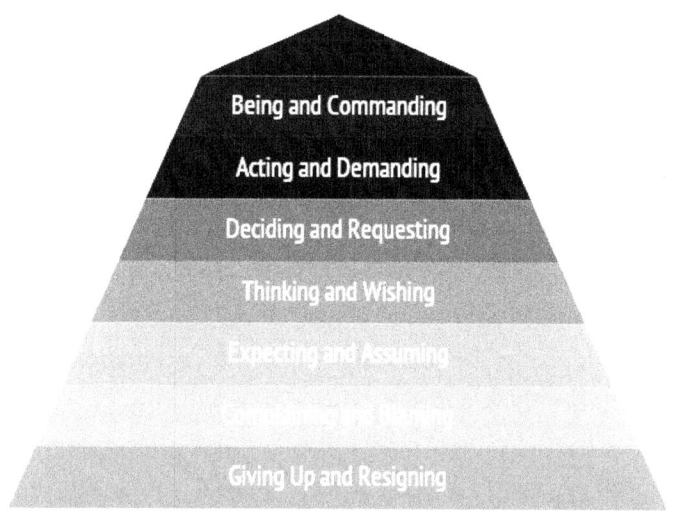

This chart, taken from my seminar slides, shows the path from victim to victor. The entry point to the scale for most people is somewhere in the middle, at the level of "thinking and wishing". If you have an idea or a thought, that thought becomes a wish or desire. From that mid-point you can either move upward and turn your desire or thought into an actual intention, an actual decision or an actual request, or you can move down the scale. The first three levels of the scale are the realm of victimhood. The top three levels of the scale are the levels of the responsible creator. The middle of the scale is the entry point. One level weaker than "Thinking and Wishing" is "Expecting and Assuming". If you have a good idea you would like to achieve then merely assuming it will come true, without having the inner conviction and belief, or expecting that the world will accommodate you and owes you something, is a weak position. Weaker still is the descent into blaming and complaining. At this level you give your power away; you give your power to the people and organizations that you blame for your situation. "It's the company's fault", "It's the governments fault", "It's my parents' fault", "It's the bankers' fault", "It's my boss's fault", "It's because of my past", "It's my partner's fault", "I blame it on the rain", "It's God's fault"…in the world the blame game comes in many variations. What they all have in common is claiming one is the victim of overpowering circumstances. The more this is done, the more disempowered and weak one becomes. At an even lower level is Giving up and Resigning which is a fall into the bottomless pit of apathy and depression. The way back up is through the levels, the first empowerment level being Deciding and Requesting. Rather than assuming something will come true or happen, you decide and request it. One level of power higher, at Acting and Demanding you actually do something about it…you take **initiative**, instead of waiting for someone to tell you what to do, and you actually insist on it coming true, no doubt about it. And one level higher still, you don't demand, which still carries a flavor of effort with it, you command. You can command if you have a certain "Beingness", namely the Beingness of Authority. If you don't radiate a high level of energy and Beingness, the world won't respond to your commands, it will laugh at them. The Universe won't respond to your commands, it will ridicule you and send you tests to see whether you're really ready for that amount of power. You may have noticed that at the very highest levels of worldly success, people don't get paid and revered for what they do (the level of Acting and Demanding), they are paid and revered for who they are (the level of Being and Commanding). This level of power isn't reactive, it's creative. It doesn't wait, it initiates. It doesn't hope, expect, assume, wish, or need. It creates or it doesn't create. It doesn't try to solve problems, it focuses on preferences. Instead of asking, "How can I solve this problem?" it asks "What would I like to create today?" Instead of waiting to act until uncertainty subsides, it acts in spite of uncertainty. That is called Courage. Instead of basing its actions on past experiences, it creates and acts out of nothing, as if there were no past that defines it.

8. The Momentous Power of Repetition

As a teenager I had bad associations with Repetition. I wanted to explore and be creative and yet schoolteachers had other views of learning. To them, learning meant rote memorization of data. I wasn't encouraged to explore or create but to endlessly repeat the data they considered important and to arrive at pre-defined conclusions After I finished school I had to re-program myself with a new definition of repetition.

Beyond boring rote memorization, repetition can be a wonderful tool for reality creation. When I speak of "focusing" in hundreds of articles on my website, I'm also speaking of repetition. The longer you focus on something or repeat it, the easier and more experiential it gets. I once assigned a student to "speed dating" events. The first time he went there, he was ill at ease. It wasn't a positive experience, but he was coaxed into going again. The second time he enjoyed it, and the third time he mastered the scene! After three repetitions a daunting and unpleasant task became an enjoyable opportunity.

Some time ago I was frustrated because I couldn't find anyone to play soccer with me where I live. Where I lived previously, I knew people I could join for a few soccer matches on the weekends. I called up a few friends but none of them were interested. Intention Repetition 1: I put an ad in an online classifieds for my new city, looking for an amateur soccer team. No response. Intention Repetition 2: I went to visit a local amateur team. Going there I found that they were *so very* amateur that I was underwhelmed and I didn't go back. Intention Repetition 3: I went for a tryout at another local amateur club. They were *so very* good that I was overwhelmed, and I didn't make the team. Frustration was mounting, but being familiar with repetition + focus + enthusiasm I wouldn't be deterred. A few days later I saw a group playing in the park. Just as in younger days I approached them and asked to join, and it worked out. I had found a soccer team at my level.

People have asked me why I like to do all kinds of things myself. "Why do you build your websites yourself Fred? I hire experts to do it. Delegation is your friend". I do it because I'm crazy about learning. I want to know how things work and gain more and more ability…in everything. It trains my focus. The more trained my focus is, the more it can be applied to *all kinds* of other things. Soccer for example. Or lucid dreaming. Or cooking. Or anything. Sustained attention can be applied to anything and then it grows.

The more you repeat something, the more expert you become at it. The more expert you become, the more "vibe" or "energy" you build around it and the easier it gets. When you're really good at something your skills in that regard seem magical to others. You get into a momentum that others can only dream of. **You make it look easy.**

The public only sees the end result, it doesn't see all the practice that preceded it. At the beginning of his career, the actor Will Smith not only learned the lines of his own roles, he learned the lines of *all the other* roles too! In an old TV show he can sometimes be seen lip-syncing other actors. To the viewer he seemed like a natural talent. What they didn't see was the amount of focus that had gone into it. In other words, years of skill building can make you look like a natural talent. Sure, we all have natural talents that come to us easily, without the need for much repetition. But even here, a little bit of focus and repetition can reawaken those talents in a fairly short time. It's good to put your focus on what you're already good at and enjoy. The union of talent + practice creates *fantastic* results.

9. The Champion's Mindset

This is a legendary motivational speech by a football coach that caused an underdog to win the championship. It teaches two vital lessons:

a) Energy and Excitement aren't generated from "out there" but from within.

b) The power of words can influence physical reality

10. Fearless

The Universe is total abundance. You have direct access to this abundance. The key to that is a fearless attitude. When I was younger, watching action movies sometimes frustrated me. They portrayed fearless heroes and adventure, but I wasn't content with just watching others experience fearless fun. I noticed that the people around me seemed to be content to watch it in movies but never try it out in their own lives. Soon I discovered that when I act without fear, no harm can come to me. Fearlessness acts like a protective shield that wards off danger.

I was 18 when I moved away from home without a penny, taking my first step into self-sufficiency. My Dad told me I wouldn't make it and I would be home within a week, but I wanted to prove to myself that I could manage. The first weeks on my own were hard. I didn't tell my parents that I sometimes slept on the streets because I wanted to "win the game" and not return home defeated. I eventually emerged out of those hard times just fine. From that point forward, taking fearless steps in defiance of others' limitations became a habit.

Some years later I was chosen to translate at a Tony Robbins Seminar on Fiji. Being at an event of this famous self-improvement coach was a dream come true back then, but in those younger days I couldn't afford the ticket from Europe, where I lived at the time, to the Pacific. If I recall correctly, it would have cost me $8,000. This was before convenient last minute booking on the Internet. I flew from London to Los Angeles for an affordable $800 trusting that I would find a cheaper flight to Fiji from there. I didn't know for sure - I hadn't even looked it up…it was just an idea I was making up in my head! I was still in the process of developing my abundance thinking that "all would be well". Sure enough, upon arrival in L.A. I "stumbled on" the ticket counter of Air New Zealand and bought a ticket to Fiji for only $1,000, soon arriving there - but I had no money left! I found myself on the other side of the world with no return ticket and no money for lodging, but I was very happy because I knew I had done something courageous. I felt like an adventurer who just ventured out with no idea how things would go – and of course, everything worked out just fine. I was kindly provided for by the organizers when I confessed my situation. Some extra translation work in the evenings got me the cash to fly home. Because I never felt afraid inside, I wouldn't end up as a beggar on the streets of a foreign country. Even if things hadn't worked out, I could imagine worse things than being stuck on such a lovely island.

Many things I have done are so outrageous that I keep them secret. Only close friends know them. This isn't because I feel uncomfortable about them but because I don't want people to emulate me if they haven't developed that degree of confidence. I've done crazy things for love, for students, for business. One of them involved secretly crossing the border of Yugoslavia (when that country still existed) to Italy through the Adriatic Sea. Another involved walking through a snowstorm at night, in the mountains, far from civilization. There are many others, but I won't go into detail because if your confidence in yourself and the universe aren't strong enough, risky adventures will certainly fail. They won't fail, however, if your faith is strong. Even without doing "outrageous" things, just a little fearlessness will help you advance greatly in daily life.

Fearlessness attracts abundance because it's rooted in the belief that you're provided for. It's irresistibly magnetic to an abundance of opportunities, relationships, people, money, experience and whatever else this vast universe has to offer. To be clear, it doesn't mean you never feel fear, it's about how you deal with your fear. Never feeling fear means that you're actually avoiding situations that could cause discomfort. That's not fearlessness, its cowardice. You postpone important decisions, avoid people you'd rather approach, and choose only the safest options. Fearful people prefer a false sense of "peace and safety", but real peace and safety can only be found within, not through the avoidance of life and following your bliss. In fearlessness you confront situations and you stay calm enough to be able to act deliberately within them. Fear strikes as a sinking feeling in the chest or stomach. A fearless person doesn't automatically resort to fight or flight but can stay centered, neither contracting nor reacting, neither fleeing nor attacking. In that peculiar state you may feel some trepidation but your actions aren't controlled by emotion, they are directed by your conscious will.

For example, you'd like to approach someone you'd like to meet. Fear will tell you not to approach them. If you approach them anyway, you're not dominated by fear. When the other person realizes you have overcome approach anxiety – something which most people haven't overcome – they will find that quite remarkable. Most fear is illusion. If you fear approaching strangers, it's because you put them on an illusory pedestal. If you would see the truth – that all people are just humans like yourself and would often like to be approached and talked to – you'd no longer fear approaching them. The truth sets you free and the fear dissolves as if it never existed. "Yes, but I have tried that and been rejected before!" the fearful person might say. So what? That's their problem, not yours. Maybe they were having a bad day and didn't want to be approached. What's it got to do with you? The fear lens sees strangers up on a pedestal, oneself as something lower and the approach as a plea for attention. The fearless lens doesn't see any of this. It just sees a normal human being who – like any other human being – could use some appreciation.

Fear will usually tell you not to try anything new. And when you continually do so anyway, you eventually transcend fear. Do it often enough and it becomes commonplace. You wake up and realize that the creative force of the universe is so **immensely powerful** that it could transport you to Alaska and back in the blink of an eye.

The fearless don't shy away from or deny anything. There's no escapism or fantasy about how things "should be". Things are as they are…for the moment. And this realism actually supports thinking positively and turning problems into opportunities. Before seeing positively, however, accept reality exactly as it's, without denial, then you can shape it to what you prefer. Put differently, you can't guide a dance partner you deny. You can't take a bull by its horns and ride it to nicer places if you run away from it. Some people are so deeply steeped in fear that they don't even want to entertain certain thoughts. They deny that such thoughts are even an option. They deny both the what-is of the here and now as well as what could be.

Fearless people may have difficulty working for others. They get restless when they have to rely on others too much. The fearful, on the other hand, are only comfortable when they work under the wings of a boss who can shelter them from an unfriendly world. Their "safety" is an illusion, as if their boss cares more about their security than they do. Hence, many fearless people are self-employed. Their highest value isn't security but freedom. They realize that true security can't be provided by the world and that true security is actually an emotional state. The fearless can handle most things on their own without dependency on employers, drugs, healers, gurus, partners, entertainment, foods, cultures, or other people. That doesn't mean that the fearless never ask for help. On the contrary, because the fearless no longer need to pretend to be self-reliant, because they **really are**, they easily ask others for support. Does it sound paradoxical? Give it some thought. Many people have been worn down by the perceived "harshness" of life and easily slip into or even embrace some form of dependency. In professional life, the fearless person strives to own what she produces. She understands her uniqueness and doesn't seek to copy what others have done before her. This fear-based society on the other hand, tends to see people who fail to conform and copy as "picky" and "difficult", when actually they are just fearless.

The fearless have a different way of dealing with resistance and challenge. External resistance doesn't equal failure. They understand that roadblocks and dark moments challenge them to be more creative and rise to the occasion. The heightened awareness in difficult situations awakens slumbering powers within. Resistance is just a wake up call to become better. If you're already getting better, then no wake up call, no adversity, is required and life will seem easy to you.

Fearless people don't delay before they take action. They don't need to be ready or receive a signal or a sign before they act. The fearless person acts before he is ready. It's as if you deliberately make things a little more difficult for yourself in order to rise to the level of energy which can handle whatever obstacle you're facing. When you're not quite prepared to move forward but do so anyway, you become more alert and inventive. You must succeed, so you will.

8

INTEGRITY TRAINING

1. 10 Factors that strengthen your Integrity:

1. Shift from "what can I get?" to "what can I give?"

2. List your strengths and weaknesses and work to eradicate your weaknesses and train your strengths.

3. When you're saying "No" on the inside, don't say "Yes" on the outside. You can also say "No" gently, while remaining true to yourself.

4. Openly communicate the issues you see. Don't hide. Go where it hurts and change that to the positive.

5. Understand before wanting to be understood.

6. Taking an Interest in others makes you interesting.

7. When you give your word, keep it. Be more careful with giving your word and with your words in general.

8. Follow a vision higher than yourself.

9. Serve others without detriment to yourself.

10. Live within the context of your values and principles.

2. Being an Upright Person

You can be an upright person physically, psychologically and spiritually. One affects the other.

Being Physically Upright

An upright body posture improves your state, presence and authority. If you have the habit of slumping or being unconscious in your physical movements you can gain extra power by correcting your posture here and there. Depending on the setting, you can also practice various deliberate poses. Stretching your arms to the sky, for example, creates an immediate openness to energy. Your mind acts in accord with your body movements. Having more control over your space will create that feeling in the mind. Tensing your muscles or crossing your arms tends to heighten concentration. Smiling deliberately tends to increase joy. Using gestures consciously makes it easier to persuade someone. The basis of conscious and deliberate movement is Uprightness. Being upright indicates that you're conscious and aware of what is happening around you. You're alert. Uprightness isn't as necessary when you're sitting at home watching a movie, but it's useful when you have an important meeting. Uprightness is a matter of straightening your spine. It only takes a second of awareness. To ensure that *Uprightness* doesn't become *Uptightness* is best alternated with phases of relaxing your posture.

Psychologically and Spiritually Upright

Psychological Uprightness is your ability to remain poised and focused on your heart's path even in challenging and difficult situations. How easy would it be to distract you from a path you have chosen? Do you sway with the winds of change or stand firm in your values and principles? Are you easily swayed by fear and desire? Can you stick to your goal even if people say you should give up? Psychological uprightness is resilience.

To be spiritually upright means to "have a backbone". When you have a backbone it means that you don't cave in at the slightest temptation, the slightest challenge, and the slightest interruption. If I offer you $5,000 to betray your best friend and this friend would never find out, and you refuse it out of a sense of integrity, it's because you have a backbone. On a soul level nothing is hidden so even if you manage to hide things in the physical, you can never truly hide anything. That's why having an upright character and integrity is incredibly empowering. Many people who are looking for "a secret" to fix things for them would be better served cultivating their integrity and thereby becoming integrated beings. "To be integrated" means to act as a part of the whole, with respect for the society you live in and your own true self.

3. How to increase the Power of your Word

To enhance the authority and power of your spoken word gains, avoid lying, chatter, and gossip. If you tell a lie it hurts you more than it hurts another. Why? Because you're teaching your body/mind/subconscious that your word is of no consequence or reality. The next time you try to use your words to create a reality, your affirmation will have no effect. After all, you have taught yourself that what you say isn't true. If however you have conditioned your body/mind to believe that your word is true, then what you say will more easily happen.

If your word is strong enough it can affect physical reality. Affirmations, Prayers and Incantations only gain traction if your word has enough power. Ways to increase it:

1. Silence

A human has two ears and one mouth for a reason. This is nature telling you that you should listen at least twice as much as you speak. If you talk too much, the power of your words isn't conserved but dissipated and wasted. If you're silent, when you finally do speak your words will carry much more weight. If you conduct presentations, make pauses throughout. It's in the empty spaces between your words that the attention of the audience is caught. The words you speak have more impact than if you had continually rambled on. Silence also allows you to gather your thoughts so that what you finally say has impact and meaning.. This rule doesn't apply to shy people who feign "Silence" because they are afraid to talk. If you're shy, do the opposite of what is recommended here so that your words begin having some impact.

2. Stop Gossip

Talking about others positively is energizing, but avoid talking badly about others because in people's subconscious this reflects badly on you. Most people are immediately game when someone starts gossiping, they love to hear it, but their innermost self is judging you for it. What they are really thinking is: "When I'm not around this person will be gossiping about me!" Gossip is one of the great energy sinks of this reality. Numerous magazines and websites thrive on it, sucking in people's attention (= life energy) minute by minute. You can choose to turn away from gossip – your own and others. When I catch myself becoming curious about someone's misdeeds I usually stop myself. When I start ranting about other people I stop myself and change the subject.

3. Keep your Word

Breaking your promises and commitments has the most crippling effect on the power of your word because you're teaching your body/mind that what you say is meaningless. You can refine the skill of keeping your word even to the smallest detail: if you say you're going to meet someone at 8 o'clock, then do your very best to show up at exactly 8 o'clock. Your body/mind/subconscious takes note of these details and assumes that your word is worth something. You can't be lying and then later expect your affirmations to come true. We want to make an impression so we sometimes promise things we have no real intention of keeping. It's best not to promise too much if you're not sure about it. Of course "I'll try to be there at 8 o'clock" doesn't sound as firm as "I'll be there at 8", but sometimes it's the better choice of words.

4. Give yourself a Vocabulary Makeover

Learn new words and new ways of expressing yourself. Notice how the words people use reveal their intentions and their current state of energy. There's a big difference between starting the day by saying "Fuck, I missed the goddamn train" and starting it by saying "I thank the most High for a miraculous day ahead". Your spoken word is a bolt of energy that leaves your body the moment you speak it. It goes out into the Universe and it returns to you. One day I heard someone use the word "Awesomeness". I had never used that word before so I decided to apply it that day. Learning and using new words keeps your mind and speech fresh and light.

5. Speak words of Appreciation

Get into the habit of praising things and people. Give words of blessing and appreciation everywhere you go. Don't do this to manipulate people or when you don't mean it, but when you do mean it, clearly express it. There are waiters, cab drivers, spouses, bosses, employees, and friends out there who will immediately lighten up when you find something about them to appreciate… but the real secret is that it benefits you even more than it benefits them. You'll light up and lighten up.

4. Don't trust the Alarmist

An alarmist is someone who grossly exaggerates a threat to mankind, to a region, to a person or to themselves. You also have an inner alarmist that goes by the name of fear, along with external alarmists who are trying to convince you that things aren't well and going downhill fast.

I don't trust alarmists and remain unresponsive to them. Here's a sampling of a few alarmist statements that I've been told in the last decade which I chose to ignore in any way:

"The swine flu is going to wipe out civilization as we know it. You'd better be prepared. Stock up and shut yourself off before it's too late!!!"

Response: No. Not gonna happen.

"We are living in the greatest economic depression the country has ever seen. It's time to stock up on foods because the end is nigh!"

Response: Back in the late 1930s they lined up to get a loaf of bread – if they were lucky. Today they line up to get the latest iPad. I don't think we have the same definition of economic depression.

"The President is going to implement a nationwide dictatorship! Better plan your escape asap!!!"

Response: Not going to happen.

"Oh my God! You have coding errors on your website! Google will down-rank you and you'll lose customers because of it!!!"

Response: I'm not Google's slave. The source of my Abundance is the Infinite Universe, not Google.

Alarmists are attention seekers who exaggerate a threat to gain someone's ear or induce worry. Some alarmists are stealth marketers who want to sell you something. Where there's an alarmist there's usually a liar, because even if something bad is happening, there's no reason to talk about it in a crazed, sensationalist way. Fear doesn't help a bad situation anyway, only action does. Don't allow alarmists to create a state of fear for you. Even if the world explodes, your soul lives on!

5. The End of Groveling

Groveling harms your integrity. A few synonyms for "groveling" in this context:

Needy, beggarly, servile, boot-licking, obsequious, slavish, submissive, false humility, spineless, cringing, squirming, craving, longing, destitute, "over-eager to please others"

And a few antonyms to make the point clearer:

Worthy, noble, royal, abundant, proud, exalted, excellent, bold, "not over-eager to please others", cool, unyielding, respectable, commendable, upright.

A few examples of groveling I've witnessed:

* A woman wanted a well known Hollywood producer to read her film script so she worked for two years in his office getting his coffee, washing his car, babysitting his kids, telling lies for him and even having sex with him any time he wanted. She did all this with the vague promise that he might "someday" read her script (and just read it, not endorse or buy it). Because she completely compromised her integrity, she'll never succeed. It turned out later he never bothered to read it, he threw it in the garbage long before.

* A guy wanted to marry a specific woman, his "dream woman" as he said. Before even getting to first base she had him pay for her vacation. On vacation she said she wanted to go jet-skiing, so he arranged it.

Shortly before the appointment, she said she had changed her mind and would rather go on a yacht, so he said "of course!" and arranged for it. She failed to show up at the arranged time and instead joined a beach party elsewhere. When she came back he didn't confront her or demand an apology. This went on for another week with him never saying "no" to any of her antics and agreeing to everything she wanted. Naturally, she grew incredibly bored with this spineless wimp and kicked him to the curb. He was heartbroken and said "I don't understand how she could leave me! I did everything for her!" That's exactly the problem…he did everything for her, regardless of whether it violated his values, principles, truth or respect. You can't possibly be interesting to someone in such a submissive state.

In a state of groveling you're profoundly out of touch with your internal abundance. You instead project too much importance on other people, bosses, superiors, celebrities, VIPs. When around them your attention becomes locked and frozen on them, not noticing or perceiving or even being interested in anything other than them and making a "good impression". Reality Creation is the extreme polar opposite of that. Your internal world is sufficient unto itself. You appreciate others' attention, but if they don't give it to you, you think "that's their loss, not mine", or you don't consider it at all. No human being is more important than the Infinite and Eternal Being of which you're a holographic aspect. The Reality Creator doesn't wait for the boss's email, for the client's praise, for the bank's money, for the world's applause, the partner's attention, the VIP's recognition or Google's ranking. The Reality Creator waits for nothing and nobody because he/she is brimming with energy and joy in the here and now.

6. Walk Away or Try Harder?

A dilemma many face in uncomfortable situations is whether they should try to improve it or focus elsewhere. "Should I stay in my troubled relationship and try to make it better or should I let go of it and look elsewhere?" "Should I hold on to my business that isn't working or should I let go and open a space for something better?" I don't have a simple answer for this dilemma but I can assure you that both paths have merit. Walking away lets go of unnecessary baggage. Trying harder makes you stronger to carry the baggage. If you drop the baggage you feel lighter. If you keep the baggage you'll become stronger. I usually tell people that life can be a fluid and balanced mix of both modes of behavior. You wouldn't walk away every time the going gets a little tough, nor would you put up with years of trouble. Knowing that both paths have merit and advantages makes the decision easier.

For more on the subject of Integrity see my book *The Leadership Course*.

7. Projected Expectations vs. Authentic Speaking

If you've ever felt awkward or not known what to say in conversation, you'll experience a major breakthrough by realizing that **you don't have to say anything.** At the root of inhibition and shyness is the idea that "you have to say something" or that the other person expects something of you. When you think this way, your words are no longer authentic, nor do they come from well being. **The idea that others expect you to say or do something is a "projected expectation". This is when you project beliefs and thoughts about what others supposedly want from you and then try to behave accordingly – instead of following your own real sense of what you want to say or not say.** Most ideas about what others expect are illusions. Even if the other person did have expectations of you, you don't need to respond to that, you're not compelled to behave in ways others want you to. Authenticity means letting go of who you think you're supposed to be, and being who you are in that moment.

To take back control of your speech, **make deliberate pauses in speaking, delay your responses to others' questions, requests and comments, and don't say anything unless it comes from presence, calm and well being.** This gives you time and space to ignore external pressures (or what you believe are external pressures), to decide whether you want to respond and to form a response that feels right to you. Many people say incessant nonsense to cover up their sense of awkwardness and because they are too concerned with pleasing and appeasing others. Changing ourselves just to be liked by others doesn't earn us their love – just the opposite. Initially, it's better if there's less talk and more presence. Later, once your words come from well being, you can say more. The words then no longer come from well being rather than insecurity.

Please Think of a Red Car

Did you do that? Did you just think of a red car? That's an example of how easily other people create your reality. Others implant thoughts into your mind all the time. If you trust or like those people, that's OK, but don't let it get out of hand. To take back your life, reduce your automatic reaction to and acceptance of others' thoughts. I'm going to ask you to think about a red car again. This time, you may decide to think about something else instead.

Please Think of a Red Car

Did you think of something else? Good for you. You just went from reactive to creative. You might have thought of white clouds, black cars, yellow birds, or millions of other things. There's nothing forcing you to react to whatever others say, unless what they say is useful, good, true or beautiful.

Please Don't Think of a Red Car

What did you do now? That one is a little trickier. "Don't think of a red car" makes you just as much aware of a red car as "Think of a red car". Because you were trying to think of something other than what I told you to think, the statement may have also locked you into a confused state as in "should or shouldn't I think of a red car?" Ultimately it's still your choice whether you focus on the red car or not. There's nothing wrong with accepting others' realities as long as you do it by choice, not automatically and unconsciously. Deliberate and conscious living is about forming your own thoughts, views and actions.

When you reduce your thought and speech reactivity to external reality, everything changes. From that point forward your speech becomes more powerful, it comes from silence and the aspects of authentic speech develop. The ability to be clear, direct and honest. The ability to state what you want. The ability to say "no" in a gentle manner, with courage rather than force. The ability to define your own rules instead of buying into whatever others say. The end of making excuses or false promises. The ability to request help. The end of blaming and complaining. The ability to think clearly and speak more creatively. The ability to enjoy other people. The release of needing to control. The ability to make mistakes and be OK with it. The ability to admit and confess to what is real. The end of silence feeling awkward. The ability to stay in the present – and much, much more.

Exercise in Projected Expectations

1. Write down the name of someone you're regularly in contact with

2. Write down what you think they want or expect of you.

3. Write down who you try to be in order to fulfill their expectations (do you change your behavior or words to fulfill what you think they expect of you)?

4. Write down who you'd prefer to be.

5. Mentally focus on the person. Focus on what you think they expect of you and who you try to be to align with that expectation. Notice the energy exchange between you. While breathing out, let go of these projections and imagine who you'd prefer to be when in the presence of that person.

An example:

1. Mom

2. She expects me to have a job and work hard.

3. I work like crazy, regardless of whether I like the work or not. On other days I'm totally lazy – which is also just a reaction to her exaggerated pressure. Both my hard work on things I don't enjoy and my laziness are reactions to what I think she expects.

4. I'd like to feel at ease and do more of the things I enjoy. I'd like to stay calm when she criticizes me about work.

Another Example:

1. Customer

2. They expect me to be available 24 hours a day.

3. I never turn off my phone and I'm available all the time.

4. I take control of my time and I'm now only available weekdays from 9 to 5.

You may continue the exercise with all the people in your life until you feel a huge chunk of relief and have taken back your true self and your life.

Published by www.realitycreation.org.

ABOUT THE AUTHOR

Frederick E. Dodson, born in the USA 1974 currently lives in Arizona. He loves viewing life from many different viewpoints and putting spiritual knowledge into the practice of everyday life rather than following the 9-to-5 routine of a "steady job". In his twenties he wrote and published 15 books and held many hundreds of workshops, talks and seminars on the topic of reality creation. Lately however, he has retreated from teaching somewhat and only conducts one course a year.

He has started viewing "experiencing joy" higher than "teaching others". Why? Because everyone has their own version of the truth and the purpose of his life is not to get others to agree with him, but to have fun. His favourite activities in the meantime include scuba diving, surfing the internet, writing, collecting movies, travelling and lucid dreaming.

If you liked this book and want to learn more, check out my website at www.realitycreation.org.

Printed in Great Britain
by Amazon